The Poverty of *R*elativism

GEMAS Studies in Social Analysis

Series Editors: Mohamed Cherkaoui, Peter Hamilton, Bryan S. Turner

This series makes available in English the best work of a leading French research group, GEMAS (Groupe d'Etude des Méthodes de l'Analyse Sociologique). The group's aim is to contribute to the production of empirical sociological knowledge and to the renewal of sociological theory. Their work is as much concerned with the relevance of classical sociology as the contemporary issues on which it can be focused, and has three interconnected elements: general sociological theory; epistemology and methodology of the social sciences; and the application of theories and methods to areas such as collective action, norms and values, culture and cultural practices, morality, debate, knowledge, and education and social stratification.

Series titles include:

INVISIBLE CODES
Mohamed Cherkaoui

BOUNDLESS YOUTH
Olivier Galland

THE POVERTY OF RELATIVISM
Raymond Boudon

http://www.gemas.msh-paris.fr/

The Poverty of *R*elativism

Raymond Boudon

The Bardwell Press, Oxford and Cambridge

Groupe d'Etude des Méthodes de l'Analyse Sociologique
Centre National de la Recherche Scientifique
Université de Paris-Sorbonne (Paris IV)

Published by:

The Bardwell Press
6 Bardwell Road
Oxford OX2 6SW
www.bardwell-press.co.uk

British Library Cataloguing in Publication Data
A catalogue record for this book is available from the British Library

ISBN 0-9548683-0-7

Typeset by The Bardwell Press, Oxford, UK
Printed in Great Britain

Contents

Preface

This new series of scholarly books — of which Professor Raymond Boudon's work *The Poverty of Relativism* constitutes the first publication — is the result of a long period of collaboration between Professor Mohamed Cherkaoui, Director of the Groupe d'Etude des Méthodes de l'Analyse Sociologique (GEMAS), Peter Hamilton (Open University) Editorial Director of the Bardwell Press and Professor Bryan Turner of Cambridge University. Its objective is to make available to the English-speaking community the significant work produced by this research group of the Centre National de la Recherche Scientifique and the University of Paris-Sorbonne.

The aim of GEMAS is to contribute to the production of empirical sociological knowledge and to the renewal of sociological theory. This work has three interconnected elements: general sociological theory; epistemology and methodology of the social sciences; and the application of theories and methods to areas such as collective action, norms and values, culture and cultural practices, morality, debate, knowledge, and education and social stratification.

The concerns of sociological theory are linked at one level to the analysis of social action and its dimensions, and on the other level to the study of the forms and consequences of understanding and of rationality.

GEMAS researchers are concerned with developing new contributions to the study of some central problems in the epistemology and methodology of the social sciences, namely:

— the dichotomy of methodological individualism and holism which is part of many contemporary debates
— the mathematical and statistical modelling of processes of social mobility, stratification, inequality, etc.
— the identification of the basic generative mechanisms of macro-phenomena
— the articulation of theories of explanation and understanding
— theories about the simulation of proof and experimental control

Empirical research undertaken in relation to these theoretical and methodological concerns have led to a number of discoveries concerning, most notably, the processes of conviction and of self-persuasion; the modes of transmission and of stability of values; the development of educational systems in relation to the problems of social mobility, development and innovation; the transformation of working conditions within the university; the redesign of secondary education and the deployment of scholastic strategies; the new problematics of collective action such as the crises in trades union organisation and the weaknesses of new social movements; the forms of public activity in France and their unintended consequences; demographic and strategic changes in scientific communities, etc.

It is important to note that the creation of a distinctive perspective on sociological theory involves a process of continual return to the classics in the field. This is why the members of GEMAS have been active in publishing a considerable body of work on the history of sociological thought and, more widely, on the history of the social sciences. Such concerns will be reflected in the choice of works that appear subsequently in this series.

Our joint intention is that the publishing programme of the GEMAS series will offer sociologists in the English-speaking world access to a new body of sociological scholarship, addressing contemporary issues in a clear and accessible manner.

Mohamed Cherkaoui
Directeur, GEMAS

Peter Hamilton
Director, The Bardwell Press

Foreword

Relativism has been a persistent feature of social science, and virtually an article of faith in anthropology and sociology. We can detect different stages and influences on contemporary relativism. In the late nineteenth century, sociological debate was influenced by historicism, where the historical context of ideas was regarded as essential for understanding the meaning of ideas and institutions. Historicism had in part grown out of the development of biblical criticism in German Protestant theology in which the Bible had been subject to intense textual criticism and evaluation. In modern terminology, we might say that biblical criticism produced a significant deconstruction of religious claims and rendered the unique authority of revelation problematic. In sociology, these developments had a profound impact on such writers as Max Weber and Ernest Troeltsch. As a legal thinker and political sociologists Weber contributed to the disenchantment of sociology as an interpretative science of the meanings of social action. Weber's philosophy of social science was understood (rightly or wrongly) as a defence of the role of value neutrality and objectivity in the social sciences. At least Weber was thought to provide a sophisticated justification of relativism and neutrality. For example, Leo Strauss in *Natural Right and History* claimed that Weber had taken from 'the historical school' the view that no social order could be said to be the *right* social order, and that Weber had contributed to the decay of natural law by showing that the theological presuppositions behind the universalistic claims of natural law no longer had any authoritative force in a period of secularisation. Strauss complained, with justification, that value-neutral sociology would, in fact, be sterile and unimportant. He gave the hypothetical example of a sociological description of a concentration camp that failed to observe that the treatment of the inmates was cruel and unjust. We need to recognise that the application of the adjective 'cruel' to the practices of the guards involves a value judgement, but its absence from any sociological description would amount to a bitter satire. A similar criticism of value neutrality was made by Alasdair MacIntyre in *Against the Self-Images of the Age* in which he complained about the absence of evaluation and criticism in American political science in which no amount of statistical manipulation of data could ever tell us whether a political regime is just or unjust.

Following MacIntyre's philosophical criticism of political science, we can also identify certain forms of functionalism as sustaining a commitment to (anthropological) relativism. This version of functionalism can be illustrated by the legacies of Emile Durkheim and Bronislaw Malinowski. In his famous and influential study of *The Elementary Forms of the Religious Life* Durkheim had attempted to provide a generic definition of religion in terms of the classification of phenomena into sacred and profane domains. The point of this definition was both to include various branches of Buddhism, which deny the existence of God or gods, in the study of religion, and to circumvent any discussion of the truth or falsity of religious beliefs. For Durkheim, all religions are 'true' insofar as they make a significant functional contribution to society. Religions are (sociologically) true if they contribute to the continuity of social systems. But Durkheim in effect indirectly demonstrated the false nature of religion by suggesting that the real object of religious belief was not 'God' but 'society'. The implication was that sociologists could safely ignore the truth content of religious belief in the explanation of human action, even where totemic beliefs appear to be bizarre. In a similar fashion, Malinowski, in *Magic Science and Religion*, rejected armchair philosophical approaches to understanding the 'primitive mind' by claiming that, for example, the beliefs of the Trobriand Islanders were not so much illogical as alogical.

These anthropological and sociological contributions by Durkheim and Malinowski represented major advances on nineteenth-century speculative philosophical accounts of the 'primitive mentality'. However, these forms of sociological neutrality can become problematic when we encounter religious or magical systems, which, for example, require human sacrifice, mutilation or suffering. If we turned to some contemporary examples of cultic religion, we can apply relativistic criteria to an analysis of the infamous Jonestown massacre of the disciples of Pastor Jim Jones in 1978 by arguing that these tragic events were a product of poverty, marginalisation and apocalyptic preaching. Those who opposed the cult at the Peoples Temple – the so-called Concerned Relatives – obviously took a different view, claiming that their relatives had been brainwashed by Jim Jones. When cultic activity involves violence towards the public – such as Aum Shinrikyo's attack on the Japanese subway in 1995 – we are less willing to embrace relativistic arguments. There are, in short, significant remaining problems with the solutions that Durkheim and Malinowski provided against the positivist criticism of religious beliefs. This problem of avoiding any scientific judgement of the rationality or validity of religious or magical belief was addressed by Ernest Gellner in an article on 'Concepts and Society', where he complained about the intellectual charity of anthropological functionalism. If all beliefs and practices – however bizarre or disconcerting – are seen by anthropologists to be meaningful in their context, then no set of beliefs or practices (however cruel or absurd) could be the subject of anthropological (or sociological) critique or evaluation.

Gellner's objections to what we might call 'functional charity' in anthropological explanations have become particularly important in the debate about cultural rights and the universality of human rights. Anthropologists have characteristically taken the view that human rights are Western, individualistic and particular. To force these human rights laws on non-Western societies is not only mistaken; it is politically unacceptable. For example, in a recent collection of essays on *Culture and Rights*, social anthropologists condemned the application of human rights notions to child prostitution in Thailand, because Western notions of childhood have no relevance to Thailand and that many villages in the Thai rural economy depend on the income of child prostitution. One problem with this argument is that NGOs operating in Thailand would themselves want to control sexual tourism. The other difficulty with these arguments from the perspective of cultural relativism is that the same relativistic arguments are used by authoritarian regimes in Asia to protect themselves from both national and international scrutiny and criticism. Despotic governments and inhuman practices can be cynically justified under the mythical umbrella of 'Asian values'.

In modern social theory, this traditional debate about relativism – that has some of its intellectual roots in Friedrich Nietzsche's assault on bourgeois Prussian values – was eventually incorporated into post-modernism. There are many forms and versions of postmodernism, the description of which need not detain us here. Suffice it to say that the advent of postmodernism in social and cultural theory was signalled by J-F. Lyotard's description of scepticism in *The Postmodern Condition* which he defined as towards 'grand narratives', especially the narratives flowing from Enlightenment rationalism. While Lyotard's postmodern theory was overtly a study of the consequences of computerisation on knowledge and education (especially higher education), it was perhaps more covertly a recognition of the failure of both the liberal model of modernisation (associated with American social science) and the Marxist version of revolutionary change. The authority of the grand narratives of liberal democracy and Marxist radicalism had been, according to Lyotard, shattered. More specifically, the computerisation of knowledge would undermine traditional norms of authority, hierarchy and completeness that had dominated the print-based forms of modern knowledge. In this respect, there was an important convergence between Lyotard's postmodernism and Marshall McLuhan's more popular insights into the workings of the global village. The reception of postmodernism into sociology, as in the social sciences and humanities generally, has reinforced the appeal of relativism. Large claims about macro-processes – modernisation, secularisation or rationalisation – are viewed by scepticism, while arguments that favour local images of postmodern society as a fragmented and diverse social reality are readily accepted. Postmodern theory has supported the view that the principal feature of the contemporary world is its unreality – or, to quote Marshall Berman's ironic adoption of Karl Marx's vision of the modern city, 'all that is solid melts into air'.

The final stage of the relativist debate is probably best reflected in the paradoxical merger of literary postmodernism, bourgeois liberalism and American pragmatism in the social philosophy of Richard Rorty. He is a controversial figure in (professional) philosophy, mainly because he argues that philosophy can no longer give an adequate account of the rational grounds upon which its assumptions about the unitary nature of Truth could be confirmed. The role of philosophy is not to illuminate the eternal foundations of Truth, but rather to be a sentimental voice alongside literature and art in the edification of young minds. The measure of philosophical progress is demonstrated by making philosophy more imaginative rather than more rigorous. As a result, Rorty tends to draw his philosophical inspiration from

Nabokov, Orwell or Proust rather than from Kant, Russell and Ayer. Because Rorty has been concerned to determine the proper limitations of philosophical knowledge in a world which is uncertain, unstable and unpredictable, his philosophical critique of knowledge and imagination has much in common with postmodernism. Whereas Lyotard, as we have seen, defined postmodernism as incredulity towards meta-narratives, Rorty in *Contingency, Irony and Solidarity* defines an ironist as somebody who has radical and persistent doubts about the final vocabulary he or she currently uses. Rorty has defended the relevance of the oxymoronic title 'postmodern bourgeois liberalism' as a broad description of his own agenda in contemporary philosophy. Rorty's philosophy and social theory can be seen as an application of, and debate with, the legacy of John Dewey. Rorty's post-professional philosophy seeks to reconcile the pragmatism of Dewey with the deconstructive ambitions of continental philosophy.

Rorty's reputation in professional philosophy was originally built on the foundations of his philosophy of science, namely *Philosophy and the Mirror of Nature*, in which he claimed that philosophers should give up the fantasy that philosophical truths could ever be an accurate mirror of nature. If there are any philosophical truths, they are not neutral representations (that is mirrors) of an objective reality (that is nature). Because Rorty holds that scientific observations of nature are theory-dependent and that the correspondence theory of truth is untenable, he rejects realism as a plausible epistemological position. In many respects, his criticisms of representational theories of truth remain his principal contribution to professional academic philosophy. The pragmatism that drives his view of the limited scope of philosophy is the same pragmatism that orchestrates his political theory and politics. Thus, his criticisms of representational theories of truth in *Philosophy and The Mirror of Nature* form the basis of his social philosophy in which his epistemological attack on correspondence theory is combined with his version of liberalism. The notion that social values and beliefs must remain tentative – because they cannot find a final or ultimate justification – is derived from the critique of the correspondence theory of truth in natural science. Relativism – or the argument that we can never have a secure, satisfying final vocabulary, but only pragmatic stabs in the dark – thus becomes a liberal virtue or antidote to all forms of ideology that claim to represent enduring Truth.

Relativism in various guises – historicism, functionalism, contextualism, postmodernism and pragmatism – has been a dominant epistemological framework in cultural anthropology and sociology for decades. It is not, however, an entirely satisfying or satisfactory position, and it has been subject to powerful criticism. While political philosophy has continued with its traditional armoury of critical concepts – justice being the most important – sociology does not possess a vocabulary that can sustain a critical evaluation of modern institutions. One illustration is the general absence of sociology from those disciplines that contribute to our understanding of human rights. Consequently, it is a pleasure and an honour to participate in the translation and publication of Professor Raymond Boudon's bold, determined but judicious attack on relativism. His radical critique of the barren legacy of relativistic thought – the moral and intellectual poverty of the relativist position – represents a decisive intervention. There is no need here to summarise Boudon's critical analysis of the limitations of relativist thought; I shall merely describe the nature and significance of his attack.

Boudon recognises the appeal and spread of relativism as a secular religion, in fact an ideology ideally suited to liberal democracies in which any belief is as good (or bad) as any other. Attacking relativism is consequently somewhat against the grain of the time. He makes the important distinction between cognitive and cultural relativism – a distinction that provides an important clarification of the debate. The word 'relativism' is automatically associated with cultural differences and with the anthropology of Montaigne who elegantly defended classical scepticism. However, Montaigne's recognition of cultural difference was set in the context of religious wars, and hence his sceptical humanism also offered an ethical position of cosmopolitan virtue. His version of cultural relativism did not entail moral relativism, and hence Boudon argues correctly that modern sociologists have greatly exaggerated the relativist legacy of classical social theory. But Boudon also points to the dangers of cognitive relativism associated with the legacy of Thomas Kuhn and the new sociology of science. The unintended consequence of any causal account of ideas – such as the sociology of knowledge – is to relativise belief. However, a causal account does not necessarily tell us anything about the truth or falsity of belief, or whether ideas are rationally held. Hence, Boudon provides us with an important defence of the rationality of science.

Finally, Boudon provides a subtle reading of the legacy of both Weber and Durkheim to defend the idea of moral evolution and progress. Relativism too easily suggests that we abandon all versions of the Enlightenment project of progress without offering any alternative. Thus, Professor Boudon defends a version of social science that does not end in pessimism or nihilism, partly by reviving the idea of moral sentiment and defending the idea of common sense knowledge. This translation and consolidation of his recent essays on sociology is an important event in the contemporary quest to find an alternative to the debilitating consequences of relativism.

Bryan S. Turner
Professor of Sociology, Cambridge University
September 2004

The Social Sciences: An Intellectual Source of Western Moral Pessimism

Every era has its favourite ideologies. In the 19th century it was historicism. It was believed that there were ineluctable historical laws of progress. Karl Popper laid this particular ideology to rest. Only a few great thinkers, who included the sociologists Durkheim, Simmel and Max Weber, were able to separate the kernel of truth that lies within historicism from the exaggerations and doubtful systematisations to which it had given birth, in the work of Auguste Comte, Herbert Spencer and Karl Marx. Historicist ideology was the background on which were drawn up the great secular religions of the 20th century. National Socialism borrowed from biological evolutionism, while communism relied on Marxist evolutionism.

Secular religions — ideologies — are more fragile than regular religions for one simple reason. Because they deny any possibility of transcendence, they are obliged to submit to the verdict of reality. Communism promised, in the words of the Front Populaire of 1936, a "joyous future" ("des lendemains qui chantent") but ended up recognising that it can only offer poverty and prisons. This fragility does not mean that once discredited such religions might disappear. The explanatory schemas offered by Marxism are still present in the work of numerous thinkers. Even the most superficial observation of political debate will show, for example, that many politicians, intellectuals and citizens still conceive of North–South relations in terms of the class struggle model: what is good for the North is bad for the South and vice-versa. Relations between North and South take the form of a zero-sum game, they insist, while in reality they are better

1

understood as a positive-sum game. The study of western societies is continually brought back to the opposition between a "dominant class" and a "dominated class" when what really characterises them is the existence of a vast middle class with above it a thin layer of the "privileged" and beneath a stratum of the "excluded". Others cling to an organicist vision of society and dream about the loss of cultural homogeneity.

The residues left by the great secular religions persist because they provide simple analytic frameworks that are easy to understand and provide meaning in one glance to a wide range of events. They make it possible to avoid cognitive dissonance on the part of the subject in relation to the world. Despite these advantages the explanatory schemas emanating from the great secular religions eventually weaken, particularly as a result of the effects of generational change: each generation is presented with a stock of explanatory schemas, but tends to reject some and accept others, while also inventing new ones. The inertia of the great secular religions is derived in part from the need for individual explanatory schemas to be integrated within one theory that synthesises them in a more or less convincing manner. The success of Marxism in the 20th century is due in great part to what it proposed doing with any social phenomenon perceived as being the negative consequence of a tacit conspiracy of the "dominant" against the "dominated" (Boudon, 2004).

It is very hard to say if a new secular religion is in process of replacing the old. One candidate, however, is emerging: relativism. It is a good candidate for several reasons. To begin with, because it is a response to the collapse of the great ideologies. And then because, as Tocqueville suggested, once everyone's opinions are adjudged to be as equally respectable as they are diverse, it will have to be accepted there can be neither truth nor objectivity. Relativism, argued Tocqueville, is the natural philosophy of "democratic" societies: liberal societies in our vocabulary. He saw that in the United States a cloud of opinions ("poussière d'opinions") forms around any subject, and his analytical instincts told him that this was linked to the "democratic" nature of American society: from the moment when all opinions count and that they diverge, it can be deduced that it is only by believing in an illusion that the actor can think that his convictions are objectively founded.

This argument is probably easier still to prove in a context of "globalisation", where the intense migratory movements unleashed by the disappearance of the two blocs that characterised the period of the cold war, the installation of culturally diverse groups within the nation-states of the western world, have increased their heterogeneity.

I believe that these factors characterising modern western societies have created a demand for theories that have made relativism fashionable. More precisely, this situation has created conditions favourable to the positive reception accorded to any theory that nourishes relativism. This demand has generated a corresponding supply from the social sciences. As a result, much of their output has helped to validate relativism.

This is how we can explain the success of what are sometimes known as the "new" sociologies. The "new sociology of science" tells us that science offers images of reality that must be understood as a range of possible constructions, and that the ideas of truth and objectivity are illusions. The "new sociology of art" sets out to disqualify the aesthetic principles which considers art works as objectively either sublime or mediocre, successes or failures. The "new sociology of norms" tends to see all norms through "culturalist" spectacles : each "culture" has its own norms and values.

Relativism argues that values have no objectivity. More exactly, it proposes that when an individual or a group puts forward a statement of the form "this or that institution is acceptable, legitimate, illegitimate, etc.", "this or that work of art is beautiful, ugly, overwhelming, etc." or "this or that theory is true, false, doubtful, etc.", and since their conviction cannot be the result of objectively established reasons (such as those which mean that two plus two equals four), it explains them by the action of socio-cultural, biological, or psychological forces. It is the common denominator of these currents of thought that traverse the social sciences and nourish relativism. Some of these currents hold that these forces emanate from cultures and that they impose on the individual his beliefs in respect of morality, aesthetics, and understanding of the world: they hold that the subject believes that "X is true, legitimate, good, doubtful, illegitimate, bad, etc." because that is what *is* believed within the culture to which he belongs. Other currents develop neo-Darwinian models and hold that cultures are made up of themes analogous to *genes*. They give these cultural genes the name of "memes" and posit a basic hypothesis, that individuals are essentially motivated by an irrational instinct of imitation. They have no hesitation in showing that these *memes* have a tendency to reproduce and diffuse themselves. As a general rule, in a number of models in use today within the social sciences, the individual is theorised as the point on which forces external to him are applied, and over which he has no control.

These explanatory models help, by their very nature, to validate relativism. If, indeed, values are the result of quasi-material forces whether these are social, cultural, biological or psychological, then they cannot be justified: they have, logically, the status of facts. It is possible to recognise their existence, but it is pointless to inquire about their causes. In the same way that a geologist determines that this particular patch of earth is clay and this other is chalk, an anthropologist observes that in one society circumcision is condemned, while it another it is approved. Such beliefs are facts for the anthropologist. No doubt the actors themselves have the impression that their beliefs are justified ; but this feeling is a cultural effect, argue the culturalists. This causalist concept of values, according to which the presence of value judgements in the mind of the social actor must be explained through the evocation of psychological, socio-cultural or biological forces, can only lead directly to relativism.

Two observations are pertinent here. The first is that if relativism is automatically produced by a causalist concept of human behaviour, this is not a concept that specialists in the social sciences employ because they are concerned to validate relativism. It is more like an unwanted consequence. If the causalist concept of behaviour tends to prevail in the social sciences, and is more general among the human sciences, it has more to do with the fact that researchers employ a narrow conception of science : they hold that all sciences, and more particularly the human sciences, since they have to prove their scientific nature, should have the objective of explaining all phenomena by material causes, or causes which can be considered as such. It is why the sociologist would prefer to explain a given behaviour by the environment of the subject, or the social structures or culture in which they live, rather than such impalpable "reasons". Indeed "reasons", that have no place in the explanation of physical phenomena, cannot, moreover, have any role to play in the explanation of human phenomena. This is why the social sciences so frequently tend to see the reasons that the actor gives for his behaviour as effects and not causes.

The second observation is that there are certainly some behaviours which can be explained in a causalist manner. The fact that I speak French better than English is of course the result of cultural forces. But it would be wrong to accept the strong if unlikely hypothesis that

I value democracy only because of my socialisation : simply because I have been taught at school and at home that democracy is a better system of government than any other. That is why I have difficulty in understanding why for example so much debate revolves around whether Dawkins' theory is preferable to sociobiology or any other "causalist" theory that seeks to account for cultural evolution. These theories might explain why the French speak French — hardly an enigmatic phenomenon — but not for instance why the death penalty has been abolished in the whole of Europe but not in the United States. I cannot see how causalist theories might explain a phenomenon of this type. They claim to be scientific theories of cultural evolution. One would expect of them that, as with any scientific theory, they would account in a convincing manner for phenomena which cannot be easily explained. Now it is easy to cite many examples of cultural data — such as the cultural differences I have just referred to — which it is difficult to believe that any causalist theory currently available in the market might be able to explain.

From relativism to nihilism and pessimism, there is only a single step. I believe that it is this relativism that explains the profound pessimism distilled in many theories put forward by the social sciences. Perhaps they also contribute to the general pessimism that seems to afflict all western nations. The secular religions of the 19th century were carriers of hope and proclaimers of progress. Today the word "progress" is filed away in the drawer marked "illusions". Even politicians avoid using it. Perhaps this is one of the causes of the "crisis of politics" that appears to afflict all of the western nations. For if the politician does not adopt progress as his objective, it is difficult to see how he can justify his actions. The word *progress* in particular is hardly ever used nowadays by sociologists, anthropologists and political scientists. This concept does not sit well with the notion that the ideas and behaviour of people might be the result of forces beyond their control. It is seen as incompatible with the generally accepted idea that a concept such as that of progress cannot be part of a theory claiming to be scientific. Perhaps not. But it is a fact that human behaviour is guided by the quest for progress: a fact that science cannot ignore. What is a science that decides to ignore certain facts? That Europeans consider the abolition of the death penalty as progress is a fact. The sociologist is obliged to take account of this and to explain it. He is also obliged to explain why such an abolition was hitherto considered to be undesirable, and why it still is today in other regions. Values are not facts. But when it is observed that a value is held in one context but not in another, this is a *fact* that can be observed, which it would not be illegitimate to try to explain scientifically.

As a result of the principles that now frequently guide the social sciences, and notably the causalist concept of human behaviour, they are involuntarily but undoubtedly responsible in part for the sense of depression that afflicts western societies.

It is understandable that the "new sociologies" of science, of norms or of art, that all present themselves as legitimations of a relativist conception of values and knowledge, should have experienced a certain success and I have just referred to some plausible reasons for such success. However, I do not believe that these new sociologies allow us to explain what they claim to explain. It is not because they are subject to socio-cultural, biological or psychological forces that social actors believe that a theory is true or false, that a work of art is beautiful or not, or that a norm is justified or not. Hence the critique presented here of "causalist" explanations of collective beliefs, particularly concerning values, from which an alternative theory can be developed that I suggest should be called "cognitive".

The "causalist" way of seeing that characterises the "new" sociologies I refer to here represents a rupture with the great lessons of classical sociology. For Weber, social actors believe what they believe, not because they are impelled by cultural forces, but because they have reasons to believe what they believe. The Roman centurion preferred the Mithraic cult to traditional religion because it seemed to be a more accurate translation, in symbolic form, of the world as he perceived it (Weber, 1920–1921). Durkheim (1979[1912]) explains that the Australian magician believes in the efficacy of the raindance because of a cognitive process with analogies to those that would make a contemporary scientist believe in this or that scientific theory. He is not impelled by any force: he has reasons to believe what he believes, given the social context in which he finds himself.

If we follow this critique of causalism to its conclusions, it is possible to find not just a more convincing explanation of collective beliefs and more generally of behaviour, but also an avoidance of relativism. Escaping relativism is also an escape from pessimism. I place a strong reliance on Weber and Durkheim to try to show this.

These writers outlined a theory of moral evolution that is hardly evident today, so great is the tendency to read them only through the spectacles of contemporary relativism. This theory of moral evolution is wholly different to the historicist theories that history itself has condemned. But the disqualification of historicism does not mean that the idea of evolution is invalid, and nor, moreover, is that of progress. This is a conclusion that I have also sought to emphasise.

If one simply returns to a point where the *homo sociologicus* of the liberal tradition, that of Adam Smith, de Tocqueville, Weber and also Durkheim, is placed at the heart of the social sciences, it is possible to provide a much more satisfying explanation of feelings, beliefs and collective behaviour. Not only is it possible to offer a coherent theory of collective feelings about a wide range of values, but also to use the data about them from a number of surveys. Many types of survey are currently carried out that attempt to explore the public's moral sentiments about a number of subjects. They are in general under-utilised and seen as purely descriptive, but sociology should, like any science, be as much concerned with explanation as observation. It should be important not only to determine how *many* persons think X or Y, but also to explain *why* they do so. Many examples of the efficacy of the cognitive theory of values will be cited here that explain the results of empirical observation.

The essential question for contemporary social science comes down, in one word, to that of the question of what method to use to explain collective behaviour, beliefs and feelings. "Causalist" explanations, those which place social, cultural or biological forces at the origin of behaviour, beliefs or feelings, are considered natural by contemporary sociology and anthropology. This causalist *a priori* may perhaps be one of the main causes of the sense of fragmentation surrounding the human sciences, and more particularly the social sciences, today. By contrast the scale of the analyses of de Tocqueville, of Weber, of Simmel, of Evans Pritchard and other great classics of the social sciences, the fact that their work indisputably increased our knowledge, is due in large part because they refused to accept that "causalism" was axiomatic. The importance and the implications of the Weberian idea of *understanding* (*Verstehen*) have not been given sufficient attention. To propose the idea that any action, attitude or behaviour is in principle understandable, is to propose that the *meaning for the actor* of his action, his attitude, or his behaviour is its *cause* : that the reasons he has to do what he does, to believe what he believes, to feel what he feels are the causes of his actions, beliefs or attitudes. All of the analyses of Weber himself, but also of Tocqueville, of Simmel or of Durkheim, if I confine myself only to the giants of classical sociology, follow this principle. Weber and Simmel apply it directly, Tocqueville does so instinctively; Durkheim even applies it against his own preconceptions.

It must be said that the relativism so naturally secreted by the social sciences is not without consequences. The ideas about humanity and society of politicians and their media commentators don't just drop from the skies. The human sciences are the reservoir from which they are more usually drawn nowadays. They fulfil today what in the past was the role of religions. The extent to which the new religious idiosyncracies are often constituted through their borrowings from the religious universe can even be measured, as shown for example by all of those intellectual movements that owe their success to combining elements taken from Buddhism, Hinduism or Christianity, and to which are added those from other sources, drawn from psychoanalysis, Marxism or other intellectual movements, that have appeared within the social sciences.

To sum up in a phrase the argument of this book, it is this: the social sciences have undoubtedly made some major contributions, but have also, in recent decades in particular, contributed to the establishment of ill-founded and questionable ideas that have not been without social and political effects.

Amartya Sen has written somewhere that the human sciences have often made the mistake of representing the social subject as a *rational idiot*. He was thinking about the *homo oeconomicus* that figures so largely in economic theory and game theory. The social sciences owe the unsatisfactory state they are in today to the fact that the *homo sociologicus* to which they devote so much attention, without being truly conscious of the fact, might on his side be described as an *irrational idiot*. Clearly, it is not without reason that economic theorists and game theorists made *homo oeconomicus* a *rational idiot*. Sensing that the model of the *irrational idiot* was inadequate, some writers have sought salvation in the application of the model of the *rational idiot* to sociology. The result of these discussions has been general confusion (Boudon, 2003a).

When confusion arises, it is best to turn to methodical critique. Perhaps it is the moment to understand that the subject that is evoked by all the social sciences in their widest sense, economics as much as sociology, may avoid the dilemma : *rational idiot* vs *irrational idiot*.

This point is even more important because the confusion evident in the social sciences is, as a result of their influence, evident in social and political life as well. It is not uncommon to see an opinion pollster use the results of a survey to see whether political corruption is an important public issue without taking proper account of its meaning. If the question is posed such as "What is most important for you? Policies for reducing unemployment, for reducing political corruption, etc." and the percentage of those choosing the former is greater than for those choosing the latter, the political scientist may deduce – scientifically, as he might think, but also somewhat naively in fact – that the public are not concerned about corruption. On the basis of this "scientific" result, and the advice of an "expert", politicians may feel encouraged to limit the legal controls on anti-corruption measures, at the same evincing surprise at the appearance of a persistent and serious "crisis of politics". In this case the citizen is, for the opinion-pollster and subsequently the politician, an *irrational idiot*. His opinions are the result, both believe, of the action of psychological or socio-cultural forces. They can only be seen as data that has been recorded but without any attempt at understanding.

The first chapter ("The Social Sciences and the Two Types of Relativism") develops the idea that the social sciences have contributed to the credibility of two types of relativism: cognitive and cultural relativism. They constitute basic ingredients of postmodernism. Why have they been seen as credible? Dubious ideas are often "hyperbolic", or exaggerated and distorted versions of true ideas. Cognitive relativism is based on the failure of the objectivity sought by the Vienna Circle and by Popper, by attempts at identifying the demarcation line between science and non-science, and on the work of post-Popperian philosophers of science, such as Kuhn. Cognitive relativism draws "hyperbolic" conclusions from these two sources. Cultural relativism has been legitimated by similarly "hyperbolic" conclusions drawn notably from certain basic concepts in the work of Montaigne, Hume and Max Weber. The influence of these hyperbolic conclusions is also due to the fact that they have been introduced to the intellectual "market" in a situation where they have been perceived by various audiences as "useful" in Pareto's sense. Once this deconstruction is made, the two forms of relativism appear as less solidly grounded than they look and as less credible than postmodernists in particular believe.

The second chapter ("The Polytheism of Values") begins with the idea according to which we live in a world characterised by what Max Weber termed a "polytheism of values". This concept is often read as supporting the relativist vision of the world, so influential nowadays. It seems to me that it would be a complete misunderstanding of the celebrated metaphors on the "polytheism of values" and "wars of the gods" to make a relativist reading of them. What must however be emphasised is that the relativism thought to be present in these metaphors is contradicted by the evidence: the observers have on many subjects strong and convergent moral sentiments. The influence of the relativist vision of the world nowadays may, nevertheless, be understood, and on this matter Tocqueville put forward some interesting hypotheses. Relativism has also emerged because of the weakness of the philosophies that attempt to oppose it: they have difficulty accounting for temporal and spatial differences in values and moral sentiments. By following Tocqueville and Weber, it is possible to set out a theory that enables us to simultaneously both avoid the relativist view according to which values cannot be objectively based and the theories that give values an objective base but are unable to account for their spatial and temporal variability.

The third chapter ("Basic Mechanisms of Moral Evolution: In the Footsteps of Durkheim and Weber") stresses the point that the issue of the evolution of norms and values is a basic one in the history of the social sciences, from Durkheim to Parsons, Hayek or Shmuel Eisenstadt. The thesis I submit here is that it is possible, by developing a number of core intuitions of Durkheim and Weber, to identify a few basic mechanisms responsible for moral evolution. Both Weber and Durkheim laid the foundations of a theory of moral evolution that is resistant to the objections raised by Popper against historicism. Also, it provides an alternative to "postmodern" relativism. To "postmodern" sociologists and philosophers, the idea of progress is clearly unfounded; postmodern sociology shows that values cannot be objectively grounded; that the idea of the "objectivity" of values is a mere illusion. The theory I propose to extract from Durkheim and Weber also has the capacity to overcome the objections raised against important modern theories of moral evolution, such as Hayek's. Eisenstadt's concept of "program" appears as implicitly present in Durkheim and Weber's theories of moral evolution as I propose to reconstruct and develop it here.

The fourth chapter ("Explaining Axiological Feelings") starts from the observation that, while moral feelings are an essential topic of classical sociology, as the work of Weber and Durkheim illustrates, this topic has to a large extent disappeared from contemporary sociology. I propose here a "cognitive" theory of moral feelings. It can also be called "judicatory": a qualification rightly given to Adam Smith's theory of moral sentiments by Max. Following Smith, moral sentiments are closely linked to moral statements that are the conclusions of systems of arguments more or less consciously present in the mind of individuals. Smith sketched a theory which is able to take into account the variability of moral sentiments: an insuperable difficulty for contractual, rational or intuitionist theories of moral feelings. The power of this theory for empirical social research is illustrated by several examples. The systems of arguments on which moral statements are grounded in the mind of individuals include empirical and decisional statements as well as principles. The question then is to identify the basis on which the credibility of these principles is grounded. Max Weber has sketched an answer to this question: these principles are fuzzy regulatory ideas, the content of which becomes more precise under the effect of a process of "diffuse rationalisation".

As the fifth chapter ("On the Objectivity of Artistic Values") shows, contemporary sociology of art is relativist. Two types of theory are dominant: the theory that holds that artistic values are explained by how they function as forms of distinction in the social class system; and the theory that the milieux known as "art worlds" have the ability to impose their artistic values on public taste. These two types of theory are relativist in character: artistic values are attitudinal phenomena created by social forces. These conceptions are put forward as alternatives to the Platonic theory of artistic values that characterises traditional esthetics. Against these conceptions, it is possible to propose a cognitive theory of artistic values. It is based on the notion that there are objectively based reasons for preferring one work of art to another, while accepting that such reasons may vary over time and space. In the second part of the chapter, a theory that explains certain particularities of contemporary art is put forward: why has Duchamp become the equal of Rembrandt in the painting hierarchy? Why are the White Squares of Malevitch considered to be significant works?

The sixth chapter ("The Devaluation of Common Sense") begins with the observation that common sense has acquired a very poor reputation in the social sciences. This devaluation of common sense can be explained to a great extent by the same causes that explain the establishment of relativism. Relativism and the devaluation of common sense are in this sense two sides of the same coin. Each derives more precisely from the attempt by a number of tendencies within the social sciences to naturalise the human being. Interpreting his

actions, beliefs, sentiments as in the first instance the effects of psychological, biological or socio-cultural forces, they can only ignore the
reasons that he gives for his actions, beliefs or feelings. More precisely
they tend to consider his reasons as effects rather than causes, and to
see those reasons as fallacious. This concluding chapter thus allows
a certain number of themes developed in the earlier chapters to be
drawn together.

Finally, it may be helpful to enlighten the reader as to the source of
these texts. As I have noted elsewhere (Boudon 2003b), I have never managed to write without being asked to do so. The starting points for these
six chapters were requests, mainly for papers to scientific congresses
and contributions and to special numbers of academic journals. The
form of the original texts was fundamentally revised during the writing
of the present volume, with the objective of clarifying the coherence of
the ideas originally appearing in a number of different contributions.
However, I also made sure not to eliminate certain repetitions, so that
each of the chapters would stand independently from the others and
would thus enable the reader to approach them in any order.

The original version of chapter 1 was published as "The social sciences and the two types of relativism", in E. Ben-Rafael (ed.), *Sociology
and ideology*, Leiden–Boston, Brill, 2003; of chapter 2 as "Les valeurs
dans un monde polythéiste", in M. de Sève and S. Langlois (eds), *Savoir
et responsabilité*, Quebec, Canada, Nota bene, 1999. The first version
of chapter 3 was a communication given at the occasion of a conference in homage to Shmuel Noah Eisenstadt, held at Jerusalem, 2–4
November 2003. That of chapter 4 was published with the collaboration
of Emmanuelle Betton as "Explaining the feelings of justice", *Ethical
Theory and Moral Practice. An International Forum*, 1999. A first version of the first part of chapter 5 was published as "De l'objectivité des
valeurs artistiques" in *Archives de Philosophie du Droit*, 40, 1995; of the
second part in *Pourquoi les intellectuels n'aiment pas le libéralisme*,
Paris, Odile Jacob, 2004. The initial version of chapter 6 was given as a
communication at the occasion of a colloquium on "Le sens commun"
organised by the University of Burgundy, Dijon, May 2–3, 2002.

REFERENCES

Boudon, R. (2003a) "Beyond Rational Choice Theory". *Annual Review of Sociology*,
    29: 1–21.

—— (2003b) *Y a-t-il encore une sociologie?* Paris, Odile Jacob.

—— (2004) *Pourquoi les intellectuels n'aiment pas le libéralisme.* Paris, Odile Jacob.

Durkheim, E. (1979[1912]) *Les Formes élémentaires de la vie religieuse.* Paris, Presses Universitaires de France.

Weber, M. (1920–1921) *Gesammelte Aufsätze zur Religionssoziologie.* Tübingen, Mohr.

1
The Social Sciences and the Two Types of Relativism

I. COGNITIVE RELATIVISM

In the last thirty years, social sciences have contributed greatly to making relativism credible, in its two main forms: cognitive and cultural. One might even assert that relativism represents one of the most basic theses of contemporary sociology and anthropology and that they owe to this thesis a good part of their influence. Relativism is a basic dimension of postmodernism. Contemporary social sciences have played an important role in the legitimisation of relativism. Should we believe cognitive relativists when they assert that knowledge is a construction which cannot aim at being objective and that theories have necessarily the character of "interpretations", always arbitrary to some extent? Should we believe cultural relativists when they assert that norms and values are culture-dependent and cannot be objectively grounded? While relativism has always been, since Protagoras, a philosophical tradition among others, it seems to have become a dominant worldview in intellectual circles. Where does the influence of these two forms of relativism come from? Are they promised to the same future? Here are the questions I would like to explore. I will deal with cognitive relativism firstly and secondly with cultural relativism. I will evidently not try to treat this complex subject in its full extension, but rather concentrate my attention on some important sociocognitive mechanisms responsible for the popularity of the two forms of relativism.

Kuhn's Role

An important source of cognitive relativism is the "new sociology of science", an intellectual tradition which was started by Kuhn's work (1962) on *The Structure of Scientific Revolutions*. More than any other, this small book has given an entirely new orientation to the sociology of science. As initiated by Durkheim (1979[1912]) in his *Elementary Forms of Religious Life* and developed by modern writers, such as Ben David or Merton among many others, the sociology of science did not convey any relativistic message until Kuhn's book was published and gave the sociology of science an entirely new turn.

The "classical" sociology of science, the sociology of science that was developed from Durkheim to Kuhn exclusively dealt with such questions as the extrascientific origin of scientific concepts, as when Durkheim (1979[1912]) wondered where the notion of force came from; it dealt with the role of institutions in scientific productivity, as when Ben David and Zloczower (1962) wondered why Germany was so important in many scientific fields in the 19th century; it dealt with the impact on the development of science of ideas developed in non-scientific spheres, as when Merton (1970[1938]) analysed the impact of Puritanism on the development of science. None of these writers held the view that the existence of an impact of non-scientific factors, intellectual or institutional, on science would imply that scientific theories would be unable to be objectively valid. All were convinced that one scientific theory can be objectively better than another; none of them contended that magical or religious explanations of the world should be placed on the same footing as scientific explanations.

After the publication of Kuhn's *Structure of Scientific Revolutions*, the sociology of science took a new turn. Kuhn's main thesis was that the history of sciences is much less linear than philosophers of science had maintained up to and including Popper. The detailed analysis of scientific discussions shows, he maintained rightly, that they are less "rational" than philosophers of science have asserted. He stressed the idea that, beside logical criteria, aesthetic, political, religious or ideological factors could also play a role in the fact that a scientist prefers one theory to another. This point had always been recognised. Thus, religious considerations have dictated in the past the attitude of many scientists toward Darwinism. This point has been studied in the case of France for instance by Buican (1984). He has shown that, in the years after the Second World War, religious considerations still affected the attitude of biologists toward Darwinism. Thus, the hostility of a well established and recognised biologist teaching at the Collège de France was still dictated by his religious beliefs in the years after World War II. It is well known that Marxism interfered with the convictions of many biologists on biological issues. The interference of religious or philosophical ideas on scientific beliefs is even more apparent in the case of the social and generally the human sciences. But nobody would have agreed to generalise Kuhn's point and to maintain that, since some individuals can, in given circumstances, prefer a scientific theory for extrascientific reasons, all scientific theories would in all circumstances be accepted or rejected on the basis of extrascientific reasons. Kuhn did not draw this conclusion himself. But it was quickly drawn by his followers.

Some years after Kuhn's work appeared, Feyerabend (1975) went as far as to maintain that scientific theories could be "fairy tales". The French sociologist Latour (1978) went even further: scientific explanations are constructions and, as we see the world through these constructions, we cannot compare the images of the world they deliver with a "reality out there" we have no access to. Latour in fact paraphrased Nietzsche's famous formula according to which there would be "no facts, but merely interpretations". But, thanks to the word "construction", the French *constructivistes* gave the impression they had invented a new insightful and well grounded theory of knowledge. On the whole, thanks to the magical character of the word "construction", constructivism in France and social constructionism in the English-speaking world became a focus of attention in the 1980's. The constructivists and the social constructionists maintained that, as "knowing" means asserting some statement about some topic using words and other linguistic tools, we have no access to reality as it really is.

Thus, Gusfield (1981) maintained in his *Driving or Drinking* that, as the relationship between drinking and automobile accidents is demonstrated by using such tools as the correlation coefficients invented by statisticians, it is "constructed" and thus should not be considered as a "fact". Rorty (1979) stressed that knowledge is not a "mirror of nature". This point had been recognised for a long time: at least since Kant, who had developed the idea that we see the world through a priori forms and categories. Rorty's very acceptable ideas were received as a revelation rather than as a well established point, however, because of the relativistic conclusions that were generally drawn from them: since knowledge is not a mirror of nature, there is no objective knowledge, no knowledge describing the reality as it is. As knowledge is a construction, several constructions can be devised of the same sectors of reality; they can be incompatible with one another and still be rightly presented as contributions to "knowledge". Hence, there is no objective knowledge. Such conclusions did not derive necessarily from Rorty's arguments, which reproduced with new words well known classical philosophical arguments from which no relativistic conclusions had been derived. My guess is that these relativistic conclusions could be drawn because Kuhn had instilled in many minds the idea that the very notion of an objective knowledge is an illusion.

Why has this cognitive relativism become common knowledge in some circles? Why has it taken extreme forms? The starting point of this process derives from the fact that Kuhn had developed his views on science on the basis of scholarly historical monographs on various controversies, such as the controversy on the phlogiston theory in the 18th century. It is true that the arguments of the believers and non-believers in the theory are far from being exclusively rational. They are far from the principles described, say, by Popper's "critical rationalism". It is true, moreover, that textbooks in the history or philosophy of science describe the scientific discussions of the past as rational: that they seem to be inspired by the rational philosophy of science developed notably by Popper; that they describe the scientists of the past as substituting a theory for an earlier theory as soon as it is falsified by some newly observed facts.

Thus, it is understandable that, although his main thesis can easily appear as common sense, Kuhn gives the impression of proposing a revolution in the current views about science. The revolution he had started rested on a robust core: the historically well confirmed fact that the selection process of scientific theories is less rational than stated by classical history and philosophy of sciences.

From the Vienna Circle to Popper

A second factor can be mentioned which helps to explain Kuhn's influence as well as the radicalisation of his ideas by his followers: the failures experienced by the philosophers of science. Kuhn appeared as revolutionary and sound, not only because he developed a view of science contradictory with the classical view and because his view was perceived as more realistic, but also because, at the time when he published his theses, the philosophy of science seemed blocked in a deadlock, as I will try to suggest with the help of a sketchy summary of a highly complex, long and dense debate.

The modern philosophy of science starts with the work produced by the Vienna Circle. The philosophers of the Vienna Circle raised in particular one question: on the basis of which criteria can a scientific theory be distinguished from a non-scientific one? Where can the demarcation line be drawn? The best known answer is Carnap's at one stage of his reflection: a scientific theory is a theory which, once it is made entirely explicit, turns out to be composed, at least in principle, of a set of statements being mere assertions on uncontroversial states of the world: empirical elementary assertions of the type "this pen is black".

This answer has been criticised. Popper (1968[1934]) proposed, as is well known, another demarcation line between science and non-science: the falsification criterion. A theory is scientific, according to Popper, if it can be contradicted – falsified – by observational data. This criterion has been widely considered acceptable, though more in non-philosophical than in philosophical circles. True, the phlogiston theory can be more easily contradicted than, say, Leibniz's monadology. The fact that the former was falsified and *a fortiori* falsifiable has to be correlated with the strong impression that, though false, it belongs to the history of science, while Leibniz' monadology does not. According to Popper, no theory can be qualified as true. The notion of verisimilitude should be substituted for the notion of truth. A theory is verisimilar when it has successfully passed all the empirical tests it has been exposed to and when it appears to have no competitor. But, as competitors may appear and as the theory can fail before a new test, verisimilitude can at best be a provisional attribute of a scientific theory.

In spite of the intellectual modesty of Popper's theory, it has been shown in the course of a long debate that it captures in an unsatisfactory fashion the distinction between a scientific and a non-scientific theory. For several reasons which can be sketchily summarised in the following way, the falsification criterion is not an adequate criterion of the demarcation line between science and non-science:

— Firstly, because many falsifiable statements will not normally be considered as scientific, such as the statement "the train from Paris to London is leaving at 8:47".
— Secondly, because many theories normally considered as scientific cannot be falsified, such as the theories produced by economists which introduce the clause "all other things being equal" without proposing any clear means on the basis of which one can be sure

that "other things" are actually "equal". For, if such a theory appears as not congruent with some data, the reason can be that the theory is false, but also that the "other things" are not "equal". As many theories, not only in the field of economics but in other fields as well, introduce currently, more or less implicitly, the clause that "other things are held as equal", most theories are in fact not falsifiable. True, the joke "let us suppose the weight of the elephant negligible, then ..." is generally applied to economic theories, but equivalent jokes have been devised in the case of physics: "let us suppose this piece of metal infinitely thin, then ..."

But more serious objections can be raised against Popper's theory. The falsification criterion cannot be considered as defining the demarcation between science and non-science:

— Thirdly, because some scientific theories do not bear on actual phenomena, but have rather the status of metatheories dealing with the question how to explain phenomena of a given class. Thus, the neo-Darwinian theory of evolution deals with the way evolutionary facts should be explained and states that they should be explained as the effects of mutation and selection. Because of their very status, such theories cannot be falsified for the obvious reason that a piece of advice cannot properly be falsified: it can be considered useful or not, acceptable or not, etc., but it cannot be falsified. Popper himself saw clearly that the neo-Darwinian theory of evolution was scientific though not falsifiable and devoted much reflection to the question, but he did not go as far, to my knowledge at least, as to recognise that neo-Darwinism is an element of a class of scientific theories which disqualified his falsification theory.

— Fourthly, a crucial point of Popper's theory is that it introduces a strong asymmetry between truth and falsity. According to Popper, a scientific theory can be falsifiable and shown to be false, but it is never verifiable and can never be demonstrated to be true. Though, as the so-called Duhem–Quine thesis states, it is not easier to be convinced that a theory is false than to be convinced that it is true. Once it has been shown that a theory is able to explain a number of phenomena and fails to explain a new phenomenon, the theory will normally not be rejected, as the history of science as well as theoretical analysis shows. It is easy to understand why. As it is impossible to know in advance which part of a theory is responsible for the incongruence between data and theory, a normal reaction of the scientist is to bet that the theory can be amended on some of its more or less minor aspects in order to reconcile the theory with the data. The scientist will be reluctant to reject a theory of which it has been shown that it explains many facts simply because a new fact is not explained by the theory. So, the normal reaction of the concerned scientist will be to forge auxiliary assumptions in order to reconcile the theory with the new fact. And this strategy often works, as the classical example of Leverrier shows, when he introduced the assumption that the deviation of a planet from the course predicted by celestial mechanics was due to the presence of a yet unknown planet. Leverrier did not reject celestial mechanics, a theory which had been immensely successful in explaining all kinds of movements of the celestial bodies. He rather introduced an auxiliary assumption able to reconcile the theory with the data: he started from the strong impression that a theory such as celestial mechanics which had succeeded in explaining so many things could not be false. So there are no simple criteria on the basis of which a scientist can state that a theory is false. It is not easier to qualify a theory as false than to qualify it as true. Hence the falsification criterion cannot as such be considered as providing a clear distinction between science and non-science.

— Fifthly, a scientific theory contains concepts which have the status of constructs. Some concepts are considered as acceptable in a scientific theory, some are not. The concept of force is considered as acceptable, and the concept of God not. Why? The falsification criterion is of no help here, since none of these concepts is empirical. Still we have no doubt that the former is acceptable, while the latter is not.

In summary, the intellectual conjuncture of the 1960's and of the following decades is characterised on the one hand by the broad attention granted to Kuhn's theory according to which the selection of scientific ideas is less rational than described by textbooks in the history and philosophy of science and, on the other hand, by a growing scepticism about the idea that it would be possible to draw a clear demarcation line between science and non-science.

Misusing the Law of the Excluded Middle
When a number is odd, it cannot be even. The two terms are contradictory. By contrast, when a pen is not black, that does not mean that it

is white. "Black" and "white" are contrary, not contradictory terms. A pen can also, say, be brown.

The "no middle term principle" is often misused in the sense that contrary terms are held as contradictory. As already noted by Pareto (1964–1988[(1916]), the confusion between "contrary" and "contradictory" is a basic cognitive mechanism responsible for many false beliefs. It is responsible for the fact that many discussions have a "binary" character: liberalism or socialism? Materialism or idealism? This is the case here: the basic question behind the works of the "new sociology of science" and behind the *constructiviste* or constructionist doctrine can be formulated: is the selection of scientific ideas rational or not? Do I believe that a scientific theory is a valid representation of the world on the basis of objective convincing reasons or not? The "new sociology of science" answers: as Kuhn has shown that the selection of scientific ideas puts into play irrational motivations, they are not rational. Another question underlying the "new sociology of science" is: can a clear demarcation line be drawn between science and non-science or not? If it cannot, then the distinction between science and non-science is an illusion. Hence some, like Feyerabend (1975) or Hübner (1985), went as far as to conclude that myths are as valid as scientific explanations of the world. The misuse of the law of the extended middle led from the acceptable views of Kuhn to much more radically relativistic views of science, such as Feyerabend's.

Scheler's Floodgates and Pareto's Distinction Between "Truth" and "Usefulness"

Another factor is responsible for the influence of cognitive relativism. Max Scheler (1926) stated that, in some circumstances, an idea can go through virtual floodgates, while in others it cannot: other things being equal, an idea will more likely be accepted if it is congruent with the *Zeitgeist* or with some collective interests. Pareto (1914–1988[(1916]) indicated in the same vein that an idea can become accepted and influential, not necessarily because it is "true", but because it is "useful". In other words, an idea can be accepted essentially because it serves cognitive and/or ideological interests. Scheler and Pareto identified through these notions and distinctions a basic mechanism through which ideological beliefs are generated.

The mechanism identified by these notions is crucial from the point of view of the sociology of ideas. Let me note incidentally that

I prefer the expression sociology of ideas to the expression created by Mannheim (1954), sociology of knowledge, which I always found unfortunate. Knowledge is a success word, in Ryle's vocabulary: in the same way as a theorem cannot be false, knowledge means valid or genuine knowledge, while ideas can be right or wrong, true or false. Now the so-called sociology of knowledge is concerned with false as well as true ideas.

Scheler's and Pareto's mechanism explains in many cases and to a large extent why false ideas are collectively endorsed. It is relevant here. The relativistic view of science produced by the "new sociology of science" (Bunge, 1999) is developed in an intellectual conjuncture when, in the US, the collusion between science, politics and the Pentagon became a strong public issue, especially in intellectual circles. This collusion would imply that the real political power is not in the hands of the democratic institutions. Consequently, Scheler's floodgates were at that time wide open to theories which, like Kuhn's or Feyerabend's, showed that the authority of scientists is less legitimate than it is generally considered. Kuhn himself was probably not clearly aware that his theory would be "useful" to those who were concerned with the anti-democratic bias in the structure of American political power as they saw it. He took, perhaps unwillingly, benefit from the convergence of his views with ideological interests.

The theories developed by the new sociology of science were not only "useful" in Pareto's sense; they also appeared "true". It seemed as clear that no criteria able to draw a clear demarcation line between science and non-science could be found, and that the selection of scientific ideas was much less rational than textbooks claimed. For all these reasons, cognitive relativism became a dominant philosophical view on science, notably among sociologists around the world.

Simple as it is, this scenario explains the growing radicalisation of cognitive relativism from Kuhn to Feyerabend in America or Latour in France and its influence. From the viewpoint of the sociology of ideas, this scenario has, moreover, the interest of identifying a typical mechanism, i.e. a mechanism which appears as being at work, not only in the particular case of the intellectual post-modern turn in the direction of cognitive relativism, but in many other cases as well. This mechanism explains the excessive credibility granted to many other ideas or theories, as I will try to show with the case of cultural relativism: the second example I will present in the second part of this chapter.

The mechanism develops according to a sequence of three phases:

— Phase 1: it starts with the mobilisation of objectively credible core ideas (as in the case of cognitive relativism the idea that textbooks give too simple a representation of the selection of scientific ideas or that it is impossible to determine precise demarcation criteria between science and non-science);

— Phase 2: these core ideas are then hyperbolised thanks to devices currently used in ordinary knowledge, such as the confusion between contrary and contradictory terms;

— Phase 3: finally, the hyperboles will probably become popular if, as well as seeming credible, they also appear as "useful" to some audiences: in this case, Scheler's floodgates will be wide open before them.

But the sociology of ideas has not only to explain how doubtful ideas or theories are born and become widely accepted. It has also to explain why and how they become rejected.

The Decline of the New Sociology of Science

The new sociology of science is no longer as influential as it was. Why? Durkheim (1979[1912]: 624) argued in his *Elementary Forms of Religious Life* that it often occurs that in a first stage an idea is accepted by most individuals because it is collectively accepted, while in a second stage it is collectively accepted only provided it can be held as objectively grounded: "we examine its claims to be objectively grounded before we believe in it" [*Le concept qui, primitivement, est tenu pour vrai parce qu'il est collectif tend à ne devenir collectif qu'à condition d'être tenu pour vrai: nous lui demandons ses titres avant de lui accorder notre créance*].

The case of the "modern sociology of science" illustrates the importance of this idea. Cognitive relativism was initially held as true because its main intuitions were collectively accepted, notably among sociologists of science. In France for instance, even at the end of the 20th century, it was difficult to have an article printed in a journal dealing with the sociology of science if the article did not pay allegiance to cognitive relativism. Doubts on the solidity of the "new sociology of science" appeared from the moment when Sokal, a physicist, had the idea of submitting to a professional journal devoted to the "new sociology of science" a paper defending the views of the "new sociology of science", but containing a number of statements and equations which were mere nonsense for any educated physicist. The paper was published without hesitation, however. Sokal's successful hoax contributed a great deal to discrediting the "new sociology of science" (Sokal and Bricmont, 1997). Today, even in France, few people beside the sociologists of science themselves care about the "new sociology of science" and its relativistic stance. This change is probably due to the mechanism described by Durkheim; thanks to Sokal's hoax, its claims appeared as ungrounded. Two arguments are essentially responsible for this disqualification.

1) As rightly stated by Kuhn, the selection process of scientific ideas is in the short term much less rational than textbook writers assume. It is true that the debates about phlogiston theory contained all kinds of arguments, some more political and aesthetic than properly scientific. But textbooks are right in the long term. Lavoisier's theory of the composition of air is objectively more solidly grounded than Priestley's phlogiston theory. But this certainty emerged in the long term, while in the short term, Priestley's arguments were credible. Priestley's arguments were not yet definitely superseded by the objectively better arguments developed by Lavoisier. If the distinction between the short and the long term is neglected, it becomes possible to ask whether the selection of scientific theories is rational or not: under this condition, middle terms are excluded. By contrast, as soon as the distinction is maintained, the question as to whether the selection of scientific ideas is rational or not becomes meaningless, since the selection can be rational in the long term and include irrational elements in the short term. I have developed this point more extensively in Boudon (1994).

2) The same argument can be developed as far as the question of the demarcation criteria between science and non-science is concerned. They were not found. From Carnap to Popper, nobody succeeded in providing clear criteria on the basis of which it would be possible to distinguish a scientific from a non-scientific theory. But, as Kant noted, a statement or a theory can be held as true, in spite of the fact that there are no general criteria of truth. There are no general criteria of truth, but we can judge that one theory is definitely more acceptable than another. Thus, Torricelli's and Pascal's theory of the phenomenon which later gave birth to the barometer is more acceptable than the theory of Aristotelian inspiration. It does not introduce the idea of the *horror vacui naturae*; it explains why the behaviour of the "barometer" depends on the altitude at which it is located. Applied to the demarcation question, this remark says that we can be confident that one theory is better than another on the basis of robust reasons and hold it provisionally as true, even though there are no general cri-

teria of truth, or of falsity. Generalising Kant's suggestion, one can state that the fact that there are no general criteria on the basis of which a theory would be considered as true or false, scientific or not, etc. does not exclude that we can be confident on the basis of particular criteria that it is true or false, scientific or not, etc. These criteria are particular in the sense that they will be used when comparing T1 and T2, but not in comparing T3 and T4. Thus, Pascal and Torricelli's theory of the barometer effect is better than the Aristotelian theory notably because it replaces a conjectural–nonempirical anthropomorphic factor (the horror vacui naturae) by an empirical factor (the weight of atmosphere). This criterion has some generality in the sense that it will be used also in comparisons between other pairs of theories, say Ti and Tj. But it is not truly general in the sense that it will not be used in many other comparisons. Thus, it is not used when we compare the theory according to which dinosaurs and ammonites disappeared because a meteorite struck the Earth to the various theories according to which they have been replaced by other better adapted species.

In other words, the fact that there are no demarcation criteria does not lead to the conclusion that the distinction between science and non-science is illegitimate. This analysis can be generalised: the fact that it is hard to provide general criteria describing the distinction, say, between classical and popular music does not imply that the distinction is illegitimate. There are no general criteria of truth and falsity, no general criteria thanks to which scientific could be nicely distinguished from non-scientific theories, no general criteria distinguishing popular from classical music. But we can decide with certainty on the basis of definite criteria whether a theory is better than its competitors, whether a given theory is scientific or whether a given piece of music is classical.

On the whole, the decline of the "new sociology of science" is probably an effect of the mechanism identified by Durkheim. We realise clearly now that the cognitive relativism it supports is ill-founded. Sokal's hoax has accelerated the process. But it worked because the "new sociology of science" was unable to defend its claims against the arguments which had been opposed to it.

II. CULTURAL RELATIVISM

Cultural relativism should be distinguished from cognitive relativism from several points of view. Cognitive relativism is a collective belief in a narrow corporation: the "new sociologists of science". Their influence is presently limited to narrow circles. Cultural relativism is by contrast much more influential. It has become a received idea that is very widespread among intellectuals. It seems that it is less influential in the general public, but also that it is not without influence on politicians.

In spite of these differences between the two forms of relativism, it is important to see that the two of them have a common feature. On this point, my diagnosis is different from Aya's (2001). In the two cases, the ideas summarised by the labels "cognitive" and "cultural relativism" have become established under the effect of the general mechanism I have described in the case of the former. To repeat, the components of this mechanism are: the existence of hard-core ideas; and the derivation of hyperbolic conclusions from these core ideas with the help of some implicit *a priori* such as the law of the excluded middle. These components have the effect of making the hyperbolic conclusions credible. A third component helps the diffusion of these conclusions: it operates when the hyperbolic conclusions appear as "useful", i.e. as congruent with collective material or symbolic interests.

I will start with the core ideas. Cultural relativism is based among other ideas on three core ideas to which three great names can be associated: Montaigne, David Hume and Max Weber. They have greatly inspired modern analysts: philosophers as well as anthropologists, political scientists or sociologists. Other core ideas will be discussed in chapter 6.

Core Idea 1: Montaigne

The prominent American anthropologist Clifford Geertz (1984) is the author of an influential article entitled "Anti-anti-relativism". The article rests explicitly on a famous chapter of Montaigne's *Essays*: the "apologie de Raymond Sebond". Montaigne's thesis in this text was summarised by a well-known formula of Pascal's, "What is this truth which mountains border, that is lie to those beyond?" (plaisante justice qu'une rivière borne, qui est vérité en deçà et mensonge au-delà). Montaigne writes in a time of religious conflicts. His objective in this chapter was plausibly above all of a political character: he wanted to suggest indirectly that, as ethical truths are different from one culture to another, there is no religious truth either. Incidentally, it can be noted that Montaigne does not write "culture", a word which did not exist in our sense in his time, but "nation", a word of his time which means approximately "culture" in our modern parlance. Montaigne's aim is probably on the whole to suggest that, since moral truths are different from one culture to another, Protestants and Catholics have no reason to fight against one another (Popkin, 1979). But Geertz is not interested by the historical context in which Montaigne wrote.

Geertz' attention has probably been attracted by passages from Montaigne like the following. It states that, to Montaigne, culture is for men second nature: "It is credible that there are natural laws (...); but as far as we are concerned, they are lost (...). A culture [une nation] considers an issue from a viewpoint (...); another culture by another viewpoint". As he often does, Montaigne illustrates this general point by many examples, such as the following.

> *Nothing is more horrible than to eat one's father. The people that had this custom in the past regarded it, however, as witnessing their faithfulness and affection, as by so doing they tried to give their parents the most worthy and honourable grave, since they placed the body of their parents inside themselves and as if in their flesh (...). It is easy to imagine how cruel and abominable it would have been to people who had internalised this superstition to throw the remains of their parents to the corruption of the earth, making it the food of animals and worms.*

> [*Il n'est rien si horrible à imaginer que de manger son père. Les peuples qui avaient anciennement cette coutume, la prenaient toutefois pour témoignage de piété et de bonne affection, cherchant par là à donner à leur progéniteurs la plus noble et honorable sépulture, logeant en eux-mêmes et comme en leurs moelles les corps de leur pères (...). Il est aisé de considérer quelle cruauté et abomination c'eut été, à des hommes abreuvés et imbus de cette superstition, de jeter la dépouille des parents à la corruption de la terre et nourriture des bêtes et des vers.*] (*Les Essais*, II, XII, Paris, Garnier, 1948, p. 289).

According to Geertz, Montaigne should be read literally. He had discovered an essential truth, consolidated by modern anthropology: the truth according to which there would be no normative truth, but only customs, variable from one culture to another. Any distinction between customs on the one hand and norms and values on the other would be illusory. The reasons mentioned by people as grounding their normative beliefs would be mere justifications rather than the causes of these beliefs. They would be rationalisations in the psychoanalytic sense:

they would be composed of reasons objectively ungrounded but subjectively, though, unconsciously endorsed by the subject because of their functional psychological value: if he is convinced that the reasons he endorses are objectively valid, he feels evidently more comfortable than if he doubts whether they are. The genuine causes of his moral feelings would lie on the side of cultural forces: people would internalise through socialisation the collective beliefs characteristic of any given culture.

This core idea is treated as a form of evidence by many anthropologists, such as Lévy-Bruhl (1960), Granet (1990), Whorf (1969), Needham (1972), Geertz (1984) or Shweder (1991). "There is no such thing as a human nature independent of culture", writes Geertz (1973, p. 49) in a formula close to Lévi-Strauss (1952). Political scientists like Goldhagen (1997) or Huntington (1996) clearly endorse the same idea. Huntington claims explicitly that the notion of universalism as well as the adjective universal is a cultural product which, far from being itself universal, is rather characteristic of a particular culture: the Western culture. All of these writers and many others are convinced that the world is made of discontinuous cultures, that each culture is characterised by idiosyncratic systems of norms and values and that these norms and values are transferred into the individuals' heads through socialisation. The collective beliefs which can be observed in a particular culture would be the exclusive causes of individual beliefs which can be registered in this culture.

In this vein, an article by Shweder (2000) describes the case of an African anthropologist. She was raised in the US, went back to her country, Sierra Leone, after graduation and submitted herself willingly there to genital mutilation. In a communication to the American anthropological society, she stated that most Kono women draw from excision a feeling of enhanced power. This was supposed to be true of men: they also draw a feeling of power from circumcision. From these facts, Shweder concludes that people consider a norm as positive or negative because they are exposed to cultural forces emanating from the cultural environment. These forces would be powerful enough to make a scholar educated in a culture and going back to her original culture experience genital mutilation as "positive" experience. According to Shweder, she had not submitted herself to excision in order to be accepted by her social environment. The cultural forces had been strong enough to make her want genital mutilation and experience it as positive. Shweder goes even further. The negative medical effects of genital mutilation have been greatly exaggerated, according to a study conducted by a Harvard anthropologist, she states. This study indicates, as Shweder suggests, that the negative feeling toward genital mutilation a Western observer normally experiences is the mere product of his or her own socialisation: (s)he has been educated in a culture where female genital mutilation is negatively perceived. Socialisation is the cause of his or her negative reaction.

Thus, Montaigne offers to cultural relativists a first core idea: the diversity of norms and values from one society to another would imply that they are mere socio-cultural unconscious conventions that are transmitted to individuals through socialisation.

Core Idea 2: David Hume

A second core idea has had a more diffuse influence: the famous theorem we owe presumably to David Hume, according to which no system of assertive statements can lead to a prescriptive conclusion. The theorem is true, beyond any doubt. The view has been drawn from this theorem that descriptive and prescriptive statements are separated by a wide gap. From this view, since it followed apparently from Hume's theorem that prescriptive statements could not, by essence so to say, be grounded on facts, they would never be endorsed because they were objectively based.

This idea has had a considerable influence. Probably because he has taken what I call here Hume's theorem literally, the philosopher Ayer (1960 [1946]) for instance put forward the hypothesis that normative statements are implicit commands. They would be endorsed and expressed by a subject because he would feel that they lead to a desirable type of behaviour. Normative statements would look like assertive statements ("doing X is good"); but the assertion would derive from a desire: the wish that X is really done. The assertive form of the statement would be illusory. Earlier, Pareto (1964–1988[(1916]) developed similar ideas: we say "X is good", while in most cases we should say "I feel that X is good and I feel so because I wish X or the outcomes of X". Ayer and Pareto assume that a prescriptive statement cannot be rationally grounded. So, they claim, prescriptive statements are irrationally grounded: they are the expression of a desire, even though they are rationalised (in the psychoanalytic sense of the word) and expressed in an assertive fashion. My guess is that, without the authority of Hume's theorem, Ayer and Pareto would not have accepted and presented such views. For their theory is complicated. It rests, moreover, on the big assumption that the subject is by nature blind with regard to his own reasons and motivations: that he is the victim of an illusion.

I shall spend some more time on anthropologists than on philosophers such as Ayer. Many anthropologists can, like the ones I have already mentioned, be ranked under the umbrella of "culturalism", in the broad sense of this term. According to culturalism in this broad sense, the social subjects would endorse normative statements under the effect of socialisation; they would accept them passively; they would normally give them a meaning which they do not have. The role of the anthropologist or sociologist would be to disentangle the true causes of the normative beliefs of the social subjects, causes which the subjects themselves are not aware of.

The anthropologists who accept Montaigne's core idea may possibly have been more or less indirectly impressed by Hume's core idea. For Hume's theorem gives, so to say, a theoretical ground to Montaigne's empirical observations. Montaigne observed that norms and values appear as highly variable from one society to the next. One draws easily from Hume's theorem the conclusion that this diversity is primarily grounded in the fact that normative statements cannot be objectively based, according at least to the current interpretation of this theorem.

Many anthropological studies aim to show, not only that norms and values appear as variable from one culture to another, but that this is also true of the norms and values which Westerners currently consider as universally valid, such as the value of equity and the norms related to this value. Thus, an impressive study, resting on an ambitious observation design (Henrich *et al.*, 2001) observes that the answers to the ultimatum game appear variable from one culture to another. The so-called ultimatum game is a game where a subject A is supposed to propose to an experimenter to share, say, 100 euros between himself and a subject B, while B has exclusively the power to accept or refuse A's proposal. The rule of the game is that, if B accepts A's proposal, the latter will be accepted, while, if B does not accept A's proposal, the 100 euros will remain in the experimenter's pocket. In most cases, while A is placed by the experiment in a position of "exploiting" B, he appears to refrain from doing so. But, interestingly enough, Henrich *et al.* show that the fifty/fifty choice does not appear with the same frequency in all "cultures". So, in some rural cultures, A appears more ready to exploit B than in urban cultures. Thus, even the feeling of equity seems not to be universal. A Western respondent A chooses in most cases to share the benefits of the game equally between B and himself, while the situation created by the experiment would make possible for him to get much more; in some other cultures, this answer appears as less likely.

Not only most anthropologists, but many sociologists seem to consider Montaigne's and Hume's core ideas as self-evident, even though they do not mention them explicitly. The difference between the two corporations is that the latter is more interested in the variation of norms and values within a given society than between societies. Sociologists observe that norms and values differ from one group to another in a society. As anthropologists, they explain this variation by causes they hold the social actors themselves to be unaware of. This kind of analysis is brilliantly illustrated for instance in the UK by Douglas and Ney (1998) or in France by Boltanski's and Thévenot's *cités* (1991): they use this term for what was earlier called subcultures.

My guess is that the big assumptions introduced by such analyses cannot be perceived as evident if one does not see them as corollaries of Montaigne's and Hume's core ideas. I am thinking notably of the assumption that the sociologist can see the causes of the convictions of the social actors, while the social actors themselves would be unable to see these causes and would see their convictions as grounded on fallacious reasons.

Core Idea 3: Max Weber

Social sciences owe to Max Weber a third core idea. Some commentators present him as a relativist on the basis of two famous metaphors: "value polytheism" and the "war of Gods" (Weber, 1995[1919]). These metaphors easily evoke the idea that societies are ruled by norms and values that can be incompatible with one another. They suggest that value conflicts rather than, as in the Marxist tradition, class conflicts would structure social life.

So, the greatest of sociologists (with Durkheim) would have insisted on the idea that values and norms are the product of social forces. He would have confirmed and elaborated Nietzsche's and Marx's philosophical theses on the origin of values.

III. DO WE NEED TO BELIEVE IN THE HYPERBOLIC INTERPRETATIONS OF THE THREE CORE IDEAS?

Montaigne

First of all, it should be noted that the distance between Montaigne and Geertz is immense. To Montaigne, norms and values vary from one "nation" to another. But Montaigne does not endorse the idea that socialisation would produce mechanical irreversible effects in the mind of individuals. He mentions on the contrary a number of cases where people change their mind even on basic issues under the action of minor factors.

Thus in a comical passage inspired by Diogenes, Montaigne shows that philosophico-religious beliefs themselves, far from expressing the indelible effect of socialisation, may on the contrary seem very fragile. A Greek member of the Stoic sect, had he recounts, "farted indiscretely while debating, in the presence of his school, and kept to his house, hiding there in his shame (...)". Such shame is indeed a socialisation effect. But this effect must have disappeared all of a sudden when one of his friends "by adding to his reasons and consolations the example of his freedom, began to fart himself in imitation, and in so he took away his shame, and moreover took him out of his Stoic sect" (*Essais*, *op. cit.*: 292).

A single fart may, then, according to Montaigne, suddenly wipe out all the effects of the mechanisms of socialisation that the culturalists see as determinant as the laws of gravitation.

Montaigne's core idea could take with Geertz a radical form thanks to the introduction of the law of the excluded middle: norms are either conventional or rationally grounded. If they were rationally grounded, they would tend to be the same everywhere. As this is not the case, they are conventional. So, when social actors see them as rational, they rationalise ideas which they owe to socialisation. By so thinking, Geertz ignores the "middle term": that some norms and values are conventional, while others are not. (Please note incidentally that throughout this book I take the word "convention" in a broad sense which does not imply that the convention is conscious and deliberate).

Ordinary language introduces, though, a distinction between the norms and values which owe their origin to "custom" and which can be considered as conventional, and the norms and values which probably cannot be held as customs. A rule can be arbitrary and grounded in tradition, while it expresses a value or a norm which derives from reasons. To take a trivial example: shaking hands is a conventional sign of politeness, while politeness itself, far from being conventional, is positively valued in all societies, even though it is not necessarily followed by all in all circumstances. There are no reasons, except conventional, to shake hands. There are reasons to be polite: the norm politeness is itself grounded on a value, i.e. the respect due to the other man in reciprocity of the respect I expect from him.

Let us now go back to the case of female genital mutilation. Shweder (2000) seems to accept, as I said, that the feeling of indignation normally experienced by any Western observer when this practice is mentioned before him is "cultural": this feeling would be an effect of the exposure of the Western observer during his socialisation to values typical of Western societies. Under the effect of "false consciousness", the Western observer would believe that this reaction is, not cultural, but rational, while it would be cultural in reality.

The expression "false consciousness" itself was created by Franz Mehring, but the concept behind the word was present in many of Marx's writings, appearing first in *The German Ideology*. I will have in this book several opportunities to suggest that the strange idea that people have in principle wrong interpretations of their own motivations and reasons would probably never have been readily accepted without the strong intellectual influence of Marx and Marxism on the social sciences. Marxism died in 1989 in its political incarnation, but it has left behind explanatory schemes which are still currently used in the social sciences by writers who seem to perceive neither their strangeness nor their origin and who often do not see themselves as Marxists.

So, it is perhaps simpler to get rid of this complicated assumption made by Shweder, to reject the idea that, when the Western observer has a negative reaction toward excision, the reaction is an effect of the values he has himself endorsed as a member of the Western culture, and to accept rather the assumption that he has some reasons to have a negative reaction against female genital mutilation.

These reasons can be described in the following way. One can easily understand that all societies tend to develop rituals, the function of which is to integrate young individuals into the world of adults and to help them developing their personal identity, and that female genital mutilation can have a function of this type. One can easily understand that the anthropologist mentioned by Shweder who submitted herself to excision wanted to be regarded in her country as a genuine Sierra-Leone citizen, in spite of the fact that she was raised in the US. But we know also that personal identity and integration can be built by other devices and that these devices can legitimately be preferred if they appear as equally efficient and less cruel than the devices generating a corporal mutilation.

When a Western observer learns that in Saudi Arabia thieves can have their hands cut off, his reaction is normally one of indignation.

This reaction can again be interpreted as an effect of his socialisation in the Western world. No anthropologists have dared though, to my knowledge at least, to extend to this other case the cultural explanation many of them treat as evident in the case of excision. Probably because the rational explanation appears in this case as evidently much stronger than the cultural one: social control is needed in all societies; but as soon as a device of social control appears as less cruel and as not less effective than another, the former tends to be selected. One does not need to assume that the Western observer follows mechanically the values he was taught and that he is the prey of false consciousness when he condemns cruel practices: strong reasons are rather the genuine causes of his reaction.

This implicit theory which I introduce into the mind of the Western observer is no other than the theory Durkheim explicitly developed in his *Division of Labour in Society*. Social control tends to rest on devices and procedures which become weaker over time, Durkheim (1960[1893]) contends. This trend is caused by a fundamental value which inspires social life in all societies: individualism. Individualism (in the moral and sociological sense), he writes, can be observed in all times and all societies; this value tends over time to become more and more respected and observed (Boudon, 2002 and below, chapter 3). For this reason, the devices and procedures aiming at facilitating social control, personal integration, etc. become weaker over time: they tend to display an increasing respect for the dignity of individuals; now, personal integrity is a basic aspect of the dignity of individuals.

Following Durkheim, we can suppose that the Western observer perceives excision negatively, not because he has been socialised to values incompatible with such practices, but because he has strong reasons for doing so. This rational explanation has the advantage that, if we accept it, it is no longer necessary to assume that the Western observer is the seat of a "false consciousness" which distorts his inner perceptions. It has the further advantage that it frees the anthropologist or sociologist from the hard if not impossible task of investigating the mysterious mechanisms underlying the notion of "false consciousness" and, moreover, from explaining the miracle thanks to which sociologists and anthropologists are not exposed to the threat of false consciousness.

In a word: it is impossible to make all normative beliefs the mere product of socialisation and of exposure to the conventions and customs characteristic of a society. It is true that mathematics is a cultural product we owe to Egypt and Greece. In that sense they are cultural; but 2 + 2 = 4 is not a cultural truth. The same could be said of many normative and axiological beliefs.

The question raised by Geertz and the other culturalists treats as obvious the assumption that it is possible to decide between two contradictory statements, describing normative and axiological beliefs respectively as conventional–cultural or as rational. This assumption actually rests on an undesirable *a priori* which is now familiar to us: the principle that there is no middle term. It gives birth to a question without answer, as in my previous examples.

David Hume

The correct formulation of Hume's theorem is the following: it is impossible to draw a prescriptive conclusion from a set of statements which are all descriptive. An alternative formulation would be: a prescriptive conclusion can be derived from a set of statements, provided one of them at least is prescriptive. A simple statement such as "traffic lights are a good thing; they should be accepted, for traffic would be even more difficult without them" shows that normative statements derive currently from a mixture of prescriptive and descriptive reasons.

Many sociologists, among them the so-called functionalists, have fully recognised this point. Thus, the functional theory of inequalities maintains that inequalities are accepted by people as long as they can believe that a lower level of inequalities would be detrimental to all. This theory argues in other words that people tend to see a level of inequality as legitimate (normative statement), if they can accept the idea that a lower level would generate negative consequences (factual statement). In the same way, people tend to see certain institutions as good when they have the impression that these institutions generate positive effects with respect for instance to some value, such as the dignity of individuals.

The pseudo-corollary currently drawn from Hume's theorem according to which "prescriptive conclusions cannot be drawn from descriptive statements" is thus a sophism and the popular image derived from this sophism which depicts a wide gap between norms and values on the one hand and facts on the other is worthless. But the influence of this sophism helps to explain that the false idea according to which normative and axiological beliefs are cultural–conventional has become widespread.

Max Weber

As I said earlier, Max Weber is represented as a hard relativist by some commentators, who say he stressed the fact that societies are endemically threatened by endless and merciless value conflicts. Bryan Turner (1992) recently, as Leo Strauss (1953) or Erich Voegelin (1952) earlier, have defended interpretations of this type of Weber's metaphors on the "war among Gods" and on the "polytheism of values" (Weber, 1995[1919]).

Weber's point is actually quite simple: every theory, including the most robustly established physical theory, rests necessarily upon undemonstrated principles. Otherwise, the statements appearing in first place in the presentation of a theory would not be principles. Simmel (1892) has a marvellous formula to express the same point: when we discuss a chain of reasons, he states, we cannot do otherwise but start from the second element in the chain. Albert's "Münchhausen trilemma" expresses the same idea (Albert, 1975). This point contradicts a common a priori, though: the apparently evident statement that a theory cannot be held as solid if it does not rest on solid principles. On the basis of this postulate, Leo Strauss believed in a "natural" right: a right whose principles would be "natural", i.e. uncontroversial. Bryan Turner believes, if I correctly interpret him, neither in "nature" nor in any other absolute entity and concludes that no theories can be held as solid. For this reason, he sees in Weber's expressions a continuation of Nietzsche's view according to which values are the product, not of reasons, but of irrational forces. Leo Strauss' "naturalism", like Bryan Turner's "relativism" or rather his relativistic interpretation of Weber's metaphors on the "war of gods" and the "polytheism of values", derives apparently from the *a priori* according to which a theory has to be grounded on solid principles to be held as solid. But this obvious statement, at first sight at least, is far from being unquestionable.

Like any well-informed philosopher of science, Weber sees principles as provisional assumptions which are deemed to be upheld or rejected according to the interest of the consequences they generate. To him, normative and descriptive theories are developed on the basis of principles which give birth to programmes, as we might say, which either are progressively developed and consolidated or are more or less quickly abandoned if it turns out that they lead to dead ends. To Weber, the selection of ideas, of scientific, but also of moral, political, philosophical and even theological ideas, follows a process of "diffuse rationalisation" (*Durchrationalisierung*). Under the effect of this process, undemonstrable principles are consolidated *a posteriori*, thanks to the interests of social actors in the outcomes and consequences they produce.

On the whole, Weber sketches in his various writings a theory of social action and social knowledge which I would qualify as "programmatic". Thus, when a political institution seems to lead to an enhanced respect for the dignity of individuals, it tends to be perceived as legitimate, to become the object of a collective approbation and, if the circumstances are favourable, to become established in the real world. One can think of the right to strike or of the existence of unions conceived as independent of both government and management. These institutions have become established in a growing number of places because they generate in principle the protection of workers and employees. The demand of these categories for protection derives from the general notion according to which every member of a community should be equally protected, notwithstanding his location in socio-professional space. This notion itself derives from the principle according to which a good society is a society where the dignity of all is respected as far as it can be. This latter principle cannot be demonstrated. It represents the first element in Simmel's chain of arguments: the element which cannot be discussed since, being the first one, it cannot be grounded on other principles. But it inspires political life constantly. This is exactly what Durkheim meant when he asserted that "individualism" has always been a central value, in all times and all societies. I will come back in more detail to these important ideas proposed by Durkheim and Weber in chapter 3.

This does not mean that political life is peaceful. The "war of Gods" is not in conflict with the "rationalisation process" Weber sees as the powerful engine leading the evolution of ideas, in all areas: political, scientific, religious or philosophical. It took a long time and many struggles before the right to strike was accepted. Before it was accepted, the "polytheism of values" ruled: many employers argued that strikes would ruin the economy, while employees maintained the economic system would run more smoothly if power was more evenly distributed among the various economic actors. Today, the "polytheism of values" and the "war among Gods" are over, as far at least as the issue of the right to strike is concerned, though it still goes on in some parts of the Western world such as the French railways. Many issues have given birth to a situation of "polytheism of values" in a first stage and to an irreversible selection of a solution to the conflict in the long term: think of the separation of State and Church, of the notion of Rechtsstaat, of the subsidiarity principle, of the right to education, of gender equality, etc. It seems to me Weber had such examples in mind when he evoked the "war among Gods" and the process of "diffuse rationalisation". In other words, Weber never drew from the idea that principles cannot be demonstrated any relativistic conclusion. This conclusion can be drawn only if an undesirable *a priori* is introduced: that a theory should be grounded on absolutely valid principles or, if not, be held as a mere conventional "construction".

IV. TOWARD THE END OF CULTURAL RELATIVISM

To conclude on cultural relativism: it results from a hyperbolic treatment of core ideas developed notably by Montaigne, Hume and Weber. It draws hyperbolic conclusions from these core ideas thanks to the introduction of some controversial a priori. In the examples I have examined these *a priori* are built on a misuse of the principle of the no middle term. This misuse and the related confusion between "contrary" and "contradictory" terms are frequent, not only in ordinary but also in scientific thinking, at least in social scientific and philosophical thinking, as Pareto has already noted and as my various examples show. This cognitive process is a crucial one for the sociology of ideas: it explains why many false or weak beliefs are endorsed by individuals. Of course, other cognitive mechanisms would in other examples explain the implantation of questionable collective beliefs.

But in order to understand why such beliefs can become collective, another element, a social one, should be introduced beside the cognitive processes. Combined with cognitive processes such as the misuse of the law of the excluded middle, this social element builds up a socio-cognitive process which is the source of many collective beliefs. As we saw, this "social" part of the socio-cognitive process was anticipated by Scheler's metaphor of the "floodgates" and by Pareto's distinction between two attributes of ideas or theories: their usefulness and their validity. These two writers identified by these notions a crucial social part of the socio-cognitive process responsible for the diffusion of ungrounded ideas or theories.

As in the case of cognitive relativism, account should be taken of the fact that cultural relativism is "useful" in Pareto's sense. If norms and values derive from mere conventions, they are incommensurable and hence all equally good or bad. Shweder's analysis of the reaction to excision will certainly please conservative people in Sierra Leone who have the impression that this tradition is an essential feature of their culture. More importantly it will be welcomed in the West, notably by intellectuals who have the impression that a moral duty of our time is to consider all cultures as equal. Colonialism was possible, they claim, because cultures were considered as unequal. This view justified the importation and imposition of Western culture on other cultures. If cultural relativism is right, no culture is better than any other and no society better than any other. So, a consistent opponent of colonialism should endorse cultural relativism: an example where Scheler's floodgates appear open to wrong views; an example, to use my other reference, where a theory is accepted rather because it is "useful" than because it is "true".

One can be a strong opponent of any institution or enterprise threatening human dignity, without rejecting the obvious observation that some cultures and some societies serve people's wellbeing and aspirations better than others.

Is this universal benevolence the most useful present the Western world can make to the rest of the world, or to use the present geographic references, the North can make to the South?

REFERENCES

Albert, H. (1975) *Traktat über kritische Vernunft*. Tübingen, J. C. B. Mohr.

Aya, R. (2001) "The Curse of Cognitive Cultural Relativism". In Lindo, F. and Mies van Niekerk (eds.), *Dedication and Detachment, Essays in Honour of Hans Vermeulen*, Amsterdam, Aksant: 33–41.

Ayer, A. J. (1960 [1946]) *Language, Truth and Logic*. London, V. Gollancz.

Ben David, J., Zloczower, A. (1962) "Universities and Academic Systems in Modern Societies". *Archives européennes de sociologie*, III: 45–84.

Boltanski, L., Thévenot, L. (1991) *De la justification: Les économies de la grandeur*. Paris, Gallimard.

Boudon, R. (1994) *The Art of Self-Persuasion*. London, Polity Press.

—— (2002) *Déclin de la morale? Déclin des valeurs?* Paris, Presses Universitaires de France and Québec, Nota Bene.

Buican, D. (1984) *Histoire de la génétique et de l'évolutionnisme en France*. Paris, Presses Universitaires de France.

Bunge, M. (1999) *The Sociology-Philosophy Connection*. London/New Brunswick (USA), Transaction.

Douglas, M., Ney, S. (1998) *Missing Persons: A Critique of Personhood in the Social Sciences*. London, Sage.

Durkheim, E. (1979[1912]) *Les Formes élémentaires de la vie religieuse*. Paris, Presses Universitaires de France.

—— (1960[1893]) *De la division du travail social.* Paris, Presses Universitaires de France.

Feyerabend, P. (1975) *Against Method.* London, N.L.B.

Geertz, C. (1973) *The Interpretation of Culture.* New York, Basic Books.

—— (1984) "Distinguished Lecture: Anti anti-relativism". *American Anthropologist,* 86(2): 263–78.

Goldhagen, D. J. (1997) *Hitler's Willing Executioners; Ordinary Germans and the Holocaust.* New York, A. Knopf.

Granet, M. (1990) *Études sociologiques sur la Chine.* Paris, Presses Universitaires de France.

Gusfield, J. (1981) *Drinking, Driving and the Symbolic Order.* Chicago, University of Chicago Press.

Henrich, J., Boyd, R., Bowles, S., Camerer, C., Fehr, E., Gintis, H. and McElreath, R. (2001) "In Search of Homo Economicus: Behavioral Experiments in Fifteen Small-Scale Societies". *American Economic Review,* 91(2): 73–78.

Hübner, K. (1985) *Die Wahrheit des Mythos.* Munich, Beck.

Hume, D. (1972[1741]) *Essais politiques.* Vrin, Paris. Tr. *Essays Moral and Political.* London, printed for A. Millar, 3rd edn., 1748.

Huntington, S. (1996) *The Clash of Civilizations and the Remaking of the World Order.* New York, Simon and Schuster.

Kuhn, T. (1962) *The Structure of Scientific Revolutions.* Chicago, University of Chicago Press.

Latour, B., Woolgar, S. (1978) *Laboratory Life.* London, Sage.

Lévy-Bruhl, L. (1960[1922]) *La Mentalité primitive.* Paris, Presses Universitaires de France.

Lévi-Strauss, C. (1952) *Race et histoire.* Paris, UNESCO. Repr.: Paris, Gonthier.

Mannheim, K. (1954) *Ideology and Utopia.* London, Routledge and Kegan Paul.

Merton, R. (1970[1938]) *Science, Technology and Society in Seventeenth Century England.* New York, Howard Fertig. Original version: "Studies on the History and Philosophy of Science", 4(2): 1938, Osiris.

Needham, R. (1972) *Belief, Language and Experience.* Oxford, Blackwell.

Pareto, V. (1964–1988 [1916]) Traité de sociologie générale. In: *Oeuvres complètes,* vol. 12. Geneva, Droz.

Popkin, R. H. (1979) *The History of Scepticism from Erasmus to Spinoza.* Berkeley, University of California Press.

Popper, K. R. (1968[1934]) *The Logic of Scientific Discovery.* London, Hutchinson. Original: *Logik der Forschung.* Vienna, 1934.

Rorty, R. (1979) *Philosophy and the Mirror of Nature.* Princeton, Princeton University Press.

Scheler, M. (1926) *Die Wissensformen und die Gesellschaft.* Leipzig, Der Neue-Geist.

Shweder, R. A. (1991) *Thinking through Cultures: Expeditions in Cultural Anthropology.* Cambridge, Harvard University Press.

——(2000) "What about 'Female Genital Mutilation' and Why Understanding Culture Matters in the First Place". *Daedalus,* 129 (4): 209–232.

Simmel, G. (1892) *Die Probleme der Geschichtsphilosophie.* Munich, Duncker & Humblot.

Sokal, A., Bricmont, J. (1997) *Impostures intellectuelles*. Paris, O. Jacob.

Strauss, L. (1953) *Natural Right and History*. Chicago, University of Chicago Press.

Turner, B. S. (1992) *Max Weber: from History to Modernity*. London, Routledge.

Voegelin, E. (1952) *Toward a New Science of Politics*. Chicago, University of Chicago Press.

Weber, M. (1995[1919]) *Wissenschaft als Beruf*. Stuttgart, Reklam.

Whorf, B. L. (1969) *Linguistique et anthropologie. Les origines de la sémiologie*. Paris, Denoël.

2

The Polytheism of Values

I. AXIOLOGICAL RELATIVISM: AN ENTRENCHED PERSPECTIVE?

Axiological relativism is strongly entrenched in modern societies. An American sociologist of law, M. Ann Glendon (1996), has demonstrated recently that lawyers and judges in the United States tend to see their roles in new ways, right up to the level of the Supreme Court. Rather than accepting the idea that a judicial decision should be founded on impersonal reasons, they are developing what Ann Glendon calls a "romantic" vision of their role. For very many of them are convinced that the question of knowing whether a decision is good or bad is fundamentally subjective and that personal conviction is the only base on which their decision can legitimately be founded.

A different example of this diffuse relativism dominant in modern societies, from another domain, is that of education: this one, also from the United States, is the development of a movement describing itself as concerned with "values clarification" (Wilson, 1993). It aims to counter the transmission of all values through the teaching system: since all values are founded solely in personal choices, to try to transmit values amounts, according to this movement, to a threat to the dignity of the human being. It is no longer a question of denouncing, as did the neo-Marxist sociologists from the 1960s onwards, the fact that the school transmits values of subordination to the established order. Here, it is the inculcation of *all* values, whatever their content or function, that is condemned by this movement.

Axiological Relativism is Contradicted by the Evidence

It is important for the sociologist to emphasise that the postmodern conception of values is in contradiction with public sentiments.

The majority of people would accept, for instance, that democracy is a better form of regime than the diverse varieties of despotism, that the abolition of *apartheid* in South Africa was a good thing, and that political corruption is a bad thing. It seems obvious that such examples can be infinitely multiplied. In other words, on many subjects, social actors have the impression – now as much as they might have in the past – that the value judgements they endorse may be considered not as private truths, as truths that they would happily accept the idea that they were the only people to hold them, but on the contrary as truths which they would have trouble admitting that others could not accept. In order to avoid the difficulties of the concept of objectivity, to which I shall return later, I propose to discuss here what I call *trans-subjective* truths, meaning by this that those who adhere to this idea would have the impression that the "generalised other" described by G.H. Mead (1934) would also endorse them. It is, of course, an empirical observation that few would contest that it is possible to find many examples of such trans-subjective truths.

Axiological relativism, the relativism of values, is not only refuted by the certitudes we witness on the part of social actors, which are easy to see in particular in the conflicts that develop in everyday social and political life. It is also refuted by many observations whose origins are scientific.

Thus, in *Le Juste et le vrai* (Boudon, 1995) as well as in Chapter 4 of the present work, I have re-analysed a group of surveys and experiments carried out by sociologists and social psychologists on feelings about justice. The main result is that the theories of feelings about justice proposed by the philosophers – from Kant to Rawls – are inadequate: they only allow us to account for a small part of the results obtained by these sociological and social-pyschological studies; but another result is that many situations and questions designed to test the axiological positions of subjects elicit from them responses whose distributions are highly structured. Such results are incompatible with a *decisionist* theory of character that treats value judgements as private matters, and just as incompatible with a *determinist* theory of character, or for that matter with a causalist theory of character that tries to explain this structuration as a consequence of socialisation.

I would clarify here that I am using the qualifications *determinist* and *causalist* to describe explanations for the holding of value judgements that refer to causes that are not reasons.

Most recently I have reanalysed the data from the international survey by Inglehart (1998) on values and shown that this data does not allow us to conclude that younger generations are more susceptible than the older to the charms of axiological relativism (Boudon, 2002). Changes may be observed from generation to generation, but they do not in any sense move towards an increase in relativism. This conclusion applies to the seven western countries that I selected in my analysis of the Inglehart data. It suggests that axiological relativism is more popular with intellectuals than with the population as a whole. More precisely, it shows that the image that intellectuals and especially media commentators have of public opinion – in its widest sense which includes both value judgements and the feelings associated with them – does not necessarily coincide with public opinion as it is actually manifested. Intellectuals and media commentators represent their contemporaries as having a conception of values that is much more relativist than is in fact the case, if we look at the evidence of the surveys. Hence the crucial importance both for sociology and for democracy of the scientific observation of public opinion, a form of observation that is rather unfashionable in contemporary sociology.

Other research deals with the feelings of legitimacy or illegitimacy produced in the minds of respondents by income distribution. This shows that in some experimental situations respondents appear almost unanimously to be "rawlsian" whilst in some other situations they are almost unanimously "anti-rawlsian". When it is made clear that income inequalities are functional, respondents accept them; when it is explained that it is not known whether they are functional or not, the respondents resign themselves to this; and when inequalities are presented as non-functional they rally to Rawls's *difference principle* according to which inequalities should be brought to the lowest level possible as long as that does not affect the weakest. I will take up these questions in more detail again in Chapter 4, but it is possible at the outset to make clear that, if the principles put forward by Rawls were principles valorised under the effect of socialisation, it would not be possible to understand why they were accepted in certain situations and not in others. The fact that in these two cases the responses were virtually unanimous also excludes them from being associated with theory of a decisionist character: unanimity implies the existence of a shared belief, and by reciprocation excludes the possibility that responses might be the result of personal motivation.

In short, a great deal of data collected in different situations appears incompatible with the two theories concerning normative beliefs and more generally axiological beliefs that are dominant today and to which I referred to at the outset: the decisionist theory and the determinist theory.

The contradiction between the theory that values are just opinions, and the fact that many values are experienced by social subjects as objectively based poses some significant questions: why is there such a contradiction? What is the source of the influence of axiological relativism? Is it indeed absurd – as many contemporary theorists would hold – to consider values as objectively based? Would it be better to posit that, when social actors evaluate them as such, they are victims of false consciousness? If values are objectively based, how do we explain their variation over time and space? There is – at least arguably – a scientific truth, but there is a plurality of moral truths and the existence of diverse cultures cannot be denied. Is not that sufficient to destroy any rational conception of values, any conception which tends to show that values are objectively based? These are the questions that I wish to discuss here.

A Question About the Sociology of Ideas

As to the first question, that of the reasons for the influence of relativism, it was Tocqueville who put forward a basic hypothesis and his analysis of this matter in the second volume of *Democracy in America* remains surprisingly relevant even today (Tocqueville, 1986b).

Modern societies, or, as Tocqueville would have put it in the language of his time, "democratic" societies, are enthused by what he called a "general and dominant passion" and what we would call a *value*, that of equality. It is important to recall that the modern meaning of the word *value* was established after Tocqueville was writing, under the influence of Nietzsche. Before Nietzsche, the word *value* had a meaning in the economic domain; in that of morality, it was essentially the equivalent of *courage*. So it is with some justification that the phrase "general and dominant passion" may be seen as the synonym of our modern concept of *value*. The "general and dominant passion" – the *value* – of equality implies that not simply all individuals but all groups and all cultures as well should be treated with equal dignity.

As a result of its moral power this value deserves the qualification of "dominant" that Tocqueville attributes to it. As individuals, groups, cultures and sub-cultures all hold, moreover, different opinions on all sorts of points and different values, it is only possible to remain faithful to this principle of the equal dignity of all by accepting that there is no axiomatic truth or objectivity. If not, then the opinions or values of some would be superior to those of the others.

Tocqueville's theorem – as I would formalise it – can be set out as follows: *when equality is a dominant value, it tends to produce a relativist or sceptical conception of the world.*

Tocqueville developed several variants of this theorem, but one of them has attracted particular attention: modern societies are characterised, he says, by the reign of public opinion. As a result of an interesting unintended consequence, equality tends to produce, according to Tocqueville, if not the destruction of values other than that of equality, then at least the appearance of suspicions regarding the ideas of truth and of objectivity, particularly as they are applied to the normative and the axiological.

By following Tocqueville, it is easier to understand the proliferation and the influence of irrational theories of moral sentiments and, more generally, of axiological sentiments in democratic societies. But it is also possible to understand why these theories are more attractive to intellectuals than to the public in general: they are more in keeping than any other theory with the dominant value of equality. But concern with the general and abstract coherence of values is of no great interest to the general public. This intellectualist concern is mainly of interest to professionals. *Common sense* rationality is more pragmatic.

In short, Tocqueville offers us a valuable route to comprehending the popularity of relativism within intellectual milieux at the same time as its minor interest for the general public. He also helps us to understand why intellectuals have so little regard for *common sense*: a subject I return to in Chapter 6.

The Silent Majority

The relativist conception of values, as I have said, comes up against both beliefs and evidence. Everyone is, in effect, convinced that it is possible to pronounce incontestable moral truths on any and all subjects.

How can the contradiction between the sentiments of the public at large and the fashion for relativism be explained? Tocqueville offers us another key that adds to that I have just mentioned. It is entirely possible that a majority of people believe *white* when *black* seems to be true. This happens when it is considered illegitimate to declare that one believes white, and acceptable to declare that one believes black. In this case, only those who believe black express themselves, and those who believe white have the impression that outside of themselves and their entourage, everybody else believes black. As Tocqueville tells us (1986a, pp. 1040–46), during the French Revolution, public opinion appeared to be anticlerical, although a big majority of the population retained the "old faith". But this majority remained silent. As it was difficult, even dangerous, to voice one's doubts, each person could easily believe that they were the only one not to have lost their faith. Similarly, it was thought that a majority of Russians had become communists, and Germans national-socialist, whilst only a minority in each case were adherents of the new faith. Tocqueville's model was recently formalised and used brilliantly by Kuran (1995). Kuran makes the point that before taking what people say as worth its weight in gold, it is essential to determine whether they are willing and able to say what they really believe. To apply these ideas to a burning contemporary issue, it is difficult to be certain that a given Palestinian mother is really rejoicing, by contrast with what she says in front of the cameras, in the fact that her son has sacrificed himself to God.

In a rather less dramatic way, Tocqueville's theory can be applied to the relativism of democratic societies. It has acquired the status of a dominant perspective. At the same time, it is in contradiction with the evidence and private beliefs. But these are hardly ever expressed. By contrast any theory that legitimises relativism is socially valued, thus advantageous for its author, and usually approved by the sounding board of conformism that is the media. Contradictory views are rarely expressed, and when they are, are rarely heard.

As a result relativism has without doubt become a sort of official truth, despite the fact that it contradicts private beliefs.

Naturalist Resistance: Its Drawbacks

At the same time relativism provokes resistance. It is felt that some forms of government are preferable to others, to offer a rather trivial example. Despite all efforts to explain that the criminal is a victim of society, there is a certainty that he deserves to be punished. We know that theft is universally considered to be a bad thing, even if the sanctions that it attracts may vary between societies.

This contradiction between common sense and the relativism that pervades democratic societies has been a motivation for the somewhat limited attempts – because of the influence of relativism – to relocate the objective basis of moral sentiments.

An American sociologist of some renown, James Q. Wilson (1993) has therefore tried to show that moral sentiments are part of human nature. On the basis of a methodical analysis of a group of social-psychological studies, he sought to defend the hypothesis that man has a natural sense of justice, an attitude of respect towards others, and a sense of duty. A Canadian sociologist, M. Ruse (1993), has also put forward the argument that this moral sense is a result of biological evolution. Some philosophers such as Alisdair MacIntyre (1981), argue from a neo-Aristotelian perspective that values have a natural source. In a more general sense it is possible to observe the re-emergence of interest in moral philosophy in its most classical forms, and a corresponding decline in the audience for the social sciences where they deal with questions relative to norms and values, probably because for many decades a great number of anthropologists and sociologists have been engaged in producing – consciously or not, willingly or not – relativist theses.

I also believe that moral sentiments and, more generally, axiological sentiments – those sentiments that lead to value judgements – have an objective basis. But the naturalistic routes often taken by philosophy nowadays are not perhaps the most promising.

It is clear that many value judgements we hold cannot be interpreted in the naturalistic way that Wilson suggests. It is not intuitions generated by human nature that produce a negative or positive value judgement about, for instance, policies for reducing unemployment or that determine whether or not one supports or opposes the death penalty.

Neither do I believe in the solution proposed by Habermas (1981) with his concept of communicative reason. His "theory of communicative reason" supposes that a value judgement can be considered to be well-founded from the point at which it is possible to assume that a community operating under the regime of pure and perfect communication would embrace it. However, a community of this type would have accepted all of the scientific errors now discredited but which were believed in the past. Before Copernicus, it would have decided that the sun circles the earth. During the 16th century in the time of the French philosopher Jean Bodin (1530–1596) it would have decided that the separation of powers was a dangerous idea, or in the 19th century that universal suffrage was bound to be disastrous. Despite its pretensions, the theory of communicative reason cannot reconcile history and reason in any way. Moreover, the notion that an idea is right from the moment it is embraced by a theoretical community characterised by absolute transparency of debate amongst its members is no more than a reworking of the old doctrine that proposes founding truth on consensus. Durkheim (1979[1912]) was much more clairvoyant and subtle – consensus may establish an idea in its early stages, but in order for it to persist, it needs to appear objectively grounded, this being as true for prescriptive ideas as for descriptive ideas, as he so rightly noted.

II. A COGNITIVE THEORY OF VALUES

The "Circular" Nature of Knowledge

I will not take up here the question of the weakness of the arguments by which relativism seeks to justify itself (cf. Boudon, 1992b), except to emphasise one point.

It is easy to see why, following Novalis, both Dostoyevsky and Nietzsche embrace the implications of the relationship "no dogmatic beliefs, no objectivity of values". "If God does not exist, anything is possible", as Dostoyevsky has one of his characters say. For Nietzsche, if God does not exist, Christian morality has no foundation.

> *If the Christian faith is renounced, then the right to Christian morality is forfeited at the same time. (...) Christian morality is a commandment; its origin is transcendant; it is above all criticism, above any right to criticise; it only has truth if God is Truth. (...)*

> [*Wenn man den christlichen Glauben aufgibt, zieht man sich damit das Recht zur christlichen Moral unter den Füssen weg. (...) Die christliche Moral ist ein Befehl; ihr Ursprung ist transzendent; sie ist jenseits aller Kritik, alles Recht auf Kritik; sie hat nur Wahrheit, falls Gott die Wahrheit ist (...)*] (Nietzsche, 1969, p. 993).

If "dogmatic beliefs", in Tocqueville's sense, or absolute truths in other terms, do indeed exist they must indeed be the bases of moral precepts.

But these "dogmatic beliefs" represent no more than one particular solution to the problem of the basis of moral sentiments, for there are three possible theoretical solutions available in this respect: that of the "dogmatic beliefs" themselves, referred to by Tocqueville, which have slowly collapsed, and in addition those of *reason* on the one hand and of *intuition* on the other. If the basis of moral sentiments is "dogmatic beliefs" – beliefs that are produced by "revelation" – then it has also been eroded as a result of the disenchantment of the world. If the basis of moral sentiments is reason this is not an answer popular in a world governed by public opinion where reason itself is seen as an outmoded idea. This is why moral theorists who want to replace relativist theories with more satisfactory ones take the route of intuition. It is that taken, for example, by J. Wilson, M. Ruse and Alisdair MacIntyre, as referred to above, when they aver that moral sentiments are imposed on us by human nature and are given to us through the evidence of our senses.

But it should immediately be pointed out that this problem of the basis or foundation of moral sentiments must be posed in terms that are strictly identical and relate to scientific facts. All scientific propositions are based on a theory, and all theories are based on principles. Now it must be one thing or another, for otherwise we are engaged in deducing these principles from other principles that must be demonstrated, and we end up in an infinite regression. The alternatives are to stop at the principles that are considered to be intuitively and absolutely true; or to shore up in a circular way the principles concerned on the basis of their consequences.

As it is easy to show, this *trilemma* has never stopped science from advancing, although it applies as much to scientific theories as others. Why? Because knowledge is "circular", as Simmel rightly saw (1892). Moreover, in the scientific domain as elsewhere, it is indeed the consequences that are drawn from the principles that are demonstrated that consolidate or weaken the principles in question.

By pointing out that scientific knowledge is a game between *conjectures* and *refutations*, Popper (1963) also emphasised that certainty is based on reasons perceived to be solid as well "circular" (in the sense just described). The principle according to which there is no movement without cause and no stopping of motion without a cause – the principle of inertia – cannot be demonstrated: if it could it would not be a *principle*. But by accepting it, theories can be generated that readily explain all sorts of observations. It grounds our interpretation of these observations whilst the observations in question strengthen our faith in the principle. There is certainly circularity, and in a sense more metaphorical than logical.

At the same time there is the impression that the principle of inertia has an *objective* validity. It has indeed an objective validity in the sense that, if it is denied, it leads to insurmountable problems. Medieval physics, for instance, was confronted with a series of dead-ends because it was not understood that all states of passage not only from rest to movement, *but also from movement to rest* required a cause that would create them. That is why it sought in vain the cause responsible for the fact that an arrow continues to fly after leaving the bow, or the cause responsible for the fact that a boat continues to glide along its path when its sails have been stowed and the wind has dropped. If the principle of inertia is put forward in the definitive form given by Galileo and then Newton, these problems disappear. It invites belief in the notion that the movement of the arrow and the boat are *without cause*. The abbreviated principle from which medieval physics started out ("all movement has a cause") led it, on the contrary, into insurmountable problems. Thus it ended up being abandoned in favour of another principle that ironed out all of the problems and dead-ends that were the result of the abbreviated principle. As a result of the new principle, some movements were deprived of a cause: a proposition which seems absurd and in any respect counterintuitive when it is removed from the context in which it appeared. This is a perfect illustration of the circularity of knowledge revealed by Simmel, and later by Popper.

In one word, dealing with the domain of the *descriptive*, the absence of absolutely valid primary principles can not in any way prevent objectivity, in the sense that I have used it here.

Assume now that it is possible to transpose this idea into the domain of the *prescriptive:* to moral theories. In other words, accept that we can look at the basic mechanism of the phenomena of appreciation in the following circular fashion:

Principle(s) $\rightarrow$ Consequence(s) $\rightarrow$ critique of the principle(s)
in the light of their consequences $\rightarrow$ eventual revision of the
principle(s)

It may be concluded that the absence of revealed first principles or of principles to which intuition would allot an absolute value do not lead in any necessary way to relativism.

Of course this is not, for me, a matter of affirming that the prescriptive and the descriptive cannot be distinguished. Axiological propositions, i.e. value judgements, are clearly distinguished from the descriptive propositions established by science, in physics for instance, in that they are certainly less unified and formalised. But they resemble them on another point: their validity is relative to the solidity of the reasons on which they are based. It is not contradicted by the fact that it might be based on principles that are *laid down* rather than demonstrated.

It is easy to see that judicial deliberation is no different in principle to scientific deliberation. In both cases it is a matter of constructing a chain of argument comprised of links that are as strong as possible. The principle of inertia is based on a chain of strong linking arguments. Moral conviction, and axiological conviction more generally, is formed in the same way.

I can now make clear what I mean by *objectivity*. This concept readily evokes the image of knowledge as a form of "mirror of nature". As soon as the word "objectivity" is uttered the impression is given of knowledge as an activity that seeks to produce images of the objects that it is concerned with that are as faithful as possible, and to be unaware of modern theories of knowledge which demonstrate that all knowledge is a construction. But it is possible to dismiss this naïve conception of objectivity without as a result falling into cognitive relativism. In the scientific domain it is possible to say that a proposition or theory is *objectively* valid from the point at which, as the consequence of a solid chain of argument, it is imperative that, potentially, it will be universally accepted. This is the case of the principle of inertia, of the Cartesian theory of refraction or any other scientific theory. These theories are not faithful images of an invisible reality of whatever sort, but irrefutable systems of argument.

If this definition of the concept of objectivity applied to a theory is accepted, it is easy to list examples showing how judicial or axiological theories may be objective in this sense.

Value Judgements are Sound to the Extent that They are Based on Sound Reasons

A banal example, but one which is difficult to refute, is all that is necessary to demonstrate this. Why is democracy considered to be a *good* thing?

Because it tries to organise a political system that seeks to answer the needs of citizens in the best possible way. Democracy requires the periodic re-election of those who govern. Why are these elections a good thing? Because they reduce the risk that those who govern will pay more attention to their own interests than to those of the governed. Naturally, it is possible that none of the candidates is attractive. The system cannot guarantee the absence of corruption. But it is a better protection than any other. Of course the principle of "one man one vote" is open to some obvious objections. It gives the same weight to the opinion of someone who has thought carefully about the issues as to that of someone who has not even understood them. But any other system gives rise to far more serious objections. Democracy contains other principles, such as that of the liberty of speech and of the independence of the judiciary. Everyone is aware that the guarantees it provides are imperfect. Politicians can use their positions to enrich themselves. But the phenomena of corruption that are normal in totalitarian regimes are more readily exposed and challenged in democratic regimes. Democratic institutions are, in other words, based on sound reasons. And it is because they are founded on a sound basis that we feel, with some evidence, that democracy is superior to all other political systems.

My objective here is not to set up a novel form of analysis of democracy, but only to bear witness as a sociologist to the collective *sentiments* that it nourishes. Democracy for me is, in other words, only one example on which it is possible to pose the question of how to explain axiological feelings. Why are we so certain that it is such a good system? Reply: because we have strong reasons for such a judgement.

I do not see how a sociologist could explain in a satisfactory way the collective belief that "democracy is a good thing" without placing in the minds of social actors an argument of the type formulated by political theory. This argument is no doubt less polished and takes a form that is more intuitive and less discursive in the mind of the ordinary social actor than it would in that of the political philosopher, but it is not fundamentally different.

The example of democracy is enough in any case to show that a value judgement *can* have the same degree of objectivity – in the sense that I propose to use this term – as a factual judgement of the type that is found in medicine or biology. If the feeling that "democracy is a good thing" was not objectively grounded, then a widespread if not general agreement with this view would not be observed. It would not be understood that, contrary to the principle of the sovereignty of states, it is thought justified to try to impose it on non-democratic nations. It would not be understood that such an enterprise is widely approved. Reciprocally, it is difficult to explain such feelings if there is a refusal to see them as based upon strong reasons.

The Historicity of Values

One objection is frequently raised against this theory of valorisation – whether it is termed *cognitive*, *rationalist*, or even by certain writers *neo-rationalist* – that I put forward here.

The majority of anthropologists, sociologists, historians, or philosophers would certainly make the objection to my analysis that democracy has not always been considered to be a good thing, that this judgement is recent, that not everybody thinks that democracy is a good thing, and that in other times other regimes were widely held to be good. I do not deny it. It is a fact that democracy in its modern sense was only discovered quite late in human history.

But that only proves that, as long as this type of system did not exist, it was not possible to have any idea about it, and that once the idea had emerged it was held that it was utopian and that as a result it was not a good thing. To be assessed, it was necessary that it had been previously conceived and theorised. It is possible to go further still: in order for it be conceived, it was necessary that it existed or began to exist in reality.

The English historian Trevelyan (1942) pointed out that the principle of the separation of powers emerged in England as a result of historical contingencies (the Civil War between Roundheads and Cavaliers). It was during this conflict that the basis of *common law* was established, and that the principle of the control of the executive by the legislature was put into place, whereas previously competition between these powers was thought to be abnormal, dangerous and something to be avoided. In a similar way the risks of emigration to the USA created, at the beginning of the history of the Union, bitter opposition between two states, Massachusetts and Rhode-Island, and it was this confrontation that was a short-cut to the emergence of freedom of speech as a fundamental right in the United States.

The significance of the institutional innovation represented by the organisation of the separation of powers was certainly perceived outside England. It was more clearly perceptible after Montesquieu than before. But Montesquieu himself would certainly not have theorised the principle of the separation of powers, or, as he often wrote "the coordination of powers" with as much conviction if it had not already been applied in England. Moreover, the importance of the new "intermediary bodies", the magistrature or the press, appeared well after Tocqueville was writing. But Tocqueville would not have emphasised their importance if he had not observed their effects.

There are innovations in the domain of the prescriptive as there are in that of the descriptive. The theory that the separation of powers is a good thing is no more intuitive than the theory of the conservation of energy. Before its initial application and subsequent diffusion, it came up against objections that no one would now dare mention, and that would be difficult to believe. Before their widespread use, both the railways and bank notes came up against obstacles that could not be lifted until reality proved them wrong. An observer of the 21st century will doubtless agree that "the separation of powers is a good thing" more readily than his predecessor of the 18th century. This variability of collective sentiments does not prove that the principle of the balance of powers is without objective foundation, but only that the first observer is situated in a different cognitive environment from the second.

Similarly, it can no longer be believed that the earth is flat. However, in earlier times the statements "the earth is round" and "the earth is flat" could be treated as equally plausible. This is not a demonstration that the truth about the shape of the earth is historical, and that it is not possible to talk about the objective shape of the earth. What is historical in this matter is the discovery of the truth, not the truth itself: history does not legitimise historicism much as sociology does not legitimise sociologism, although such distinctions are often forgotten. The fact that mathematics has a history does not count against the validity of mathematical truths. The fact that morality has a history is no more of a proof that moral values are lacking in objectivity.

The example of the separation – or as it seems more apt to say, the balance – of powers is typical of the process of establishment of values. Quite frequently, as in this example, axiological innovation has a contingent origin. The wars between Cavaliers and Roundheads might never have happened or could have taken a different course. But once the system of the balance of power is put in place it is easy to see that it improves the operation of the political system. By institutionalising conflict, it decreases the chance of it taking a violent turn. It allows divergent interests to be expressed and to display their merits. It rationalises the processes of collective decision-making by subjecting them to opposing debates. To use the language of the evolutionists, the mutation represented by the positive evaluation of the separation of powers has thus been "selected".

This is a classic example of the interplay between "historical forces" and "rationalisation", so often referred to by Weber.

It should also be recognised that the interplay between historical forces and rationalisation ensures that irreversibility is never guaranteed in reality: a democracy may become corrupted, certain democracies being caricatures of good government and others are monarchies, some even dictatorships in disguise. But the processes of rationalisation of which Weber writes – and that illustrate the emergence of belief in the worth of the balance of powers – leads to an irreversibility of values. Democracy can be weakened or corrupted. The idea will persist that its principles are a good thing. This idea, in itself, can never be reversed. This is why the members of parliament who, in France in 1940, agreed to the destruction of democracy in favour of a corporatist state were so heavily condemned in the public mind.

An institution or an idea may indeed be established as irreversibly "good" in the public mind, while their realisation is made difficult by the interplay of contingencies and interests. This is why, at a time when nobody doubted the principle of the independence of the judiciary, it took so long in France to put it into effect: memories of the role played by the parliaments of the *Ancien Régime* meant that the political class for a long time was suspicious of a "government of judges". For this reason the constitution of the Fifth Republic allows an "authority" but not a "power" to the judicial system. The innovation is contingent or at least it can be: the selection of ideas is rational but it has to work with the irrational interplay of historical forces.

Another important point: although established value judgements are based on sound reasons, that does not mean that an axiological truth exists for all subjects. It is necessary, on the contrary, to insist on the fact that – in the case of the normative as much as for the positive – there are indecisive situations where the competing systems of reason lead to divergent conclusions and between which it is impossible to make a choice. Moreover, the same problem can and frequently does have several solutions. It is possible to design an aircraft, even one destined for a well-defined task, in several ways. Equally, there are many different ways in which the balance of powers can be organised: there are specific examples in all the nations of the western world.

To sum up, there is a history of prescriptive truth as much as there is a history of descriptive truth. There are innovations, real innovations, in the domain of the prescriptive as much as in that of the descriptive. There are certainties in the domain of the prescriptive as much as in that of the descriptive. But it is necessary to guard against too close an association of the rational with the real. The emergence of innovations depends on contingencies and if their selection is tendentiously rational, events may lead to wrong choices and to some backward steps. Contingence and necessity, "historical forces" and "rationalisation" are continually interlinked.

Examples of Axiological Irreversibilities in Contemporary Societies

It is not hard to see the interplay between historical forces and mental irreversibilities that I have just been emphasising. The case of the death penalty seems to me to be exemplary here. Some "historical forces" have led to its reintroduction in a country with a liberal and democratic tradition: the United States. However, since it has been shown that it has no deterrent value it has tended to be seen as barbaric.

In a more general fashion and following a trend that Durkheim had clearly noticed when, in *La Division du travail social*, he notes that over the long term civil law tends to expand at the expense of penal law, it can be seen that contemporary societies have a tendency to seek mechanisms of "social control" that respect the principles of both retributive justice and the dignity of the individual. See, for instance, the development of sentences of "substitution", such as community service work, which are coming to replace older penal sentences when the minor nature of the crime permits.

In the realm of morality, it is possible to see an evolution of a similar type: in the place of an earlier and more rigid moral code, has emerged a morality that respects individual liberty whilst it balances the necessity of coexistence between people. There is a tendency, in other words, towards a morality based on a unique prohibition: do not do what is damaging to others; do not injure the dignity of others; recognise the equal value of everybody. The convulsions of the 1960s were a stage in this moral evolution. As both Durkheim and Weber saw, the emergence of Protestantism was a stage in this evolution. Inglehart's (1998) research cited earlier confirms this trend towards the "rationalisation of morality". In western societies, younger generations are no less demanding about morality than older generations, but their morality tends to reject any rule that might be seen as a *taboo* based on tradition alone, and to privilege in an almost exclusionary manner the principle of respect for the dignity of others (Boudon, 2002).

Consider also the evolution of our sensitivity towards war. Only a few decades ago, war was thought to be a normal phenomenon. Today, it is seen to be pathological. The same is seen in the evolution of our sensitivity to international relations. Hitherto, it was thought normal that international relations had a Hobbesian nature. Nowadays, the ideas of international solidarity, of international aid, and of the "right to interfere" are widely flaunted.

All of these changes correspond to mental irreversibilities. I do not see how sociologists can account for these irreversibilities without seeing that a process of rationalisation lies behind these evolutions.

III. WHY THE SIMILARITIES BETWEEN THE COGNITIVE AND THE AXIOLOGICAL ARE NOT UNDERSTOOD

Why are the similarities between the cognitive and the axiological not understood despite the fact that it is easy to find many cases that confirm them?

Because they run counter to the traditions of thought to which I have just alluded, and that exert a discreet but determinant influence on our everyday philosophy.

These traditions are to a degree mutually incompatible in their principles, but at the same time convergent in certain of their consequences: they all support the concept of an insurmountable discontinuity between the axiological and the cognitive, the normative and the positive, between practice and theory.

Let us attempt to complete the list outlined above. Firstly, there are modern *empiricism* and *positivism*, movements for which the "is" and the "ought" represent two distinct worlds, as held, for example by Ayer (1960 [1946]) or Urmson (1968).

Sociologism holds for its part that values are factual data ("to each society its values"), but also and complementarily that the mode of the "ought" through which they are normally understood by the social subject is the result of an illusion. A moral judgement can never be correct in itself; it is always uttered from a given point of view, that of the culture to which the subject belongs; thus no one point of view is able to dominate any others. The *culturalism* of anthropologists, for whom the incommensurability of cultures is thought to be unquestionable, has been a major source of sociologism.

Decisionism holds for its part that the individual chooses his values as the result of an inexplicable inspiration.

Followers of Marx hold that moral sentiments are distortions in the minds of social subjects due to their *social* interests.

Those of Nietzsche hold that they are distorted and unconscious expressions of the *psychological* interests of the subject.

Those of Freud see values as the sublimations of urges that come from the deepest recesses of the personality.

Postmodernism holds that the concept that certain values could be objective and universal is an illusion: indeed it is its principal hypothesis. According to one of the most eminent representatives of the post-modernist club (Rorty, 1989), the feelings of horror that Auschwitz creates in us are the product of historical conditioning. This position has at least the merit of being coherent: it would be difficult to see how relativist theories could lead to any other conclusion.

Outside these systems of thought, the varying postulates adopted, often without discussion, by the human sciences add to the difficulty they have in explaining moral feelings adequately. I am thinking in particular here of the *causalist* postulate to the effect that human behaviour can be explained as the result of non-rational causes.

Some even more vague postulates have also been put forward: such as that according to which the variability of beliefs in time and space is evidence of their contingent character, and would indicate that they have no basis in reason.

An example such as that of the separation of powers is enough however to refute all these theories. It is not a result of socialisation alone, nor because of an inexplicable decision, nor because of the influence of class interests, nor because of dominant groups that the separation of powers is currently thought to be a good thing. Contingency presided over its genesis; rationality over its selection.

Inadequacy of Responses to Irrationalist Models

The irrationalist models of moral sentiments have also been reinforced by the inadequacy of the responses that have challenged them; thinking here of the *naturalist* theories that are content merely to affirm the existence of a moral sense inherent in human nature. Such theories are clearly incapable of accounting for the variability of moral sensibilities. It is not very enlightening to declare with the *formalists* that values – the *good*, the *beautiful*, the *true* – are eternal in their form and historical in their content. No doubt many value judgements are variable in time and space. But others are invariant: deception has never been thought of as having a positive value. Won't it be for all eternity that a government which serves the interests of those who are governed is seen as better than one that serves the interests of the governors? The "good" here is not *formal*, but to borrow from Scheler (1955), *material*. This example is enough on its own to refute any formalist concept of values. But Scheler's *intuitionist* theory which holds that values may be perceived by a mysterious value sense is not really very persuasive.

It only remains to discuss the rational theories of moral sentiments proposed by sociologists. Although less popular than irrational theories, they do exist. *Functionalism*, in certain respects is one example, alongside *contractualism* or *rational choice theory*.

The basic principles of the *functionalist* explanation of norms can be seen in the example of the game of marbles so beloved of Piaget (1985[1932]). Children do not like cheating in marbles, Piaget tells us, because they love to play marbles and cheating destroys a game in which they take pleasure. Here the negative value attributed to cheating is analysed as the result of its negative effects on the social system constituted by the marbles players. It is why young children spontaneously dislike cheating, without the necessity of being taught that it is wrong. Here as in other cases, socialisation only has an effect if the principles which it tries to teach the subject find an echo in him: if he has the feeling that they are valid. At base *functionalism* argues that a situation is thought of as good by individuals when it helps the functioning of a system to which they are attached. Thus the members of a club will monitor who can join it, such a device being necessary if they want to keep out those candidates who have little interest in it or are incapable of contributing to its proper functioning. This is why elite academies and sports clubs select their members. In its best versions functionalism is, without question, a theory that is very useful where it deals with normative phenomena.

With the exception of the theory outlined by Weber and that I am trying to develop here, all of these theories – despite their importance – do however suffer from a serious weakness that leaves the field open to irrationalist theories. They have the advantage of positing that normative beliefs are produced by sound reasons, but they have the disadvantage of positing that these reasons are always exclusively relative to the *consequences* created by an action or a given state.

Moreover, they rarely emphasise the "circular" nature of the rationalisation process that I described above, the process by which the axiological novelties generated by historical contingencies or by innovators become the object of a process of social selection. Before discussing these weaknesses it is important, I feel, to underline the usefulness of these theories.

The Consequentialist Dimension of Axiology

Inspired by utilitarianism, the rational theories that I have just referred to with the example of functionalism have attempted to make *consequentialism* the motor of morality and more generally of axiology. They have tried to show that moral and social norms may always be explained in a consequentialist way (Opp, 1983 and Oberschall, 1994), and that moral and social norms are evaluated as good or bad according to the *consequences* to which they lead. There are examples for which one need go no further. Policies that threaten the lives of citizens will be seen as wrong, without having to add anything further to the matter.

The generally "consequentialist" nature of the rationalist theories of morality in the social sciences can be explained by the fact that many beliefs, attitudes, and decisions common to private or work life that involve value judgements may readily be analysed in a consequentialist manner.

Why do we think that majority rule is – usually – a good method for forming collective decisions that have the force of law from the divergent opinions of individuals? Why do we feel that this way of doing things is *right*? The wide acceptance of majority rule may be explained, as Buchanan and Tullock (1965) have shown, by the fact that it minimises in many cases the *costs* that would otherwise occur. The more it is required that a large number of participants in collective decision making accept measure X before it becomes law, the longer the debate will last. The less it is required that this number should be large, the more the number of people grow who are at risk of having a law which they do not want imposed on them. Thus, majority rule is the solution that minimises both types of drawback, if it is accepted that the two graphs are convex, as is normally done. For this reason it is "naturally" accepted as *right*. The judgment, "majority rule is a good thing" is therefore based on *objective* reasons.

Leo Moulin (1953) showed that in the history of western societies these rules were first identified and selected by monks of the Benedictine order, for the same reasons as in Buchanan and Tullock's work, although they were expressed in a different language.

The Buchanan and Tullock model not only explains the spread of majority rule, but many other facts. It explains why it is that the fact that certain decisions are taken by a single responsible person is considered normal, for instance, when the costs of the decision increase very rapidly with the time it requires to take them. Such is the case on the battle field, and here a slow decision-making process can lead to high risks for the combatants. In this case, the costs generated by the time taken to reach a decision have major importance. To use the jargon of decision theory, even the most committed democrat would readily accept that in such a case the decision-making should be of a "dictatorial" type. Not only would he accept it, but he would demand it. Thus, public opinion quite justifiably considered it to be scandalous that the prevarication of Europe and the United States should have allowed the Serbs the freedom to destroy Gorazde during the Bosnian war. Public opinion felt strongly that there was a contradiction between the importance of the stakes at issue and the organisation of decision-making, for the latter involved a slow process in a context where the costs of the decision appeared to be growing exorbitantly over time. By contrast, it would seem that the autonomy given to the military commanders during the Anglo-American campaign in Iraq in 2003, may have been largely responsible for its exemplary character from the military standpoint. Decentralisation of decision-making ensures its rapidity (and also its efficiency and relevance from a military standpoint).

Within the same society it is readily accepted that on certain questions a "dictatorial" organisation of collective decision-making is *right*, whilst on others it is usual to expect a "democratic" form. But it is important to note that the *variability* of these value judgements, far from being explicable in an irrationalist manner, is completely compatible with a rationalist theory of value judgement. What is right in one context is wrong in another, and it is by applying the *same* principles that reasons can be found for why what is *right* in one context is *wrong* in the other.

By contrast with a common misconception, the contextual variability of value judgements does not mean the absence of "objectivity" in the said judgements. This variability often means, as in the present example, that in contexts with different parameters there are correspondingly different evaluations. A procedure might be execrable as a military decision, but excellent as a political one.

These examples also, however, share another trait. They are consequentialist. The reasons for which such a rule is considered right here and wrong there have to do with the *consequences* that the rule involves. The rule of unanimity leads to good consequences in autarchic societies where subsistence is the economic regime, whereas it would lead to the breakdown of institutions in a modern society.

The Non-consequentialist Dimension of Axiology

Some examples do, however, exist which should be more strongly empha-sised here and concern the reasons – implicit or explicit, conscious or what I would call, following Hayek, meta-conscious – on which axiologi-cal beliefs are based and whose character is *non-consequentialist*.

The example I have referred to concerning majority rule points to the inadequacy of any theory of moral feelings that only refers to *conse-quentialist* reasoning. The way in which Buchanan and Tullock pose the problem of the transformation of individual preferences into a collective rule accepts without question the principle of "*one man, one vote*". Now this principle is rather questionable from the point of view of consequen-tialist reasoning, as has often been remarked. It has been noted many times that it is absurd and could be very harmful from a consequentialist viewpoint to base collective decisions on this principle. Is it not absurd and dangerous for instance that decisions on complex technical issues are taken by a majority of individuals whose knowledge is variable and generally quite lacking on the questions that are posed? A somewhat coarse (and untranslatable) pun of Bismarck bears witness to the state of collective sensibility in respect of universal suffrage at the beginning of the 20th century: "*vox populi, vox Rindvieh*". A rough translation, that ignores the alliteration but renders the crudeness of the formula socially acceptable is "people's voice, bovine voice".

It is understandable then that there have been interminable debates about whether, from the standpoint of their consequences, universal suffrage is really the best way of taking decisions which aim to serve the general interest. How then is it that we now accept this idea without discussion? Why do we consider universal suffrage to be such a good thing? Moreover, wouldn't we be shocked if it was replaced by a system where for instance the voter had to sit an examination or a test of interest before being allowed to vote? Because the principle "*one man, one vote*" expresses the equal value of each citizen. The only people who may be excluded from the polls are those who have lost their civil rights. The principle expresses, therefore, a fundamental trait of democratic organisation: that all should be admitted to a common table. But we should also recognise that it is much simpler to admit the imprescriptible nature of universal suffrage in a society where the citizen is required to follow an obligatory period of education.

On the one hand the same principle recognises that there is no unimpeachable competence on complex questions. In some ways it is odd to suggest to the citizens of the European Community that they vote on the question of whether they approve or not of the Treaty of Maastricht, a very complex text. On the other hand, the results of such a treaty are so complex that they are in reality unclear to everybody. It is by no means certain that the opinion of an expert would be clearly more enlightened than that of the average citizen. And furthermore, it would be difficult to deny the principle that associates all citizens with decisions concerning the future of the society of which they are members.

The "consequentialist" objections to universal suffrage that Docteur Bénassis voices in Balzac's *Médecin de Campagne* (*The Country Doctor*) are repeated almost exactly by American critics such as Blumer (1969[1930]), or French critics such as Bourdieu (1980[1973]), with regard to opinion polls. Their critiques are based on an excessive dramatisation of the problems raised by the interpretation of opinion polls, and which have been known to specialists in the field for a considerable time. They reproduce the same suspicions of such fictional tests of public opinion that Balzac, Marx, Lenin or Bismarck, held concerning universal suffrage. It is not by chance that, in the second half of the 20th century such suspicion of public opinion should be so marked among the Marxists; for "formal democracy" is, according to the teachings of Marx, an underhand method through which the "ruling class" oppresses the "working class".

Opinion polls are no more than developments of the *straw polls.* They have become common because they allow the sampling of public opinion between elections. Modern critiques of opinion polls commit, moreover, the same error as the assailants of universal suffrage that proliferated in the 19th century, as they do not distinguish between *consequentialist* and *axiological* rationality. It is true that opinion polls do not necessarily produce results that conform to the general interest. But even if they come up against *consequentialist rationality*, opinion surveys are an expression of *axiological rationality* in the sense that they crystallise the principle that in a democracy, everybody's opinion should count.

Thus the proposition that "universal suffrage is a good thing", one of the best established and most irreversible collective beliefs, is in part rational and on the other hand is *not* based on *instrumental rationality*, or at least does not exclusively rely upon it. It is not because beneficial consequences are necessarily brought about that the same weight is given to the opinions of competent or incompetent actors, of interested or disinterested actors, but because of the principle that in the good society, everyone counts. To deny this principle would be to introduce a value difference between individuals, it would be to negate the essence of democratic organisation.

To prove that practical rationality can take a non-consequentialist form, another example can be cited, almost a classic example: that of the feelings of rejection usually provoked by *theft*.

The English writer Mandeville (1728–1729) put forward a demonstration via the absurd of the fact that theft cannot be condemned because of the consequences to which it leads. In fact theft really only hurts a minority of people, that is, its victims, as Mandeville tells us rather humorously. For it also provides work to locksmiths and lawyers. Insurance companies could be added to this list. It is easy to reinforce Mandeville's theorem in general terms with some other arguments. Theft, for instance, creates a dual market with positive consequences. The market that is supplied by pilferage and theft allows the least well-off – who do not always know that they are buying stolen goods – to acquire the products much sought after in the "consumer society", electronic products especially, that the well off buy at market prices. Here, *the rich pay more*, and redistribution occurs in the "right" direction. The theory of Caplovitz (1967) according to which "the poor pay more" is in opposition to another and contradictory theory which seems no less true. But theft is not just a good thing for lawyers, insurance companies and the poorest social classes. It also increases demand, and stimulates supply. Without theft, the unemployment rate would be higher than it is. *From a strictly consequentialist viewpoint theft has some positive effects.* The demonstration by taking the case to its absurd extreme outlined by Mandeville is quite convincing. It shows that it is not possible with any moral certitude to use a consequentialist argument to draw the conclusion that theft is wrong.

In other words a consequentialist analysis would lead in this case to conclusions that contradict moral sentiments. These regard theft as wrong. However, its consequences are mitigated. So it is not because of the consequences to which it leads that theft is thought to be wrong.

To show that theft is wrong - that is, to account for the common sentiment that is expressed by the value judgement "theft is wrong"

– it is necessary to invoke non-consequentialist reasons. In fact theft is wrong because the social order is based on the fact that all remuneration should in principle correspond to a certain level of contribution. If not, then the very principle of social relationship itself would be called into question. Now theft is a positive remuneration that the thief gives himself at the expense of the victim, by resorting to an illegitimate duress. By doing so he violates the very idea of social exchange in the same way that the single-party system violates the idea of democracy. The certitude that accompanies the *judgement-sentiment* that "theft cannot be tolerated" cannot be explained by the consequences of theft, because they are opposing signs. The negative sign only prevails if the sole consideration is the consequences of the theft for its victim. However, the only justification for ignoring these particular consequences is by applying a *principle*: that by which it is not possible to give oneself a unilateral advantage at the expense of others.

This explanation offers a rational explanation of the negative sentiments engendered by theft. In effect, it accounts for these feelings by seeing them as emanating from sound reasons. At the same time, it points to reasons of a *non-consequentialist* character. It offers not merely an explanation of the universal nature of the condemnation of theft, but also of easily observed everyday phenomena. It may account for the apparently paradoxical fact that a theft which is without *any major consequences for the well-being of the victim* is widely felt by him or her to be intolerable, or for the fact that somebody who observes a theft will feel indignant that the theft has happened, quite independently of the loss suffered by the victim. In the final analysis it is because theft attacks the very heart of the social system that its advantages cannot make up for its drawbacks: the *consequentialist* reasons that might be advanced for choosing to steal or for the single-party system are subordinate to the *axiological* reasons which convince us to reject them.

The theoretical question that I investigate here is not without practical consequence. A consequentialist-type analysis will not, in fact, help to understand why "petty" crime is so hard for people to accept. It is however very easy to understand as soon as the existence of a non-consequentialist rationality is accepted.

It is possible to analyse many manifestations of everyday morality in the same way. The *plagiarist* provokes a feeling of distaste, not so much because he puts on a mantle that is not his own, but more because he violates the principles that preside over the arts of invention and creativity. The *impostor*, who manages to get work accepted as science that negates the elementary principles of scientific method, destroys the very essence of the game of science. But it is not because of the damage they cause that the plagiarist and the impostor are held in such low regard. The consequences of their misdeeds are quite often short-term and restricted, and they are usually unmasked in the end. The revulsion that they inspire comes more from the fact that they violate certain principles.

In the same manner it is difficult to accept that two people, who perform the same functions and who have equal seniority, should be paid differently. This is because payment is not simply the remuneration for a given contribution, but its recognition and its acceptance. Someone who receives less than his colleague will deduce from this that his contribution has not been recognised, and that there is an injustice. He will, on the other hand, accept that a colleague who performs a similar function might be better paid if he has greater seniority, because it is usual that an adjustment of contribution–remuneration might take place over time. He will also accept the possibility of some eventual incommensurabilities between contributions, of a lack of clarity about their evaluation and of contingencies that will render an alteration in contribution–remuneration more difficult. But in situations where none of these complications occur, he will usually demand equality between contribution and remuneration. Because this principle is constitutive, at a very abstract level, of all social exchange. The reciprocal of this is that social exchange is devoid of meaning if this principle is violated.

The preceding examples have been taken from everyday life. Others could easily be found. The pressure put on South Africa by the western democracies to end *apartheid* was *ex ante* questionable from a consequentialist standpoint: the transition might have been painful. But it was not questionable from the axiological standpoint: the benefits of democracy cannot without contradiction be reserved to one category of citizens alone; by their very essence basic human rights apply to everyone. Here, the axiological dimension of rationality is so clear that it would seem simply incongruous to put forward the consequentialist standpoint.

This example draws attention to an important point: it is usual to represent the "ethic of conviction" and the "ethic of responsibility" as the two alternatives of a choice that is irrational (not justified) and always open. If in fact these two terms may sometimes signify options that are equally legitimate, it is only because they are isolated examples. In other situations one of these two dimensions has primacy over the other, as evidence of the existence of a global rationality. Medical advances, by reducing infant mortality, have contributed to under-development: as the decline in the birth rate lags behind such progress, it leads to a population growth that feeds the vicious circle of poverty. But who would deny that this reduction in infant mortality, which is negative from the consequentialist standpoint, should be seen as progress?

IV. MORAL PROGRESS?

What results from all this, and however strange the proposition may seem, is moral progress. I do not mean by this that human beings become better and that they are less capable of cruelty today than in earlier times. Everything says this is not the case. I only mean that from the moment that an axiological innovation appears it has a tendency, if it appears to reinforce the dignity of man, to be socially selected. It creates, then, a modification in the prescriptive universe, somewhat akin to how a scientific innovation creates a modification in the descriptive universe.

To cite Tocqueville once more, he refers to the delight shown by Madame de Sévigné at the spectacle of an execution and draws from it the evident conclusion that our moral sensibility has changed (Tocqueville, 1986b, 540-542). This change is not short of causes. It comes from these innovations that carry irreversibilities that I have referred to earlier. It instigates restructurings that are analogues of those produced by certain scientific discoveries (heliocentrism, the theory of evolution, for instance) or certain major works of art (the music of Beethoven, Impressionism, for example). From the point at which it was possible to show by experience that universal suffrage did not necessarily lead to chaos, it was *definitively* more difficult to argue for regimes that dispensed with it, and not to feel a sort of distaste for them; much as the abolition of judicial torture did not paralyse the search for judicial truth, it became difficult to return to it and even less to think it was acceptable. Historical accident will doubtless ensure that regimes might appear to reinvent and even perfect it. But this practice would be universally perceived as a sign that they represented the worst. War is nowadays seen as abnormal (although this is not enough to prevent it, nor that anyone might lift a finger to stop it). Even if they are ridiculous, hypocritical and contradictory, expressions such as "clean war" or "surgical strike", do at least bear witness to the abnormality of bloody war. In the same way, it is not possible to go back to Aristotle's theory of motion, or to the idea that numbers and quantities inhabit distinct spheres, as the Greeks believed. These ideas had their own meaning in their time; they were justified by sound reasons. That is no longer the case now. But who would draw from the fact that science has a history, i.e. from the fact that we don't get immediately to the truth on all subjects, the conclusion that objectivity is a lure, a deception?

To reiterate once more, if this "rationalist", "neo-rationalist", even "cognitive" theory of values may appear shocking, it is because we are used to thinking that value judgements and fact judgements may be represented by two unconnected spheres. We don't know how to draw the imperative from the indicative, the *ought* from the *is*. From "this is" we do not know how to deduce "this is good". The "disenchantment of the world" has enlarged this gulf even further. The unintended consequences studied by Tocqueville that I referred to at the beginning, have reinforced the effects of disenchantment and make of relativism an unreachable horizon. The sociologist can only recognise that this relativism is in contradiction to what he observes, in the sense that this relativism is not shared at all by social actors themselves. They do not experience values as illusions or as purely personal convictions.

REFERENCES

Ayer, A. J. (1960 [1946]) *Language, Truth and Logic*. London. V. Gollancz, 2nd edn.

Blumer, H. (1969[1930]) "Science without Concept". In: *Symbolic Interactionism: Perspective and Method*. Berkeley, University of California Press: 153–170.

Boudon, R. (1992a) "Le pouvoir social: variations sur un thème de Tocqueville". *Revue des Sciences Morales et Politiques*, 531–558. Reproduced in *Études sur les sociologues classiques, I*. Paris, Presses Universitaires de France, 1998.

—— (1992b) "Should we Believe in Relativism?". In: Bohnen, A., Musgrave, A. (eds), *Wege der Vernunft. Festschrift zum siebzigsten Geburtstag von Hans Albert*. Tübingen, J. C. B. Mohr (Paul Siebeck): 113–129.

—— (1995) *Le Juste et le vrai, Études sur l'objectivité des valeurs et de la connaissance*. Paris, Fayard.

—— (2002) *Déclin de la morale? Déclin des valeurs?* Paris, Presses Universitaires de France and Québec, Nota Bene.

Boudon, R., Betton, E. (1999) "Explaining the Feelings of Justice". *Ethical Theory and Moral Practice. An International Forum*, 2(4): 365–398. Reproduced in Boudon, R., Cherkaoui M. (eds.). *Central Currents in Social Theory*. London, Russell Sage Foundation, 2000, Vol. VI: 453–484.

Bourdieu, P. (1980[1973]) "L'opinion publique n'existe pas". *Les temps modernes*. Reprinted In: *Questions de sociologie*, Paris, Minuit, 1980: 222–235.

Buchanan, J. and Tullock, G. (1965) *The Calculus of Consent*. Ann Arbor, University of Michigan Press.

Caplovitz, D. (1967) *The Poor Pay More*. London, Macmillan/New York, Free Press.

Durkheim, E. (1979[1912]) *Les Formes élémentaires de la vie religieuse*. Paris, Presses Universitaires de France.

Glendon, M. A. (1996) *A Nation under Lawyers*. Cambridge (Mass.), Harvard University Press.

Habermas, J. (1981) *Theorie des kommunikativen Handelns*. Frankfurt, Suhrkamp.

Inglehart, R., Basañez, M., Moreno A. (1998) *Human Values and Beliefs: A Cross-Cultural Sourcebook*. Ann Arbor, The University of Michigan Press.

Kuran, T. (1995) *Private Truths, Public Lies: The Social Consequences of Preference Falsification*, Cambridge, Mass., Harvard University Press.

MacIntyre, A. (1981) *After Virtue*. London, Duckworth.

Mandeville, B. de (1728–1729) *The Fable of the Bees, or Private Vices, Public Benefits*. With an essay on charity and charity-schools, and a search into the nature of society [by Mandeville]. The 5th edition, London: J. Tonson (J. Roberts).

Mead, G.-H. (1934) *Mind, Self and Society. From the Standpoint of a Social Behaviorist*. Chicago, University of Chicago Press.

Moulin, L. (1953)]) "Les Origines religieuses des techniques électorales et délibératives modernes". *Revue internationale d'histoire politique et constitutionnelle*, avril–juin: 106–148.

Nietzsche, F. (1969) *Götzendämmerung*. Werke, Bd 2, Munich.

Oberschall, A. (1994) "Règles, normes, morale: émergence et sanction", *L'Année sociologique*, (44: Argumentation et Sciences Sociales): 357–384.

Opp, K. D. (1983) *Die Entstehung sozialer Normen*. Tübingen, J. C. B. Mohr.

Piaget, J. (1985[1932]) *Le Jugement moral chez l'enfant*. Paris, Presses Universitaires de France.

Popper, K. (1963) *Conjectures and Refutations: The Growth of Scientific Knowledge*. London, Routledge.

Rorty, R. (1989), *Contingency, Irony and Solidarity*. Cambridge/New York, Cambridge University Press.

Ruse, M. (1993) "Une défense de l'éthique évolutionniste". In: Changeux, J.-P., (ed), *Fondements naturels de l'éthique*. Paris, Odile Jacob: 35–64.

Scheler, M. (1955) *Le formalisme en éthique et l'éthique matériale des valeurs*. Paris, Gallimard, 6ᵉ éd.

Simmel, G. (1892) *Die Probleme der Geschichtsphilosophie*. Munich, Duncker & Humblot.

Tocqueville, A. de (1986a) *L'Ancien Régime et la Révolution*. In: *Tocqueville. De la démocratie en Amérique, souvenirs, l'Ancien Régime et la Révolution*. Introduction and notes by Lamberti, J.-C., Mélonio, F., Paris, Laffont, Bouquins.

—— (1986b) *De la démocratie en Amérique*. (1835–1840). In: *Tocqueville. De la démocratie en Amérique, souvenirs, l'Ancien Régime et la Révolution*. Paris, Laffont.

Trevelyan, G. M. (1942) *English Social History: A Survey of Six Centuries, Chaucer to Queen Victoria*. London, New York, Longmans, Green.

Urmson, J. O. (1968) *The Emotive Theory of Ethics*. London, Hutchinson.
Wilson, J. Q. (1993) *The Moral Sense*. New York, Macmillan/The Free Press.

3

Basic Mechanisms of Moral Evolution: In the Footsteps of Durkheim and Weber

I. MORAL EVOLUTION: AN OBSOLETE IDEA?

The evolution of norms, values and institutions is a classical sociological issue from Durkheim to Parsons, Hayek, Eisenstadt or Dawkins. The thesis which I will try to defend here is that some basic mechanisms making social evolution more intelligible can be identified by developing some basic insights of Durkheim and Max Weber – to a point, however, where professional historians of sociology would possibly protest. It seems to me the two classical sociologists have sketched a theory of moral evolution which overcomes the objections rightly raised by Popper (1957) against historicism. Neither of them introduces the idea that there are such things as *laws* of historical development. As Pareto has written, when an idea is discredited, this situation tends to generate the view that the contrary idea is true. This figure is clearly illustrated by the case of evolutionism. From the moment when the evolutionary theories appeared as discredited, the idea that the notions of progress and even evolution are obsolete tended to acquire the status of an evident *truth*. Postmodern thinkers tend to adhere to what I might call an absolute or integral version of relativism, which sees the notion of progress as a mere illusion. Weber and Durkheim reject the idea that there are laws of history. But they would also have vehemently rejected the idea that the notions of progress and evolution are empty notions.

The evolutionary theory which I propose to draw from some central insights presented by Durkheim and Weber provides, it seems to me, an alternative to postmodern relativism and avoids the objections which have been raised against current evolutionary theories. Thus, Hayek's (1973–1979) theory pays much attention to innovations with an adaptive function and little attention to ideas which represent absolute innovations; he has also to some extent neglected the role of contingency in political and social life. As to Dawkins (1989), his attempt to build up a theory of "cultural evolution" which would have the same scientific attractiveness and solidity as the theory of biological evolution is certainly brilliant. But I perceive it as a scientific regression when it is compared to the theory which can be drawn from Weber's and Durkheim's insights. Not only are Dawkins' *memes* loose metaphors, the attractiveness of which rests rather upon their evocation of the scientifically uncontroversial genes than on their intrinsic explanatory value, but, furthermore, we do not need them if we follow Durkheim's and Weber's hints. I would say the same thing of Sperber's (1996) theory about the "contagion of ideas". His theory does not succeed in *explaining* cultural change: it provides rather, if I rightly understand it, an elegant system of concepts to *describe* it.

II. A CRUCIAL INSIGHT OF DURKHEIM AND WEBER

Durkheim on Individualism

I will insist first on an essential insight proposed by Durkheim (1960 [1893], p. 146). He writes in his *Division of Labour in Society*:

> *individualism, free-thinking appeared not in our days, nor in 1789, nor during the Reformation, nor with Scholasticism, nor with the decline of Greek and Roman polytheism or of oriental theocracies. It is a phenomenon which begins nowhere, but which develops continuously through the course of history*

> [*l'individualisme, la libre pensée ne datent ni de nos jours, ni de 1789, ni de la réforme, ni de la scolastique, ni de la chute du polythéisme gréco-romain ou des théocraties orientales. C'est un phénomène qui ne commence nulle part, mais qui se développe, sans s'arrêter tout au long de l'histoire*].

The rhetorical tone of the passage, stressed by the sequence of "nor" which brings us to the dawn of history, was certainly meant in Durkheim's mind to stress the importance he attached to the idea that "individualism begins nowhere". Many commentators on *The Division of Labour in Society* stress Durkheim's thesis that "individualism develops continuously through the course of history", but most of them disregard the first part of the sentence, which states that "individualism begins nowhere". In contradiction with this passage, current comments on *The Division of Labour in Society* maintain that Durkheim would have regarded individualism as a consequence of the growth of the division of labour and would have seen it as beginning with the protestant reformation. The same comments see individualism as a particular doctrine which has the status of one philosophical viewpoint among many others. The text which I have just quoted entirely contradict this current interpretation. It is true that in Durkheim's mind the increasing complexity of the division of labour, because it has favoured an increasing diversification of social roles and qualifications, has helped to reinforce individualism; more precisely, it has given birth to institutions facilitating the expression of individualistic values. It is true that Protestantism indirectly testifies to the development of individualism during the Renaissance: as it stresses the freedom and responsibility of the believer in the interpretation of Holy Scripture, Protestantism expresses, on a theological register, the fact that the development of the division of labour has increased in individuals' minds the sense of their singularity. These statements, which textbooks and comments emphasise, are indeed present in Durkheim's *Division of Labour in Society*. But they constitute only one part of his theory.

Durkheim makes as clear as possible, as I have said, that, to him, if individualism grows continuously through history, it should also be recognised that *it begins nowhere*. My guess is that the reason why so few commentators pay attention to this part of Durkheim's sentence lies in the fact that it appears to them as contradictory with the evolutionary theory developed in *The Division of Labour in Society*. How can individualism possibly have *begun nowhere*, both be present in all societies and increase continuously?

The meaning of this formula seems to me very clear, however, and in no way conflicts with Durkheim's evolutionary theory. It indicates that individuals as such have always represented the reference point, if not unique at least fundamental, from which the relevance and legitimacy of norms and generally of institutions in the broadest sense of this latter notion can be appreciated: the tacit norms which regulate small informal groups, as well as the norms which take the form of official collective decisions legally enforced, or the norms illustrating intermediary cases.

The formula indicates that in all societies, archaic as well as modern, institutions are perceived by individuals as more or less legitimate, as more or less acceptable. As to the criteria according to which they are judged as more or less acceptable or legitimate, they are the same in all societies: people appreciate or reject them depending on whether they have the feeling that they respect their dignity and vital interests.

The notion of *individualism* should obviously not be confused with the notion of *atomism*. It does not assume that societies are made up of a mere juxtaposition of individuals, but rather that, in any given society, people tend to consider an institution, a norm or a value X as *good*, or an institution, a norm or a value Y *better* than Z if and only if they have the impression that X is as *good* or that Y is *better* than Z for all individuals in the society or for some groups they belong to, or even do not belong to, without being detrimental to any.

In the same way as individualism should not be confused with atomism, it should not be confused with *egoism*. As individualism attributes an equal dignity to any individual, it assumes that a particular individual will tend to consider an institution as good or bad depending on whether s(he) has the impression that any other individual would also have a tendency to judge it so. We can check immediately that it is difficult to state or even to believe that an institution is good or bad if one does not have the impression that other people or at least some other people would also tend to judge so. This does not mean that there are no conflicts between opinions. Like conflicts of opinion in science, conflicts of opinion on moral, legal or political issues also divide adversaries who hold different views; but they all believe their reasons to be sound. An individual cannot consider a statement true or an institution good if he does not feel other people would also find the statement true or the institution good.

Briefly, I propose to read the half sentence "individualism begins nowhere" as indicating that, once an institution is proposed or imposed on a collectivity, a member of the collectivity will tend to consider it as acceptable or not, good or bad, legitimate or illegitimate, etc. depending on whether s(he) has the impression that it tends to be good for some groups of people and in the most favourable case to all. That actual institutions in all societies tend to be evaluated, judged good or bad, legitimate or not, on the basis of this ideal principle does not mean of course that individuals are entitled or permitted to express this evaluation nor that they are in all cases explicitly conscious of it; nor, as we just saw, that there are no conflicts of opinion.

The objection which can be opposed to this interpretation of Durkheim's thesis that *individualism begins nowhere* is the conjecture of *historicism*, according to which individuals have become conscious of their singularity only in modern societies: a controversial idea which Durkheim's formula directly contradicts. This controversial idea rests upon the doubtful metaphor which sees individuals as the *product* of the social environment they are embedded in. It derives from a rough confusion between categories. The social context determines the *parameters* individuals have to take into account when they behave or act in such and such a fashion; it does not *determine* their feelings, beliefs, actions or behaviour as such, even less whether they are aware or not of their dignity and vital interests. The fact that some societies are more coercive than others is indubitable; as is the fact that individuals are more respected in some societies than others; or the fact that the conception people have of their rights or dignity varies from one society to another. But the fact that there are no societies where people do not have a sense of their dignity and of their vital interests and of the dignity and vital interests of other people and notably of the people close to them is equally clear. It seems advisable, as Durkheim proposes to do according to the quoted sentence from *The Division of Labour in Society*, to take both these facts into account – the fact that individualism begins nowhere as well as the fact that it is more developed in some societies than in others – rather than to oppose the former to the latter, as historicism and culturalism wrongly propose.

Under the influence of positivism, Marxism, culturalism and structuralism in particular, the essential distinction between the notion of *cause* and the notion of *parameter* has been erased. The distinction is fundamental and simple, though. In order to go from a street A to a street B, I have to cross either street C or street D. This fact is a constraint I have to accept: a *parameter* I have to take into account but which does not *determine* my decision of going from A to B, nor my choice of crossing, say, street C rather than D. In the same way, the fact that I belong to a society where I am not allowed to express my sense of dignity does not mean that I am deprived of this sense. When the notions of *cause* and *parameter* are confused with one another, individuals are *naturalised*: their behaviour, their feelings, etc. are analysed as the mere effect of outside forces, while they are in fact actions and reactions taken under constraints. Though Marxism and structuralism are now rightly widely considered as obsolete, some of their principles are still active in many minds.

Durkheim's Insight Empirically Confirmed

Many studies provide an empirical confirmation of Durkheim's statement according to which in all societies, traditional as well as modern,
individuals have a sense of their dignity and vital interests. Popkin's
(1979) *Rational Peasant* seems to me particularly illuminating in this
respect. Against a received idea defended by many anthropologists,
he has shown in a convincing fashion that, in the village societies of
South-East Asia or Africa, the rule of unanimity is a widely accepted
constitutional rule because it is perceived as the rule most likely to
generate respect for the dignity and vital interests of all. Against this
interpretation, anthropologists have contended that the diffusion
of the unanimity rule reflects the fact that individuals in archaic
societies have little or no self-awareness, little or no sense of their
singularity and of their personal dignity and see themselves as mere
parts of the collectivity. The interpretation reveals the importance of
the metaphysical representation according to which the sense people
have of their dignity and vital interests is a dependent variable: it
would be present in some societies, absent in others. To Popkin by
contrast, the constitutional unanimity rule was devised and accepted
because any other decision rule would entail serious threats to the
economically weakest members of the society. The village societies
of Africa or South-East Asia, he explains, are societies of small size,
based on a subsistence economic system, with few exchanges with the
outside environment. In such societies, the weakest members would
be heavily threatened if collective decisions were taken, say, on the
basis of majority rule. Consequently, such a constitutional rule would
not be considered legitimate. Popkin's interpretation, in contrast to
the current interpretation among anthropologists, recognises the
obvious fact that the unanimity rule maximises the power of each
individual, as shown by the fact that it has another name: the right
of veto. Moreover, Popkin's interpretation accounts for the fact that,
in village societies with the unanimity rule as a basic constitutional
rule, decisions generally take a long time and occur in a climate of
confrontation and institutionalised conflict. On the whole, this type
of study shows convincingly that the everyone's sense of their individuality and singularity is characteristic as well of societies where
solidarity is mechanical, to use Durkheim's terms, as well as of societies with organic solidarity. Individualism meets more favourable
conditions in the latter, i.e. modern societies; but it characterises
the former as well.

Possibly without being aware of Durkheim's statement according to which individualism begins nowhere, Simmel (1900) considers as evident the fact that the individualistic virus is already present at the dawn of history. It explains the abolition, in Anglo-Saxon and early German law, of the *Wergeld*, a judiciary practice which indexed the penal sanction on the social rank of the victim. Once the *Wergeld* was abolished, the abolition became irreversible because it represented a step forward in the establishment of individualism: the abolition introduced the idea that any human life, the King's life just as the life of the poorest peasant, has in principle the same value. So, to Simmel as to Durkheim, individualism begins nowhere, but it leads the selection of ideas and institutions and explains that some ideas and institutions are irreversibly adopted.

Such studies illustrate the powerful of the social sciences. Once they follow a scientific *ethos* and care about looking scrupulously at data, they display their capacity to eradicate the ethnocentric representations of ordinary sociology. Durkheim, Simmel and nowadays Popkin and others show that the view according to which individualism (in the sense where Durkheim takes the concept) is exclusively characteristic of modern societies is the product of an ethnocentric illusion. Popkin's powerful study shows that ethnocentrism can be pronounced even among professional anthropologists: many of them seem to believe that, since the people they observe *behave* and seem to *feel* differently from the way they themselves behave and feel, they should *be* different from themselves. The imagery of the fusional community where individuals have no consciousness of their own self and exist exclusively, so to say, through the group is treated by many anthropologists as going without saying, while it is a mere ethnocentric illusion. Equally ethnocentric is the representation that people in the past submitted to collective representations and values they passively accepted, while in modern and postmodern societies, they pick up the representations and values they please. Ethnocentrism can be historical as well as geographic, vertical as well as horizontal, so to say: it leads to misrepresentations, not only of individuals belonging to other cultures, but also of individuals belonging to the past of our own culture. Unfortunately, studies like Popkin's are too rare: a lasting ethnocentric bias leads on the contrary to the current view that individualism is a distinctive cultural feature of modern Western society. Like Durkheim and Adam Smith before him, the economist Amartya Sen (1999) has rightly stated that the first value for any individual, Indian or European, is to be able to consider oneself with respect.

I may perhaps note incidentally that I feel confirmed in the inter-pretation I propose of Durkheim's statement according to which "indi-vidualism begins nowhere" notably by the fact that he was strongly influenced by Kant's philosophy. Stating that individualism begins nowhere amounts to stating that the effects of institutions on the vital interests of individuals represent the only reference point which can possibly be used to evaluate them. If I am right when I stress the influence of Kant on Durkheim, individualism, in the sense where Durk-heim takes the notion, is comparable to a Kantian *a priori* category: it represents the frame within which institutions would are evaluated. It should moreover be noted that, by introducing this neo-Kantian cate-gory, Durkheim proposes an *a priori* more acceptable than the *a prioris* by means of which Kant had proposed to ground moral evaluations. Durkheim's *a priori* is clearly less mysterious than Kant's *a prioris*.

An objection can be opposed to this *a priori*: that it presupposes the existence of a "human nature": a notion which many sociologists consider unacceptable. But is it a serious objection? The idea accord-ing to which the social sciences would have irreversibly discredited this notion has the status of a received idea. That an idea is broadly accepted does not demonstrate that it is valid, though. Wilson (1993) has shown on the contrary that it could be used to explain a number of moral facts observed by historians, sociologists, anthropologists and psychologists. But it should immediately be made clear that the notion of "human nature" can be accepted only if it is reduced to a number of undetermined principles such as the principle of *individualism* in Durkheim's sense.

More precisely, to Durkheim as to Weber, men are similar in all cultures, but they are embedded in various social and historical con-texts. Men are everywhere self-conscious, self-interested; they have objectives, intentions, projects; they evaluate rationally in particular the institutions in the context in which they live. But they make use of their autonomy in the framework of the context in which they are embedded. The features of this context constitute, as I proposed to call them before, the *parameters* to which their feelings and actions are subjected, but which in no way *determine* these feelings and actions.

A wide gap separates Weber and Durkheim from many sociolo-gists in this respect. To Comte and Lévy-Bruhl, the culturalists or the structuralists of complete obedience, the people's behaviour should be analysed as *determined* by the socio-historical context in which they are embedded. To Durkheim and Weber, their behaviour must be seen by contrast as reflecting their *autonomy*, given that the latter is bounded by the parameters defining the context. Both sociologists have greatly emphasised the existence of a long-term trend toward the extension of individual autonomy. Both took their inspiration in great part from Kant. This is not only true of Durkheim, but also of Weber. The two knew and appreciated the importance Kant had given to the notion of autonomy. Both saw that recognising the existence of a socially bounded autonomy is a condition to be met if sociology is to be scientific: to describe reality as it is.

By contrast, positivism, structuralism and culturalism see the autonomy of individuals as an obstacle: as the main reason why the social sciences have a hard time becoming genuine sciences, sciences as scientific as the natural sciences. Positivism, structuralism and culturalism share the impression that mechanics is the model of science. From this impression they have drawn a principle: that genuinely scientific social sciences should attempt to picture people as *determined* by the social structure. Applying this principle, they try to explain human behaviour as the mere effect of *forces*. Weber and Durkheim define science rather by the old notion of the equivalence between things as they are and the way the intellect sees them: by the old notion of the *adequatio rei et intellectu*. And, as they see autonomy and the ability to behave rationally as basic features of men, they are careful to take these features into account in their sociological analyses.

Weber's and Durkheim's Insights on Individualism

Although he used other words, Weber put forward some ideas that are strikingly close to those of Durkheim, just examined above.

In his *Essays in the Sociology of Religion*, Weber (1920–1921) comments on a passage of Paul's *Letter to the Galatians* where Paul reprimands Peter: the latter had suddenly taken his leave from a group of Gentiles because he had seen Jews coming towards them. Weber sees in this anecdote, he writes, a crucial episode in the history of Western civilisation. "It signals the birth moment of the idea of citizenship in the West" [*Die Geburtsstunde des Bürgertums im Okzident*]. Peter had not dared to remain in the company of the Gentiles when the Jews appeared, while Paul would have expected that, by remaining seated, Peter would have meant that all men are of equal worth beyond their differences; that consequently they are all entitled to sit at the same table; that a legitimate political order must recognise this equal dignity; briefly, that *individuals* should be regarded as *persons* and that a necessary condition for them to be treated as persons is that they are treated as *citizens*. The realisation of this idea, says Weber, was considered from this moment in the West as a basic objective; this objective was bound to direct the history of the West for centuries. Where does the strength of this idea come from? From the fact that the crucial innovation represented by the notion of *citizenship* that underlies the idea of *commensality*, the idea that all should be entitled to sit at the same table, appears immediately as giving expression to the idea of the intrinsic value of every individual, with the corollary that good institutions are institutions that would be approved by all.

Weber puts forward in other words a *programmatic* view of moral evolution: a view that sees moral evolution as led by "programmes", a familiar concept notably in Eisenstadt's evolutionary theory. Weber's work is in other words an invitation to see the history of political institutions, the history of religions or the history of morals as guided by a diffuse *programme* aiming at defining institutions, rules, etc. which would respect most efficiently the dignity and vital interests of all. The invention of the notion of *person* is a crucial step in the realisation of this programme. Already in the first century, writes Weber, this *programme* was advanced in a spectacular fashion thanks to the creation of the notion of *citizenship*. For, if the *word* is not used by Paul, the *notion* is present in the anecdote reported by Paul's letter to which Weber attributes such historical importance.

In order to make clearer the interpretation I propose of Durkheim's and Weber's suggestions, one can, as Weber often does, emphasise the analogy between the history of morals and political philosophy and the history of science (Boudon, 2000, Ch. 5). Science is born from a vague programme which can be defined as: *describing the real world as it is*. The value of this programme cannot be demonstrated, for ultimate values cannot be demonstrated acceptable or not, legitimate or not: an obvious statement well stressed by Weber's (1995[1919]) famous conference on *Science as Vocation*. Weber simply meant that any theory starts from principles which cannot be demonstrated, if not by other principles which would have to be demonstrated and thus *ad infinitum*. Once this programme is proposed (if one can say so, since, like individualism, it *begins nowhere*), it has inspired and still inspires a constant flow of speculations and researches.

In this lecture, Weber states clearly that, not only science but the other domains of thought, are governed by a process of rationalisation:

Scientific progress is beyond doubt the most important fraction of this intellectualisation process to which we have been the subject for millennia.

Der wissenschaftliche Fortschritt ist ein Bruchteil, und zwar der wichtigste Bruchteil, jenes Intellektualisierungsprozesses, dem wir seit Jahrtausenden unterliegen (Weber, 1995[1919], p. 18).

So, the history of science illustrates a fundamental process which also appears in other aspects of human thought.

Like the history of science, the history of morals and of political philosophy is the history of the realisation of a programme, the objective of which is to conceive institutions able to respect as far as possible the dignity and vital interests of individuals. Like the validity of the programme of science, the validity of such a programme cannot be demonstrated. And this programme is as fuzzy as the programme of science: the notion that science should describe the world as it is really is unclear; as unclear as the notion of the dignity of the person. The validity of the two programmes cannot be demonstrated; and they are equally vague. They are even necessarily vague, one might add, since they are defined by a regulatory idea which requires that their meaning is made more precise. They are never completed; they guide human action in several of its dimensions. An indirect proof of the fuzzy character of the programme described by the notion of science can be seen in the fact that, while many works in the philosophy of science have tried to identify the demarcation criteria between science and non-science, have never been found (see chapter 1).

The success of Christianity and later, in an entirely different period, of socialism is due to the fact that the two movements may be seen as major steps in the realisation of the programme described by Weber and Durkheim. As Simmel (1892, 1900) rightly noted, the two movements, as different as they are in many respects, have one point in common: they owe their influence to the fact that they have been perceived as advancing the individualistic programme; in other words, as stressing the respect owed to each individual independently of his or her competence and merits. In order to avoid possible misinterpretations, it should be noted that Simmel is obviously referring to the *socialist movement* in the form it was in his own time, when it had not yet taken power anywhere.

It can be noted on the occasion of the association made by Simmel between Christianity and socialism that *regular* religions have a crucial advantage over *secular* ones: given the symbolic character of their doctrine, the former are immunised against criticism, while the latter are not, since they claim to be "scientific". This explains, say, that Christianity seems to be today in better health than socialism.

Before sociologists, philosophers well understood that programmes can be proposed that include their own definition among their objectives. Thus, Hegel saw that many ideas can become clear only once they are put into practice; he had also seen that ideas can be opposed by social forces, and that they could however survive in human minds. As Popper (1945) rightly states, though, Hegel did not escape the fallacy of historicism. With Max Weber, this undesirable feature is eradicated. To him, some ideas appear irreversible because they are the product of rational selection; but historical forces can always have the consequence that they are not really inscribed in the real world. I will come back to this central element of Weber's insight shortly.

If the elaboration I propose of Durkheim's and Weber's insights is accepted, one should see in the moral and political evolution of the Western world the realisation of a diffuse *programme* defined by the leading idea to which Durkheim has associated the notion of *individualism*. Its objective is to define norms and institutions aiming at satisfying the dignity and moral interests of individuals. Again, it should be made clear that these interests are by nature undefined and depend on the state of societies.

In the case of modern societies, the deployment of this programme is particularly remarkable. "We have", writes Durkheim (1960[1893], 147), "a cult of human dignity which, as every cult, already has its superstitions" [*Nous avons pour la dignité de la personne un culte qui comme tout culte a déjà ses superstitions*]. As can be readily confirmed by this argument, the cult of "human rights" did not start in our time.

Max Weber could have written the same statement by Durkheim. The notion of the dignity of the person, he claims, is present throughout the history of the West. But this idea is more or less active and of course defined in various ways: fuzziness is characteristic of the notion of the *dignity of the person* as it is of *individualism*. And the fact that it is more or less present and defined in various ways depends on structural factors, but also on contingencies and on innovations. These factors affect not only the more or less intense awareness that people have of this notion, but its very realisation. There is consequently no guarantee that regressions will not appear. "Historical forces" are able to generate and have effectively generated such regressions.

Of course, historical forces are also able to slow down and generally to make unpredictable the path of the diffuse rationalisation process explicitly described by Durkheim as well as by Weber. Because of the interference of these "historical forces" in Weber's sense and of the structural factors described by Durkheim, the basic principle of individualism (organising society in order to respect as much as possible the vital interests and the dignity of each) has been permanently thwarted. Thus, the Greeks devised institutions which have been justly praised and imitated because they aimed at respecting the dignity of citizens. But they considered slavery legitimate, for they were convinced of its functional interest for society as a whole. Aristotle did not conceive a society without slaves. By contrast with Aristotle, Montesquieu did not see slavery as functional. He held slavery as "against nature" (*contre la nature*). He thought, however, that the economic circumstances of his time did not make the abolition of slavery possible for, he contended, if slavery was abolished in the West Indies, the price of sugar would rise too much. This situation, where slavery was to be "against nature" while it was at the same time considered dangerous if not impossible to abolish it, lasted until slavery was abolished by force in the areas where, as in the South of the US, it had played an important economic role. Only then could axiologically rational arguments dominate the instrumentally rational arguments which had long prevailed.

Today, slavery has been abolished almost everywhere, but it reappears again under the effect of "historical forces" (e.g. child prostitution in South-East Asia). But these modern forms of slavery are condemned and clandestine, for a negative value is irreversibly associated with this institution: nobody would dare today to legitimate slavery. This example stresses the important point that institutions are reversible, while the value attributed to institutions can be irreversible. Slavery reappeared in our contemporary world, but not the idea that slavery is a good institution. This idea was already held unacceptable in Montesquieu's time. It remains unacceptable in our time.

III. A THEORY OF MORAL EVOLUTION

The Diffuse Rationalisation of Political, Juridical and Scientific Ideas

The programme defined by the notion of the dignity of the person is governed, like any programme, by a process called by Weber "diffuse rationalisation" (*Durchrationalisierung*). This process is essential.

It explains that certain ideas become irreversibly accepted by public opinion. It explains, as Durkheim states, that individualism "develops constantly throughout history".

The notion of *rationalisation* is widely used by Weber, as shown by Sukale (2002), but never defined by him in an explicit fashion. It describes on the one hand the process through which, given a programme or a project, better means are sought to promote it: this dimension of the process mobilises the *instrumental* type of rationality. Thus, legal notions such as *habeas corpus* or the principle of *freedom of opinion* are associated with legal instruments that are crucial as far as the enforcement of individual rights is concerned. In the same fashion, the abolition of the above mentioned *Wergeld* represents a crucial instrument in the realisation of the individualistic programme.

The notion of rationalisation designates on the other hand the process through which the nature of a programme is made more precise and theories are developed which advance its realisation: this dimension of rationality can be called *cognitive* (Boudon 2003). Cognitive rationality is at work in a particularly clear fashion in science. It guides the production of scientific theories. The activity described by this notion aims at devising better explanations of the phenomena the scientist is concerned with; at realising the goals of the programme *science*: explain better; explain more; explain in a more coherent fashion, etc. The advances of science depend on external conditions and on structural factors; but they are also produced by an endogenous process of diffuse rationalisation, in the cognitive sense of the word.

This rationalisation process characterises, according to Weber, the history of law and legislation, as well as the history of morals or of political philosophy and even of religion (Boudon 2000, Ch. 5; Sukale 2002). All these activities are inspired by the objective of finding better rules and better explanations of the phenomena under their jurisdiction: rules and explanations which aim at being more effective, simpler, more coherent with one another, at arousing more clearly a feeling of legitimacy or of validity in the public. The idea that rationalisation is at work in all areas of human thought is possibly one of the most important ideas developed by Max Weber. Its importance is not always emphasised, probably because it contradicts the common view according to which the progress of science is essentially endogenous, while law, politics or religion are primarily if not exclusively affected by exogenous factors, either contingent or structural. This contrast between the way the development of science on the one hand and of law, morals or political theory on the other hand is commonly seen reflects the received idea according to which a wide gap separates *is* and *ought*, norms and facts, values and facts.

The similarities between the rationalisation processes at work in the history of science, morals, law and religion do not mean of course that there are no differences between these activities: science rests upon the principle that all its statements and notions can be criticised, while religion considers some of its statements and notions as immunised against criticism: religion entails faith, while science rejects it, in principle at least. Religion accepts to explain visible phenomena by the action of supernatural forces; science does not. But, beyond these obvious differences, the procedures of verification, falsification, generalisation, simplification, etc., characteristic of scientific thinking are also characteristic of moral, political or legal thinking. This crucial idea inspires the most path-breaking studies of Weber and Durkheim in the sociology of morals, law, religion and magic (Boudon 1999, 2000, 2001).

Legislation tends to create systems of norms as efficient and as compatible with one another as possible; adapted to the demands of the public as the legislator sees them; likely to be considered legitimate by public opinion. For rules perceived as illegitimate are a source of social tensions and conflicts. Taking this implicit requirement of legitimacy into account is essential: it disqualifies at once so-called juridical positivism. Goyard-Fabre (2002) has shown that an endemic tension between natural right and positivism characterises the philosophy of law from Greek Antiquity to the present time. This permanent tension shows that it is impossible to understand the evolution of law if one does not see that a new norm can only be accepted by the public if it arouses a feeling of legitimacy, while on the other hand such feelings of legitimacy or illegitimacy can only appear in the presence of concrete laws.

The political theories inspiring the construction of institutions are equally subjected to the same process of rationalisation. Thus, Montesquieu's principle of the separation of political powers projects a type of political organisation aiming at guaranteeing the rights of citizens. It has been accepted with difficulty. Its history has not yet come to an end and will probably never come to an end. Thus, in France, as I mentioned in chapter 2, when an important politician is condemned, many voices in the political class would regularly bring up the risk of a *gouvernement des juges* and recall the role played by the judiciary institutions at the beginning of the 1789 Revolution. But, in spite of this resistance, the validity of the idea according to which a good political system should make the powers independent of each another appears to have been widely accepted. Like scientific ideas, it has been rationally selected. It has been retained in the course of this selection process because it has the consequence that it gives birth to a more efficient form of political power; that it reduces the probability of a violent solution of social tensions and conflicts; that it offers citizens a greater guarantee that their rights will be respected by the authorities; that consequently citizens will accept the latter more easily.

At the same time, social evolution has the consequence that working out the principle of the separation of powers constantly meets new questions, challenges and obstacles. Thus, the growing power of the media in communication societies has inspired new institutions such as the regulatory bodies attached to newspapers, TV or radio stations.

In spite of this permanent adaptation of the principle to new situations, the principle itself has been irreversibly selected; the idea according to which each power should be balanced by a counter power is considered sound. The reason for this selection lies in the fact that the principle definitely generates positive outcomes. Simple and well known as it is, this example shows that the processes by which ideas are selected in the field of political theory, legal theory or moral theory are not different in nature from the processes by which ideas are selected in the natural sciences.

It is essential to note in this chapter on rationalisation processes that they obviously do not automatically generate happy outcomes. They can also produce undesirable effects. Thus, many contemporary societies are afflicted by what has been called in the case of France a symptom of *legislative inflation*. As soon as a group has a nuisance power, it can be tempted to use it to impose hastily devised legislative changes which will be likely to produce negative effects. The new law will restore social peace in the short term, but produce negative effects in the long term.

The Origin of the Irreversibility of Ideas

The origin of the irreversibility of a new idea lies in the fact that, when competing ideas are presented on the market of ideas the best one tends to be selected in preference to the others. This process is readily observed in the history of science. When the phenomenon of optical interferences was discovered by Fresnel, it disqualified the corpuscular Cartesian theory of light.

The same kind of process can be observed as far as, not only scientific, but also axiological ideas are considered. The principle of the separation of political powers has been irreversibly selected against the principle defended in particular by Beccaria or Bodin, according to which political power should be concentrated in order to be effective. As a result of this selection process, totalitarian or even authoritarian regimes are currently considered illegitimate. The irreversibility of the basic principles defining democratic regimes explains why the communists decided to call the types of regimes they established after World War II "people's democracies". Though the Marxist tradition had long condemned democracy as serving the interests of the bourgeoisie, the communists well saw that the idea that democracy is preferable to other types of regimes had been irreversibly selected. They decided for this reason to label the totalitarian regimes they set up in such a way as to suggest that they were democracies carried to a higher level of perfection: they were more than "democracies"; they were "people's democracies".

The fact that irreversible ideas can be easily found in the domains of law and political philosophy derives in part from the fact that axiological rationality and instrumental rationality, as Weber stated, though distinct, are currently mixed with one another in practice. In simpler terms, a system of reasons leading to the belief that "X is good, legitimate, fair, etc." includes in most cases factual statements beside normative statements. Now, factual statements can be compared with data, for instance when they state that some means are better given that some objective is aimed at. In still simpler terms, law and politics have technical aspects: some measures are objectively more effective than others to lower the rates of unemployment or delinquency, say. Now, technology is a type of activity where the notion of progress can be defined in entirely unambiguous terms, as clearly stated by Weber.

It can be noted that these remarks refute the idea according to which *ought* cannot be derived from *is*. We can very well draw a conclusion of the *ought* type from a system of reasons where all reasons are of the *is* type, while only one is of the *ought* type; in other words, we can often draw a normative conclusion from reasons all of which except one are factually grounded. So, though popular, Hume's theorem according to which an *ought* statement cannot be derived from an *is* statement or the notion made popular by Moore (1954[1903]) of the *naturalistic fallacy* is a wrong one. *Ought* is not separated from *is* by an unbridgeable gap. As I have discussed this idea more thoroughly in Chapter 1 and will come back to it in chapter 6, I will content myself here with this short notation on a crucial point.

The current impression that the evolution of ideas would be rational as far as knowledge is concerned and contingent as far as morals, political theory or law are concerned is grounded on the fact that political, moral or legal discussions are held on the public stage, often in a context of sound and fury, while scientific discussions take place in the confined atmosphere of scientific colloquia or of laboratories. But, behind this apparent contrast, all ideas are indistinctly affected, as Weber has rightly stated, by a process of diffuse rationalisation.

The Irreversibility of Moral Ideas Revealed by Contemporary Empirical Research

The rationalisation process I have just mentioned appears to be at work in contemporary societies. One can verify it in many surveys and notably in the famous inquiry on world values conducted by Inglehart *et al.* (1998).

By comparing younger respondents to older, it is readily verified that the younger tend to have a *rationalised* conception of moral values in the sense that they tend more frequently than the older to consider that the ultimate and unique ground of moral rules is the basic value of respect for other people; that any rule which does not give the impression that it is rationally grounded should be considered with scepticism; that authority is legitimate and hence acceptable exclusively when it is rational; that charismatic and traditional authority should be regarded with scepticism; that a rule grounded on tradition and giving the impression of not being rationally grounded is of weak validity: it is perceived as a *taboo* and tends to be rejected.

In the same fashion, the younger respondents tend to have a more rational view of religious beliefs: they tend to reject the elements of religious doctrines which cannot easily receive a symbolic interpretation; when they believe in God, they believe much less frequently than the older in a personal God. They believe less frequently than the older in a life after death. They tend on the whole to develop an immanent view of religion. They are attracted by religious doctrines which, like Buddhism, are practically devoid of transcendent elements.

As regards political values, they would like to see politicians as more respectful of the wishes of citizens; they want new rights to be defined, to the effect of protecting minorities and respecting the right of all to define their identity freely; they push toward the development of an opinion democracy beside the representational party democracy; they believe less often than the older, other things equal, that political problems have easy solutions. For this reason, they reject extremist political programmes more often than the older respondents. These various data are illustrative of what I called following Weber a *rationalisation process*. A more detailed presentation of this interpretation of Inglehart's data is presented in Boudon (2002).

The same process of *diffuse rationalisation* is present, more generally, in many trends characterising modern societies. Reciprocally, the basic insights sketched by Weber and Durkheim and which I propose to develop here are crucial tools for the understanding of modern societies.

Thus, "the decrease of social control" (*la diminution du contrôle social*) described by Durkheim appears as a permanent objective of criminal policy: misbehaviour must be punished but in ways as compatible as possible with the dignity of individuals. Contemporary moral sensibility cares about the dignity of criminals to such an extent that it has welcomed the idea that prevention should be substituted for repression. The utopia "prevention instead of repression" has been so popular in Western societies in the last decades of the 20th century that the notion of dissuasion itself seems to have disappeared altogether, probably because, as it includes the notion of threat, it was perceived as being as unpalatable as repression itself. This preference for prevention generated unwanted effects: it played a role in the increase of misbehaviour. This example offers the opportunity of stressing the fact that rationalisation should not be equated with progress. It can produce unwanted beside desirable effects.

On the whole, modern morality tends to be restricted to a single leading principle: that the forms of behaviour which are exclusively qualified to be forbidden are those which entail a negative impact on others; conversely, if it can be demonstrated that a given type of behaviour does not cause a nuisance to others, it should be allowed. One tends to consider taboo the prohibition of any form of behaviour entailing no detrimental effect on other people. It is generally considered that holding opinions considered shocking by some people cannot be forbidden, since such a prohibition would contradict the notion of freedom of opinion, which is itself a corollary of the principle of respect for the dignity of all.

This rationalisation process explains why sensationalist porno-graphic literature is sometimes promoted to the status of an important literary event (see e.g. the cases of Houellebecq or of Catherine Millet in France). The seriousness of this literature makes it entirely distinct from the erotic tradition: it has attracted a great deal of attention thanks, not to its literary quality – it displays a minimal power of seduction – but to its ideological meaning: it stresses the right of individuals to choose their sexual practices with complete freedom provided only they entail no undesired nuisance on others.

The Extension of Rights in Modern Societies

The same phenomenon of diffuse rationalisation explains why rights tend to multiply. T.H. Marshall (1964) identified this process a long time ago. It is still at work. New rights are constantly identified which have the property – curious if not shocking from a legal viewpoint – that they are enforced by no laws or regulations. See as an example the French *droit au logement* (literally: the right to housing). The notion has been part of the language for decades, while this so-called *right* is legally not enforced. Some lawyers have proposed calling *rights of the third generation* rights such as *the right to peace* or the *right to right*, i.e. those rights which have little chance of ever being legally enforced since it would imply the aboli-tion of force in national and international processes (Cohen 1999).

This uneven, almost stuttering character of the development of new rights is unavoidable. It confirms the characteristics of any *pro-gramme* in the sense in which I use this concept here. The notion of the *dignity* of the person is fuzzy; hence its content is unstable; hyper-bolic interpretations of the notion are consequently unavoidable: see for instance, in the US notably, the hyperbolic views developed by the feminist movements or by the movements struggling for the defence of minority rights. Utopias are a normal component of the rationalisation processes through which new rights are identified and defined.

But it should also be noted that, at the same time, these utopias and hyperbolic interpretations are exposed to a process of rational selection. Obviously, this selection process does not result from a dis-cussion between experts; it results rather from a confrontation between actors; among them: public opinion, social movements, intellectu-als and lawmakers. That such rational selection processes currently develop in a context of conflict should not obscure their underlying rationality. Unfortunately, such an obscuration is typical of the so-called sociological theories of conflict and domination.

The inflationary extension of rights which can be observed today is a symptom of the development of the programme defined by the notion of respect for the person, as are many other features characteristic of contemporary societies: the development of the right of interference with the sovereignty of other nations (the french *droit d'ingérence*), or the creation of international penal tribunals. Episodes such as the arrest of Pinochet in the UK or the indictment of Milosevic by an international court of justice are easily explained by the rationalisation processes I have described. Their importance lies in the fact that they illustrate the case where the rights of individuals are perceived as having priority over the principle of national sovereignty. The constant attempt to devise means of social control aiming at minimising criminal acts and at the same time expressing maximum respect for the person of the criminal is another example of the action of these rationalisation processes. As I have mentioned, this type of rationalisation was identified by Durkheim (1960 [1893]).

The identification and analysis of the dynamics thanks to which a necessarily fuzzy programme gives birth to various interpretations which are submitted to a process of rational selection in which various collective actors take part is, it seems to me, one of the major theoretical findings of the social sciences. They have made obsolete the static Kantian notion of the *dignity of man*. Kant's formalism forbade him to give the question of the *content* of this notion the crucial importance which it has.

Once elaborated, the evolutionary theory sketched by Weber, Durkheim and contemporary writers, such as Eisenstadt, seems to me also more convincing and clearer than the brilliant theories of cultural evolution proposed by modern writers, like Dawkins' (1976) theory of *memes* or Sperber's (1996) theory of the contagion of ideas. These theories are currently popular – in some social scientific circles at least – for two reasons: they naturalise the human subject and thus give the impression of being more "scientific" than the theories which treat the human subject as an agent with projects, intentions, emotions, sentiments, who is able to develop scenarios, etc. They use pseudo-technical concepts (such as Dawkins' *memes*). These concepts are unclear; but they suggest that the theory of cultural evolution can be as *scientific* as the theory of biological evolution.

This case illustrates, as can be incidentally noted, a current view most adverse to the progress of knowledge in the social sciences: being scientific means being pedantic, if I may say so, notably by creating neologisms. While being scientific means trying to describe reality as it is. Now, an obvious indubitable fact is that men have intentions and projects. When this essential feature is forgotten, no credible theory of human action can be produced. Unfortunately, a false conception of science starts from the idea that, if the human sciences aim to be "genuine" sciences, they have to eliminate any consideration of the states of mind of human actors. This basic error explains the failure of structuralism, culturalism or Marxism and generally of all the movements which have attempted to naturalise the human actor. As to Dawkins' or Sperber's views of cultural evolution and the other theories of the same type, they also have the consequence of making human evolution blind and meaningless. That should not be a surprise, since they consider human projects and intentions as facts which can be disregarded.

Rationalisation Does Not Mean Standardisation

An important caveat should be introduced at this point: that one should not draw from the evolutionary theory I have developed on the basis of some insights of Durkheim and Weber the conclusion that the various "cultures" should be deemed to become progressively more standardised. Five types of reasons lead to the opposite conclusion:

1) The idea that organisation of political power in the style of Montesquieu is better than organisation in the style of Bodin is irreversibly established for instance. It derives from the process of rational selection that governs the choice among ideas. But it should also be noted that in most cases there are many ways of putting the same idea into practice. Thus, the organisation of the separation of powers is not the same in France and in the UK. The legal system is not organised in the same way in France and in Germany: the prosecutors' decisions have a jurisdictional character in France and an administrative character in Germany. They are taken by magistrates in France and by civil servants in Germany. The conception of law is inquisitorial in the UK and accusatory in France or Germany. In the former case, the State is supposed to have the function of arbitrating conflicts between parties and to determine what is right or not, fair or not, on the occasion of these conflicts; in the latter case, as having the function of prosecuting misbehaviour.

2) On the other hand, many norms derive from *customs*. There is no other basis than custom for the fact that politeness is expressed

in one way here and in another way there. This derives from the fact that the relation between a symbol and its meaning can be arbitrary; whence the same meaning can be translated in various ways.

3) Technical objects themselves show that, while technical progress produces irreversible constraints, it also leaves a wide margin of freedom to those who develop them. One cannot put a plane on the market today which is too noisy or too wasteful of energy nor a fountain pen which leaks; but, once these constraints are taken into account, there are many ways of conceiving a plane or a fountain pen. The same could be said of all the domains where the "diffuse rationalisation" process described by Weber is at work.

4) Some competing ideas cannot be ranked against one another for basic reasons. The case of religions illustrates this point. All religious explanations of the world have the common feature that some of their components are held as immune to criticism. All religions have their theologians, though theology is more developed in some religions than in others. Even in the case where theology is very developed, the identity of a religion is protected against criticism by the immunisation of some points of the doctrine. For this reason, religions are deemed to coexist. Rationalisation processes can only make this coexistence more peaceful. It must be added on this point that, under the effect of these rationalisation processes, the principle of freedom of opinion has become more firmly established. Consequently, atheism tends currently to be treated as one of the possible worldviews among others. On the other hand, the dominant religion of the Western world has finally accepted that it cannot consider itself as better than others; what matters is, in Durkheim's words, that individuals recognise the existence of the sphere of the *sacred*. I have submitted in Boudon (2000) that Durkheim's notion of *le sacré* can be translated in our modern vocabulary by the notion of *values*. Durkheim himself could not use this word since, in his time, it was not currently taken in this sense. The modern sense is due to Nietzsche. It became current only after World War I.

5) Different societies can be behind or in advance on such and such point with respect to one another. Democracy became established later in South than in North America or Western Europe. Western Europe has abolished the death penalty in all countries and one has the general feeling that it is very unlikely that it will ever be

restored. The death penalty has not been abolished in the US. But I would be ready to bet that it will be in a more or less distant future, because, once it has been recognised that the death penalty has no deterrent effect, it appears mere cruelty. It is retained in the US probably under the effect of a religious consideration: redemption. Raskolnikov had a feeling of redemption that made him happy once he got his punishment for his crime. All surveys show that the public is much more religious in the US than in any other Western nation, and Adam Smith, Tocqueville and Weber have explained why. But, if the death penalty is considered acceptable by many Americans because it produces redemption, the contradiction between this reason and universal principles should appear sooner or later. Religion rests on faith, whence it follows that nobody can be forced to believe or disbelieve in any particular religion and that no institution concerning the general public should be grounded on religious principles. Now, if the notion of redemption, being a religious one, cannot be accepted as a justification for the death penalty, and if the death penalty cannot be validated by a purely imaginary deterrent effect, it should be sooner or later perceived as being merely a cruel institution which should consequently be abolished. I am ready to bet that this argument will be made by some intellectuals, prophets (as recognised by Weber, even modern secularised societies have and need their prophets) or more or less spontaneous or organised social movements. *Laïcité* is a French notion, inaccurately translated into English by *secularisation*. The very difficulty of the translation provides another illustration of my point. The notion of *laïcité* is grounded on the fact that religion rests on faith and that people cannot be forced to believe or disbelieve without contradicting the principle of freedom of opinion. Now, this notion can be institutionally translated in various fashions: it can give birth to various types of institutional relations between the State and the Church(es). In some countries, such as France or the US, Church and State are separated. England and Denmark up till now or Sweden until recently had by contrast a State religion. But none of these countries allows that politics should be dictated by religion or that people should be forced to belong to a religion.

This example suggests that the evolution process I have delineated is solid enough not only to explain, but even to generate some predictions. *To explain*: no Western European government has pro-posed to reintroducing the death penalty in spite of the polls that have shown repeatedly that the public opinion would in many countries be favourable to such a reintroduction. The same governments have shown that on many issues they are ready to follow the polls, even against their convictions. In this case, they were not. Why? Because the reasons justifying the abolition of the death penalty are strong ones. *To generate predictions*: as these reasons are strong, they should lead to the abolition of the death penalty even in a country where, as in the US, *historical forces* have until now dominated these reasons and thwarted the rationalisation process that led to the abolition of the death penalty in Europe.

The culturalist-relativistic assumption according to which no dif-ference should be made between cultures and societies is widespread today: it belongs to the code of "political correctness". But the same people who hold this culturalist view would not hesitate to declare that, with regard to the question of the death penalty, the US is backward in comparison to Europe. They would be right. But they should also recognise that this example where a society can be declared backward or in advance in comparison with some other in such and such respect is not unique. The world is waiting for the Islamic world to discover the advantage of the separation of religion and State.

The five basic reasons I have listed explain how, although ration-alisation is at work in all societies, they maintain a strong identity and singularity. The existence of rationalisation processes does not entail that societies are fated to become standardised. Conversely, the persistence of various "cultures" does not imply that processes of rationalisation are not at work in most of them, or that there are no universal values. A permanent debate opposes those who believe in the existence of universal values and of processes transcending the singularity of societies to those who insist on the singularity of societies and cultures. The philosophers of law have always hesitated between a *natural* theory and a *positivist* theory of law. Many anthropologists see the world as made of a juxtaposition of singular cultures. Once it is realised that institutions should be interpreted as deriving from the realisation of a "programme", these false dilemmas disappear: among the norms enforced in a given society some express their singularity; some are the outcomes of processes of diffuse rationalisation.

Finally, the evolutionary theory I propose to draw from Durkheim's and Weber's insights is *open* in the sense that it does not claim that evolution tends toward some end. Evolution results from the realisation of programmes led by a rationalisation process. The cases of ethics, law or political theory are not in principle different from the case of science. Like the evolution of science, the evolution of these other dimensions of thought is doomed to never reach an end.

IV. ADVANTAGES OF A PROGRAMMATIC THEORY OF MORAL EVOLUTION

It seems to me the *programmatic* theory I propose to derive from the sketchy insights taken from Durkheim and Weber has a certain number of distinctive features when it is compared to other theories of moral evolution. It emphasises the importance of *ideas* in social evolution; the importance of innovations; the unpredictable character of many new ideas; the role of contingencies; the fact that new ideas can reflect the realisation of a "programme"; that for instance the notions of *citizenship, person, right-to*, belong to a widely undefined programme which they helped to deploy progressively; it emphasises the fact that ideas tend to be rationally selected; that a selected idea can be put into practice in an indefinite number of fashions; on the fact that many norms are unaffected by these rationalisation processes, because they are connected with some values in an arbitrary fashion (as in the case of *customs*); the fact that evolutionary processes cannot always be interpreted as adaptation processes, but are often generated by innovations with no adaptation function in fact; that the notion of *rationalisation* combines the *cognitive* and the *instrumental* dimensions of rationality.

These various features characterise the theory of social evolution proposed by Eisenstadt (2002). Eisenstadt uses explicitly and abundantly the notion of *programme*. He shows well how collective identities are generated by *programmes* made up of a mixture of singular and universal features; resulting from the interplay between rationalisation and singularities.

The well-tempered theory of moral evolution which I propose to derive from the insights of Durkheim and Weber and which I identify in Eisenstadt's work must be distinguished from other evolutionary theories, notably from Hayek's theory. Hayek's evolutionary theory is certainly one of the most interesting modern theories of cultural evolution. But, probably because it is essentially inspired by Hayek's reflections on the history of economics, it appears incomplete to the sociologist's eye. The process he qualifies as *group selection* is but one of the selection processes at work in social evolution. Hayek refers here in particular to the ineluctable victory of liberalism over socialism (Nadeau 2003). Now, the *selection of ideas by such and such group* is another essential mechanism beside *group selection*. An example of such a process can be drawn from Weber and was mentioned in the introduction: monotheistic cults born in the Middle East, such as Mithraism, were preferred by Roman civil servants and military personnel to the traditional Roman polytheistic religion. This selection process had immense consequences. Among them, the fact that concepts such as that of *person* or of universal *citizenship* were offered on the ideas market. As Hayek pointedly stressed, unanticipated consequences of intentional actions are an essential component of social evolution; but equally essential is the idea that the selection of ideas results from individual choices and the individual choices from reasons. Thus, the Roman military had strong reasons for preferring the monotheistic cults to the Roman polytheistic religion. As stated by Nadeau (2003), Hayek's version of methodological individualism is *synthetic*: it insists on the non-intentional effects of individual actions. They are essential: the conversion of Roman soldiers and civil servants to monotheistic cults made easier the penetration into the Roman empire of the idea of citizenship, as we saw: a definitely unintentional effect. But methodological individualism has also an *analytical* side: it insists on the logic of individual actions, and especially of these essential actions that lead to the endorsement or rejection of an idea: the Roman soldiers and civil servants had understandable reasons to leave the polytheistic traditional Roman religion for the new monotheistic cults. The addition of such actions creates a *collective belief*. Moreover, it is essential to emphasise, if in many cases competing ideas can be ranked with respect with one another and can give birth to a rational selection process, this is not true of all ideas, however. This distinction helps to explain why all societies include universal and singular features.

The fundamental notions I have introduced here (*programme, rationalisation, rational selection*) can be used in various circumstances. I have described in the above examples very general *programmes*: the programmes underlying the history of morals, science or political theory. These notions can also be applied to narrower subjects. In everyday political life, programmes are developed which begin with *slogans*, for the content of these programmes is often reduced to a more or less vague idea that has to be made more precise in the course of action:

decrease the consumption of tobacco, reduce the rate of unemployment for instance. These narrower programmes are also subjected to the *rationalisation process* described by Weber.

One question remains. It belongs to the history of sociology. According to Durkheim, "individualism begins nowhere", while it seems that, to Weber, the central role given to the notion of citizenship is a feature characteristic of Western culture.

In fact, the two authors can be seen as very close to one another on this question. The demand for respect for the dignity of all is universal, even though it is currently thwarted by *historical forces* and though the diffuse rationalisation process develops over time. Cicero, Seneca and the Stoic thinkers had a strong feeling of human dignity, but accepted slavery. Seneca was very severe against the masters who used slaves as sexual tools or used to beat them. Weber's emphasis on the meaning of Paul's reaction to Peter's behaviour, whereby the latter divided people into the two categories of Jews and Gentiles, indicates that he read in this reaction the fact that Paul's *Letter to the Galatians* stated for the first time that all men have, as men, an equal dignity independent of their ascribed or achieved features, their status or their beliefs. The elaboration of the idea of human dignity from the Stoic thinkers to Paul was probably in Weber's mind an example of "diffuse rationalisation". Historical contingencies have caused the demand for respect for dignity to be satisfied earlier and more constantly in Europe than in other parts of the world.

But it can easily be seen that this demand is present today in all societies. The veils worn by young Iranian women from the bourgeoisie become more elegant and more personal; a satirical press emerges in Iran; jokes are circulating; as in the communist countries during the Cold War, they are directed against the political authorities: never queue up at a taxi station close to a mullah, since no taxi would stop. Other jokes, in the style of black humour, indicate a preference at least for certain features of Western culture: the September 11th attack against New York could not have possibly been carried out by Iranians, for they would have landed the aircraft in Hawaii.

REFERENCES

Boudon, R. (2000) *Études sur les sociologues classiques, II*. Paris, Presses Universitaires de France.

—— (1999) "Les *Formes élémentaires de la vie religieuse:* une théorie toujours vivante". *Année sociologique,* 49(1): 149–198.

—— (2001) "La rationalité du religieux selon Max Weber". *L'Année sociologique,* 51(1): 9–50.

—— (2002) *Déclin de la morale? Déclin des valeurs?* Paris, Presses Universitaires de France and Québec, Nota Bene.

—— (2003) *Raison, bonnes raisons.* Paris, Presses Universitaires de France.

Cohen, D. (1999) *Le Droit à..., Mélanges offerts à F. Terré.* Dalloz, Presses Universitaires de France: 393–400.

Dawkins, R. (1989) *The Selfish Gene.* Oxford, Oxford University Press.

Durkheim, E. (1960[1893]) *De la division du travail social.* Paris, Presses Universitaires de France.

Eisenstadt, S. (2002) "The Construction of Collective Identities and the Continual Construction of Primordiality". In: Malešević S. and Haugaard M. (eds), *Making Sense of Collectivity: Ethnicity, Nationalism and Globalisation.* Pluto Press: 33–87.

Goyard-Fabre, S. (2002) *Les Embarras philosophiques du droit naturel.* Paris, Vrin.

Hayek, F. von (1973–1979) *Law, Legislation and Liberty.* London, Routledge and Kegan Paul.

Inglehart, R., Basanez, M. and Moreno, A. (1998) *Human Values and Beliefs: A Cross-Cultural Sourcebook.* Ann Arbor, The University of Michigan Press.

Marshall, T. H. (1964) *Class, Citizenship and Social Development.* Garden City, New York, Doubleday.

Moore, G. E. (1954[1903]) *Principia ethica.* Cambridge, Cambridge University Press.

Nadeau, R. (2003) "Cultural Evolution True and False: a Debunking of Hayek's Critics". *Cahiers d'épistémologie,* Montréal, UQAM.

Popkin, S. L. (1979) *The Rational Peasant: The Political Economy of Rural Society in Vietnam.* Berkeley, University of California Press.

Popper, K. R. (1945) *The Open Society and Its Enemies.* London, Routledge and Kegan Paul.

—— (1957) *The Poverty of Historicism.* London, Routledge and Kegan Paul.

Sen, A. (1999) *Employment, Technology and Development.* Oxford, Oxford University Press.

Simmel, G. (1892) *Die Probleme der Geschichtsphilosophie.* Munich, Duncker & Humblot.

—— (1900) *Philosophie des Geldes.* Leipzig, Duncker & Humblot.

Sperber, D. (1996) *La Contagion des idées.* Paris, Odile Jacob.

Sukale, M. (2002) *Max Weber: Leidenschaft und Disziplin.* Tübingen, Mohr Siebeck.

Weber, M. (1920–1921) *Gesammelte Aufsätze zur Religionssoziologie.* Tübingen, Mohr.

—— (1995[1919]) *Wissenschaft als Beruf.* Stuttgart, Reklam.

Wilson, J. Q. (1993) *The Moral Sense.* New York, Macmillan/The Free Press.

4

Explaining Axiological Feelings

I. PHILOSOPHY AND SOCIOLOGY ON AXIOLOGICAL FEELINGS

Feelings of justice and axiological feelings more generally are some of the most important social phenomena and some of the least mastered scientifically. One reason for this unsatisfactory situation is that the most important theories of justice are philosophical. Their aim is in other words mainly normative: it is to determine what is good or bad, right or wrong or what should be done, rather than to explain why people see some state of affairs as good or bad, right or wrong or as congruent with what should be or should not be done. A philosophical axiological theory is obviously expected to be congruent with people's axiological feelings, but how far it should be congruent remains unclear. Kant (1797) considered that lying can never be treated as being good, against B. Constant's view, according to which lying is actually in some circumstances normally perceived by people as a good thing. If Kant's theory was a descriptive theory, it would be disqualified by such a fact, since it would appear as contradicting the theory. As it was rather meant by its author and is rather perceived as a prescriptive theory, it is unclear whether the fact disqualifies it. Generally, while it is hard to accept that a prescriptive theory is incompatible with people's axiological feelings, it is hard to determine to what extent it is invalidated by data on actual axiological feelings.

Empirical sociological research on justice and axiological feelings generally seems keen to collect data on people's axiological feelings rather than to explain them. Exceptions can of course be found, such as the work of the Swiss sociologist J. Kellerhals (Kellerhals *et al.*, 1995), among other examples. Thus, Frohlich and Oppenheimer (1992) conducted an original experiment with the objective of checking whether people endorse some leading theories of justice such as Rawls' (1971) or Harsanyi's (1977). They found that people are for the most part neither Rawlsian nor Harsanyian: doubtless an interesting finding. But they made little effort to explain this fact, nor to construct an alternative theory which would aim at reproducing people's feelings of justice. This is surprising, since they explicitly hold Rawls' or Harsanyi's theories as explanatory theories, i.e. as theories aiming at reproducing people's actual feelings of justice.

But the unsatisfactory state of the social scientific art about axiological feelings is mainly due to the fact that the available theories of justice and more generally of axiological feelings are themselves unsatisfactory. To take some major examples: Kant's theory is contradicted not only by the already mentioned fact that people would normally consider it good for a prisoner to lie, for instance, when a Gestapo officer asks him the names of his fellow resistance fighters, but by a host of other observations as well; while there are many other facts which the theory fails entirely to explain, such as the fact that inequalities are accepted in some circumstances and not in other circumstances. The utilitarian theory is contradicted by the fact, well observed in particular by Durkheim (1979[1912]), that people can be genuinely altruistic. Rawls' theory is contradicted, not only by the Frohlich and Oppenheimer experiment only, but also by the fact that social and political actors seldom appear as Rawlsian. Habermas' (1981) "communication" theory is contradicted by the fact that pure and perfect communication can generate false theories as easily as true, as the history of science shows; why then would "communicative rationality" be immunised against errors as far as normative questions are concerned? Or let us mention a final example, the relativistic theory for which all axiological feelings are local: "truth this side of the Pyrenees, falsehood the other side" ["*vérité en deça des Pyrénées, erreur au-delà* "], as Pascal wrote (1977[1670]). It is contradicted by the existence of axiological universals: stealing is held everywhere to be bad in principle and tolerated only in specific circumstances. Corruption is treated as bad in principle by all cultures.

II. A COGNITIVE THEORY OF AXIOLOGICAL FEELINGS

My claim in this chapter is that axiological feelings and feelings of justice in particular can be more satisfactorily explained if we start from an intuition I see as contained in Weber's notion of "axiological rationality" (Weber, 1922).

Many interpretations have been given of this notion. In general, it is held to be controversial. Thus, Lukes (1967: notably 259–60) contends that it is meaningless, while Sukale (1995), one of the best contemporary commentators on Weber, sees the concept as misleading (*irreführend*). Sukale writes (1995, 43):

Weber's distinction between axiological and instrumental rationality, as though there were two types of rational action, is extremely misleading.

[*Damit ist Webers Einteilung des rationalen Handelns in zweckrationales und wertrationales, als gäbe es zwei verschiedene Arten rationalen Handelns, aüsserst irreführend*].

To Sukale, as for Lukes, rationality, simply, and instrumental rationality are synonyms. Hence, they reject the very notion of a type of rationality which is not instrumental. Lukes' or Sukale's rejection of "axiological rationality" as a genuine form of rationality is possibly a projection of the dominant contemporary definition of rationality rather than a convincing interpretation of Weber's notion. This sceptical interpretation of Weber's "axiological rationality" is presumably reinforced by the fact that Weber is often described as supporting a decisionist theory of values, namely a theory according to which ultimate values cannot be grounded. But if values were endorsed without ground by social actors, how could their behaviour be understandable? How could Weber insist on the crucial importance of the notion of *Verstehen* in sociology, i.e. on the idea that the ultimate causes of behaviour lie in the reasons and motivations of social actors, and that these ultimate reasons and motivations can in principle always be reconstructed by the analyst?

My own proposal is to take the notion of axiological rationality seriously, rather than to introduce the debatable conjecture that Weber had committed a *lapsus calami*, so to speak.

If so, what does the notion mean? One can start from the remark that rationality is currently used as a major concept by two disciplines, namely economics and philosophy of science. To economists, rationality means instrumental rationality, in other words: adequacy between means and ends. To historians and philosophers of science, being rational has an entirely different meaning: I am rational if, to the best of my knowledge, I endorse a stronger rather than weaker theory. Thus, it became irrational to believe that the earth is flat once proof had accumulated showing that it is round. Let us qualify this form of rationality as cognitive.

In a brilliant essay, Radnitzky (1987) has tried to build a bridge between these two basic meanings of the notion of "rationality". He uses an example to illustrate his point: it became irrational to believe that the earth is flat from the moment when it became more difficult, in other words more *costly*, to defend this theory than to accept its competitor. But the costs of defending an obsolete theory T are higher than the costs of defending an alternative theory T′ if the latter explains more easily observed phenomena than T. Without knowing and understanding the arguments used by T and T′ to explain, say, why the sails of a ship disappear at the horizon after the ship itself, I cannot evaluate the *costs* of endorsing respectively T and T′. So, the reduction proposed by Radnitzky of cognitive to instrumental rationality appears artificial. What matters is that T′ explains more convincingly a number of phenomena P, P′, P″, etc. than T. Little is gained by translating "T′ explains more convincingly..." into "T′ explains in a less costly fashion". In other words, "cognitive rationality" (the type of rationality which historians and philosophers of science spontaneously refer to) cannot be reduced, except artificially, to instrumental rationality.

A more natural bridge relates cognitive and instrumental rationality, though it retains the distinction between the two types of rationality. When an actor follows a goal G, he can be convinced that M is an adequate mean because a solid theory T shows that G can be reached via M. The actor believes T because he is cognitively rational; and, as he uses M in order to reach G, he is moreover instrumentally rational.

My contention in this paper is that Weber had this distinction in mind when he coined the expression "axiological rationality" (*Wertrationalität*). In other words, I interpret this notion as indicating that what I call here cognitive rationality can be applied, not only to descriptive, but to prescriptive questions; not only to representational, but to axiological questions.

I will leave aside the question whether my interpretation of Weber is correct: I have discussed this point elsewhere (Boudon, 1997a;

Boudon 1997b). Rather, my aim is to develop a theory of axiological feelings in general and feelings of justice in particular starting from this interpretation. This theory rests on three postulates. *Firstly*, on the postulate that theories can be built on axiological as well as descriptive questions; that, moreover, prescriptive theories can, like descriptive ones, be stronger or weaker. *Secondly*, that people tend to choose the theory they see as stronger. *Thirdly*, that they tend to endorse a value statement and to experience the feeling that "X is good, bad, legitimate, fair, etc." when it appears to them – more or less vaguely depending on the circumstances – as grounded on strong reasons. My claim is that this theory is useful to explain axiological feelings generally and feelings of justice in particular, as they are observed by sociological and psychological empirical research.

It is often contended, by application of the theorem attributed to Hume which I discuss in chapters 1 and 6, that axiological theories are basically different from descriptive ones, because an *ought* statement cannot be deduced from an *is* statement. This is true. Still, prescriptive arguments can be evaluated: some prescriptive arguments are clearly weaker or stronger than others. Thus, to take a trivial example, under general conditions, people prefer driving a car faster rather than slower in city traffic, and for this reason consider traffic lights as a good (though unpleasant) thing. The value statement "traffic lights are a good thing" is the conclusion of a strong argument based on the indubitable empirical statement that traffic flows better with traffic lights than without. Though simple, this example is typical of many normative arguments. It shows that a normative argument can be as convincing as a descriptive one. Whether A is a cause of B is a non-normative question. Now, I will accept the statement "A cause of B" if it is a consequence of a strong argument. If, moreover, I prefer B to not B, A is demonstrated to be a good thing for me. If all prefer B, A is demonstrated a good thing for all. So, the gap between ought and is undoubtedly exists. But, when axiological statements can be interpreted consequentially, i.e. when "A is good" means "A leads to consequences considered as good by people", their validity can be demonstrated as solidly as the validity of descriptive statements. As "A leads to consequences considered as good by people" can be translated into "A is an appropriate mean to reach a state of affairs considered as good by people", the argument can be called instrumental as well as consequential.

However, as Weber observed so well, axiological statements cannot always be considered as the conclusion of consequential arguments. By creating his notion of "axiological rationality", he possibly wanted to emphasise that people may have strong reasons for believing that "A is good, bad, legitimate, illegitimate, fair, unfair, etc." in some circumstances without these reasons belonging to the instrumental–consequential category. My contention is that by doing so he introduced a powerful idea, crucial to our understanding of axiological feelings and of feelings of justice in particular. I will disregard here the point made by Sukale (2002) in his brilliant book on Weber that Weber only used the expression "axiological rationality" (*Wertrationalität*) twice, for he used the notion underlying the expression repeatedly in his empirical analyses.

To summarise, I would define a feeling or a statement as "axiologically rational" if people consider it as founded on strong arguments which *can be but are not necessarily* of the consequential–instrumental type. I propose in other words to define axiological rationality as a form of cognitive rationality characterised by the fact that it deals with arguments where at least one statement is axiological, since *ought* cannot be derived from *is*, or, more precisely, since an *ought*-statement cannot be exclusively derived from *is*-statements.

While Weber was probably the first author who proposed conceptualising the notion of "axiological rationality" as we understand it, he was not the first one to use it.

This reference to Weber should not be misunderstood. By associating "axiological rationality" and "cognitive rationality" and making the first a species of the second, I introduce a strong thesis, not only as far as the interpretation of Weber is concerned, but still more as regards the theory of moral feelings. It proposes in fact to reorient to a large extent sociological theorising about justice and axiological feelings more generally.

Adam Smith's Example

An example drawn from Adam Smith (1976 [1776]) may illustrate concretely Weber's notion of "axiological rationality", as I interpret it.

In his *Wealth of Nations*, Smith (1976 [1776]) wonders why his fellow men have the collective feeling that miners should definitely be paid more than soldiers. Why the collective agreement on the value statement "miners should be paid more than soldiers"?

His answer consists in showing that this feeling is based on strong reasons, which can be reconstructed in the following fashion:

— A salary is the remuneration for a contribution.
— Equal remunerations should correspond to equal contributions.

— Several components enter into the value of a contribution: the investment required to generate the type of competence required to produce the contribution, the risks involved in the realisation of the contribution, etc.

— The investment is comparable in the case of the miner and of the soldier. It takes about as much time and effort to train a soldier as a miner. The two jobs are characterised by similar risks. The two cases include above all a risk of death.

— Nonetheless, there are important differences between the two types of jobs. The soldier serves a function which is central in any society. He contributes to preserving the identity and the very existence of the nation. The miner by contrast fulfils an economic activity among others. His function is no more crucial to the society than, say, the function fulfilled by textile workers.

— This difference and others have the consequence that the death of the two men has a different social meaning. The miner's death will be identified as an accident, the death of the soldier on the battlefield as a sacrifice.

— Because of this difference in the social meaning of their respective activities, the soldier should be entitled to symbolic rewards, in terms of moral prestige, symbolic distinctions, funeral honours in case of death on the battlefield, etc.

— For symmetric reasons, the miner is not entitled to the same symbolic rewards.

— As the contribution of the two categories in terms notably of risk and investment is the same, the equilibrium between contribution and remuneration can only be restored by making the salary of the miners higher.

— This system of reasons is responsible for our *feeling* that the miner *should* be paid a higher amount than the soldier.

Lessons from Smith's Example

Max Scheler rightly saw that Smith's theory of collective moral feelings and values is "judicatory" (*urteilsartig*). He disagreed deeply with Smith, he developed an intuitionist phenomenological theory of values. But he saw in full clarity that Smith's theory was of utmost significance and he identified accurately its "judicatory" character: that in this theory collective values are analysed as the consequence of systems of arguments more or less implicitly perceived as valid by the members of a group.

The approach used by Smith could be easily illustrated by examples taken from modern writers. A contemporary theorist of ethics, M. Walzer (1983), proposes several analyses of our moral sentiments following the same line as Smith's analysis. Why do we consider conscription a legitimate recruitment method in the case of soldiers but not of miners, he asks? The answer is again that the function of the former, but not of the latter, is vital. If conscription could be applied to miners, it could be applied to any and possibly to all kinds of activities, so that it would lead to a political regime incompatible with the principles of democracy. In the same fashion, it is readily accepted that soldiers are used as garbage collectors in emergencies. But it would be considered illegitimate to use them to carry out such tasks in normal situations. In these examples, as in Smith's example, collective moral feelings are based on solid reasons. These reasons can be called "trans-subjective" since they would probably be considered strong by most people.

So, Smith's analysis implicitly proposes a general theory of axiological feelings and of feelings of fairness in particular. His analysis suggests that axiological feelings are based on reasons and that these reasons are not necessarily instrumental. Smith namely offers here, not an "instrumentally rational", but rather a "cognitively rational" explanation of the collective feeling he examines: "X (that miners are paid more than soldiers) is fair". The feeling that "X is fair" is collective and strong because it is based on strong reasons in individual minds. Thus, the collective feeling that "X is fair" is not a feeling in the personal idiosyncratic sense of the word. It illustrates rather a type of feeling a social actor cannot experience without having at the same time the impression that everybody would and should feel like him.

The connection between the feeling "X is fair" and the feeling that all should judge so becomes clear as soon as one supposes, as Smith does implicitly here, that we experience this feeling as a consequence of strong reasons. In other words, he assumes that feelings of the type "X is fair, legitimate, etc." are the effects of reasons, exactly like feelings of the type "Y is true". Prescriptive statements, like descriptive ones, are produced by reasons. Consequently, I naturally expect the "generalised Other" in Mead's sense to judge (Mead, 1934), as I do myself, that "X is fair" exactly as I expect him to judge that "Y is true" if I do so.

It is easily checked that the individual statements used in Smith's argument as I reconstruct it belong to several types, and more importantly, that all have in common to be strong in the sense that they can be easily accepted.

Some of these statements are empirical. For instance: it takes as long to train a soldier as a miner; both occupations are exposed to deadly risks. These statements are indubitable. Uncontroversial too is the statement that reinforcing the security of a nation is a central social function, while mining is rather a particular economic function. Some of the statements derive from sociological theory: thus, classical sociological functional theory, as developed after Smith, says that remuneration should be the higher the more central the function; exchange theory says that people expect the remuneration they get to reflect the contribution they provide. These statements can hardly be rejected. Some statements are rather sociological observations: death is not perceived as having the same meaning when it is the effect of an accident rather than of self-sacrifice; symbolic rewards can be used to reward the latter but not to compensate the former, etc. Such statements can also be easily accepted.

On the whole, all the individual statements used in Smith's argument are acceptable. For this reason, the conclusion "X is fair" is normally perceived by people as strong. In other words, Smith suggests a "cognitive" explanation of the collective axiological feeling "X is fair".

Moreover, it should be noted that the *consequences* of paying the miners more than the soldiers are not mentioned in Smith's analysis with the exception of the fact that doing so is likely to generate public approval. So, the reasons underlying the statement "X is fair" are not consequential, except indirectly. In other words, the rationality inspiring the belief in the statement "X is fair" is not instrumental but axiological: it is rational to pay miners more, not because of the possible consequences of paying them more, but because paying them more is congruent with strong principles, such as the principle of equality between contribution and remuneration.

That Smith's analysis is axiological rather than instrumental–consequential is worth emphasising, since it is extracted, not from his *Theory of Moral Sentiments*, but from his other main book, *The Wealth of Nations*, a book generally considered, not only as founded on but as founding the utilitarian paradigm: the paradigm in which rationality is defined as instrumental–consequential.

Obviously, Smith does not and need not assume that the reasons explaining the feeling "X is fair" are explicitly and clearly present in everyone's head, but he clearly assumes that they are present in an intuitive fashion.

III. WHAT ARE THE BASES FOR THE FEELINGS OF JUSTICE?

The cognitive explanation of axiological feelings illustrated by Smith's example can build a bridge between theory and empirical studies on axiological and particularly feelings of justice more easily than other models. Some examples, among which one will be presented in detail, will show that, with the help of this model, the interpretation of the findings from empirical studies can be made clearer, while the model suggests at the same time more efficient observation – and research procedures.

The Frohlich–Oppenheimer Study

The first example has already been alluded to: the Frohlich–Oppenheimer (1992) study aimed at determining whether current theories of justice, such as Rawls' and Harsanyi's in particular, are able to reproduce the people's actual feelings as to which distribution of goods is fair or not. A sample was asked to choose a fictitious income distribution among a set of distributions. I need not describe the ingenious experimental procedure used by the authors of the study. It suffices to say that the set of distributions was built in such a fashion that the choice of a given distribution among those that were proposed allowed it to be inferred which of four principles of justice the subjects had in mind when they made their selection. The four principles were the following:

— The principle drawn from Harsanyi's utilitarian theory (Harsanyi, 1955), namely: select the distribution with maximum mean.
— The "difference principle" drawn from Rawls's theory of justice: select the distribution maximising the floor income.
— The principle: maximise the mean and define a minimum floor. By contrast with the "difference principle" derived from Rawls' theory, this principle requires that the floor should not fall below a given value, rather than the value of the floor be maximised.
— The principle: make the mean as high as possible, provided the variance does not exceed a given value.

The first two principles are founded on well-known theories: Harsanyi's and Rawls'. The third is not actually derived from a formally developed theory of justice, but reflects the distribution policy generally enforced by political authorities in most democratic countries.

The fourth is a corollary drawn from sociological functionalist theory. Well before Rawls, sociological theorists asked under which conditions inequalities are held to be acceptable or not. The functionalist theorists' answer is that inequalities tend to be accepted as long as they are perceived as having a function. They should, in other words, be limited to the amount necessary to fulfil this function. Thus, if we suppose that the worst paid would be demotivated above a certain difference between the best and the worst paid, a degree of inequality above this threshold would be regarded by most people as too great; it would be dysfunctional with regard to the system. In the same way, if, below a certain difference, the best paid would be demotivated, people would normally consider that this other threshold should not be crossed. The Frohlich–Oppenheimer study introduces the assumption that respondents, having in mind a theory of justice more or less inspired by these functionalist ideas, should pay attention to the standard deviation of the distributions proposed.

Rawls' assumption about the "veil of ignorance" was simulated in the experiment by the fact that the subjects were told they would be located in a random fashion, once their choice was made, into one of the income classes and that they would get a reward proportional to the income of the class. Thus, they were led to consider that their choice would affect their reward. But their judgment as to which distribution is fairest could be held as unprejudiced in the sense that it could not be inspired by their interests, since they did not know whether they would belong to the highest, to the lowest, or to one of the intermediary classes of the proposed distributions.

The study was conducted on a sample of Americans and on a sample of Poles. It is illuminating for our discussion. It shows namely that people reject the Rawlsian principles of justice. In other words, Rawls' theory cannot be held as a valid reconstruction of the axiological feelings of people about the distribution of primary goods. By far the most frequent choice of the respondents was to maximise the mean and to define a minimum income. Harsanyi's principle (maximisation of the mean without any constraints on floor and deviation) comes next, but far behind; the maximisation of the mean with a constraint on deviation is quite unlikely to be chosen. To be precise, of the 81 experimental groups, the principles were chosen with the following frequencies:

— Constraint on the floor and maximisation of the mean: 77.8%.
— Maximisation of the mean: 12.3%.

— Maximisation of the mean and constraint on the deviation: 8.64%.
— Difference principle (Rawls): 1.23%.

Another interesting finding from the experimental study should be noted: that the same structure of answers characterises the American and the Polish samples. In the two cases, the first choice is far more frequent than the three others.

Cognitive Interpretation of the Frohlich–Oppenheimer Study

When, as here, the distribution of answers is highly structured, one can suppose that strong causes are responsible for the distribution. Moreover, when the structure is similar from one cultural context to another, it can be assumed that these causes are trans-contextual. Finally, it can be supposed that the high structuration of the answers and their trans-contextuality is produced by the fact that the respondents' choices are inspired in their minds by strong reasons.

The study proposes to the respondents a very abstract decision-making situation. They have to answer the question whether one distribution is fairer than the others. They have no information as to how the income inequalities have been generated. They know nothing about the occupations of the fictitious population represented in the distributions. Now, the discussions which were conducted with the respondents have shown that they accept the idea that income inequalities should reflect functional inequalities: I am entitled to get a higher income if the tasks I am supposed to carry out given my occupational role are functionally more important. But, given the context of the experiment, they could not answer the question whether the income distributions reflected functional inequalities or not: they missed the relevant information which would have been necessary to make the question meaningful.

It can be assumed on the whole that the respondents considered questions they could answer and tried to give them the best grounded answer: is it a legitimate goal for a government to try to make the mean of an income distribution as high as possible? They obviously answered yes to this question. Is it a good thing for a government to try to make the standard deviation lower? The respondents endorsed the idea that inequalities are legitimate when they are functional. But, as they did not know whether the inequalities reflected by the distributions were functional or not, the most reasonable assumption open to them was that they were and that consequently an effort to reduce the standard deviation could be unjustified and dangerous. On the whole, given the cognitive conditions created by the experiment, an attractive answer was to reject any constraint as far as the standard deviation of the distribution was concerned. On the other hand, the respondents considered that it was a good thing to introduce a constraint on the floor, since it is normally expected from a government that it tries to establish some protection against the hazards of life the citizens are exposed to. On the whole, the solution the most widely chosen for understandable reasons was: maximise the mean, guarantee a minimum income, do not attempt to minimise standard deviation, since it is produced by multiple unknown mechanisms and since it can be counterproductive to lower it.

In other words, the highly structured statistical distribution of the answers can be analysed as being the effect of strong reasons. It can be noted, incidentally, that the same strong reasons presumably explain why real governments make more or less generally (though implicitly) the same choice as the respondents. They usually consider decisions likely to increase the mean of the income distribution, in other words to enhance growth as good. On the other hand, most of them consider that people should be provided with insurance against the hazards of life: even the less "social" governments care about poverty and about making the proportion of the poor as low as possible. Moreover, all care – though of course to various degrees – that nobody should, ideally at least, be "excluded" from society. Finally, all recognise that inequalities are the product of complex micro-phenomena; that they are partly functional; that it is impossible to determine what the ideal standard deviation of the income distribution would be, etc. They also consider that a lower standard deviation is not necessarily better. For these reasons, most governments are very prudent in this respect. Their efforts to reduce the standard deviation of incomes are in many cases marginal when they are not merely symbolic.

In other words, governments, like people, probably have more or less diffuse minimal theories as to the fairness of income distribution. This theory includes a set of arguments which they consider strong. From these arguments, they draw conclusions as to whether it is good or not to try to make the standard deviation as low as possible, the mean as high as possible, etc.

Reciprocally, the strong rejection of Rawls' difference principle by governments as well as by the samples in the experiment considered is due to the fact that there are strong reasons to reject it: in particular, it is impossible to determine effectively the threshold below which a reduction of the standard deviation of the income distribution would have a negative effect on its mean.

It should be added that the system of reasons at work in the answers of the respondents would presumably have been different if the experimental conditions had been different. Suppose, for instance, that the distributions suggested to the respondents had been presented as reflecting, not fictitious unidentified global societies, but salary distributions in organisations, that the organisations had been described as similar to one another, and that information had been given to the respondents on the types of occupations and functions corresponding to the income classes. In that case, the respondents would have probably considered the standard deviation and tried to see whether it reflected functional inequalities. For, while it is impossible to determine what the best standard deviation would be as far as a global society is concerned, it is not impossible in the case of an organisation.

Checking the Importance of Contextual Effects

The previous example suggests that people's feelings of justice cannot be considered as deriving merely from an application of general principles. This does not say, though, that we can avoid raising the question of the relation between the theories of justice and actual feelings of justice. Indeed, if we come to recognise that people, when they endorse a moral judgment, express, not only subjective preferences, but rather objective judgments which can potentially be shared by others, it is hard to accept that the theories of justice cannot teach us anything about their feelings of justice.

Taking into account the contextual dimension of moral judgments allows us to clarify that question. More precisely, it can be claimed that the "philosophical" theories of justice have an explanatory value in a given situation as soon as the contextual assumptions they introduce implicitly can be considered as effectively satisfied in the situation.

In order to make this idea more concrete, I will compare Frohlich's and Oppenheimer's (F&O) findings with those of another experiment, quite similar in its orientation, but explicitly introducing a contextual variation. This latter experiment is by Mitchell, Tetlock, Mellers and Ordonez (Mitchell *et al.*, 1993) (MTM&O).

As they did not use the cognitive model, F&O did not attempt to reconstruct the system of reasons induced by the experimental context.

Furthermore, they did not succeed in using their findings to build a bridge between general theories of justice and the observed actual feelings of justice. Indeed, the greater popularity they observed of the "combined principle" (maximise the mean and define a minimum floor) does not mean that it should be considered as generally valid, i.e. as able to predict people's feelings of justice in all contexts. As to the weak success of Rawls', Harsanyi's and the functional theory among F&O's subjects, it does not say that these theories cannot have an explanatory value in other contexts.

According to Rawls' postulate, a hypothetical situation can be identified, such that the principles chosen in that situation can be considered relevant, whatever the context may be. F&O interpreted Rawls' philosophical postulate as a sociologically valid postulate, simulated the "veil of ignorance" situation and checked whether people actually endorsed Rawls' "difference principle". As we saw, it turned out that a very small minority appeared to endorse this principle.

The study by MTM&O is interesting because it introduces an explicit variation of this crucial contextual dimension. Briefly, MTM&O's experiment consisted in asking people's opinion about the fairest economic reform in a society which was described to them as more or less meritocratic.

More precisely, the subjects were requested to choose between economic policies guided by the same alternative principles as in F&O's study: The "difference principle" drawn from Rawls' theory of justice: maximise the floor income; the "combined principle": maximise the mean and define a minimum floor; the principle drawn from Harsanyi's utilitarian theory: maximise the mean; the principle of equality: minimise the standard deviation.

The alternative policies were presented as efficient: they were supposed to generate income distributions congruent with the principles. The subjects' choice was supposed to depend merely on the degree of morality and political acceptability of the alternative principles of justice. Moreover, the subjects were encouraged to avoid projecting themselves into one of the classes of the stratification system when evaluating the alternative economic actions. By contrast with F&O's experiment, they were not motivated by an actual gain in money. On the whole, MTM&O sought to avoid subjects taking into consideration their personal interests, either real or imaginary.

As in the case of F&O's experiment, the subjects were led by the experimental situation to answer the following implicit questions:

How have the income inequalities been generated? Do they reflect merit and/or achievement inequalities? Can income inequalities be considered as functional? Is it a legitimate goal for a government to try to make the mean of an income distribution as high as possible, to make the standard deviation lower, to define a minimum floor, or to maximise the base income?

Plausibly, the subjects devoted special attention to the first question, since, in contrast to F&O's experiment, they were informed as to the functional character of inequalities: they were informed whether they had to consider a society where inequalities were broadly, moderately or weakly meritocratic.

In the low and medium meritocratic conditions, the subjects know that income inequalities do not reflect their efforts, merits and achievements. So, income inequalities will probably appear to them as dysfunctional and, hence, as arbitrary. In such a context, we can assume that individuals would not allow the government to maximise the mean without constraints, since this would possibly lead to an excessive enrichment of some individuals to the detriment of others, who would also have contributed to the creation of wealth. Moreover, a constraint on the floor will possibly be considered as sufficient if an income distribution can be considered as functional. But if it cannot, such a constraint will be unable to eradicate the feeling of unfairness raised by the distribution. In other words, when the inequalities appearing in a distribution are perceived as afunctional or dysfunctional, people will be encouraged to endorse Rawls' "difference principle", since it is the only one – among the proposed principles – which is able to compensate for the feeling of arbitrariness aroused by the distribution. Indeed, as the "difference principle" maximises the floor income, it should naturally generate a major redistribution. Moreover, given that the distribution is supposed afunctional or dysfunctional, the best way to restrict its arbitrariness is to impose a constraint on the ceiling or at least to make the ceiling lower. Finally, the Rawlsian principle is more attractive than the principle of equality, since it ensures a higher mean. MTM&O's experiment supposed namely that the principle of equality is associated with a lower mean than the other distribution principles.

On the whole, in a context where inequalities are supposed afunctional or dysfunctional, the subjects tend to wish for protection against risk, and a constraint on the standard deviation to the effect of correcting the arbitrariness of the distribution, with the provision that this constraint should not lower the mean. In agreement with this reconstruction of the reasons of MTM&O's subjects, one of the two main findings of MTM&O is effectively that in low and medium meritocratic conditions, a majority of the opinions appeared as effectively endorsing the Rawlsian "difference principle".

The second main finding of MTM&O is that, in a hypothetical high meritocratic context, a majority chooses rather, as in the F&O study, the "combined principle" (maximisation of the mean, definition of a minimum floor). If an income distribution is perceived by individuals as reflecting adequately their merits and achievements, and if we suppose that most individuals have in mind some rough version of the functional theory, trying to make the standard deviation lower would appear to the subjects unjustified and dysfunctional: it would have the effect of demotivating social actors. As to the principle of equality, it is hard to see how it could be preferred in such a context. But Rawls' principle will probably not be attractive either: when a distribution is perceived as functional, the subjects have no reasons – except in the case where they are exclusively motivated by envy – to see a reduction of the standard deviation as justified. As in F&O's experiment, the subjects have strong reasons though to wish for protection against the risks of life, provided it does not lead to a distortion of the functional character of the distribution and has no negative effect on the mean. On the whole, in a highly meritocratic context, the subjects have strong reasons to choose the "combined principle" (maximise the mean and define a floor income).

It can be noted incidentally that the principle of equality is almost never chosen in the experiments where individuals are asked to select a distribution principle for the society. Plausibly, because it is difficult to find the strong reasons that could support this principle.

To sum up, Rawls' "difference principle" adequately describes the feelings of justice actually experienced by people notably in a context where the distribution of goods is perceived as arbitrary. When it is not perceived as arbitrary, but rather as functional, the same principle is rejected by a strong majority. Maybe people would appear as Rawlsian in other contexts, beside the context where the distribution of goods appears arbitrary. Identifying these other contexts would be an interesting goal for further sociological research on feelings of justice. But the main conclusion to be derived from the analysis of F&O's and MTM&O's study is that no single theory of justice is able to reproduce the feelings of justice which people experience.

This is due to the two complementary reasons that 1) all these theories are implicitly contextual (though they are generally presented as not contextual) and that 2) the feelings of justice experienced by people is aroused in them by reasons taking the parameters of the context into consideration. With these reasons in mind, it becomes easier to understand why people appear for instance as Rawlsian in some circumstances and anti-Rawlsian in others. No single criterion or theory of justice can predict in all contexts the feelings of justice as they actually are. The "general" theories of justice are actually special applications of the "cognitive model", valid in special types of contexts.

IV. WHICH CRITERIA OF FAIRNESS, LEGITIMACY, ETC.?

The previous examples suggest that collective feelings of type "X is fair, legitimate, good, unfair, illegitimate, bad, etc." can be explained fruitfully as the product of strong reasons. This raises the question what makes a reason strong or weak. In other words: on the basis of which criteria can I judge that a reason is weak or strong? As paradoxical as this may appear, I would contend that most theories of justice and more generally most axiological theories fail because they naïvely tend to associate simple criteria with the ideas of goodness, fairness, legitimacy, etc. and their opposites.

It is almost unnecessary to accumulate the examples. Against the Kantian criteria of universalisation, it has been objected that lying and other deviant types of behaviour can in some circumstances be moral. Against the utilitarian criterion, it has been objected that people can be very hostile to a state of affairs without any consequences or even with positive consequences for their well-being. Axiological theories such as the Kantian and utilitarian theories owe their success to the fact that they start from the principle that a criterion of morality, fairness, justice, etc. could be easily defined (Taylor, 1997). But this reason for their success is also a major cause of their weakness.

It is surprising that Kant tried to propose a general criterion of morality. For this appears to contradict with a just and profound remark he makes in his *Critique of Pure Reason*. I have already mentioned the crucial importance of this remark in chapter 3. Those who look for general criteria of truth, he writes (Kant [1787] n. d., I, I, 2nd part (*Die transcendentale Logik*), III (*Von der Einteilung der allgemeinen Logik in Analytik und Dialektik*), p. 93), remind us of these two idiots of whom one attempts to milk a male goat, while the other one holds a pail under the animal's belly. The joke stresses an important point. There are effectively no general but merely particular criteria of truth. Thus, there are criteria, defined by Tarski (1936), of the truth of observational statements: "snow is white" is a true statement, if and only if snow is white. But there are no general criteria which could be mechanically applied to evaluate the strength of a theory or generally of a system of arguments. Take a scientific theory considered as wholly uncontroversial, such as Huygens' theory of the pendulum. On which criteria do we hold it to be true? Popper (1968) would have said that we hold it to be true because, to date, we have failed to discover facts which would contradict it: all the pendulums we can observe under a variety of circumstances behave in a way congruent with the predictions derived from Huygens' theory. The theory appears as not falsified up to now and in that sense as true. But we do not accept Huygens' theory as true only because it leads to predictions congruent with observations. We also accept it specifically because it does not introduce concepts we would consider unacceptable in a scientific theory. But on which criteria do we consider a concept scientifically acceptable? The movement of the pendulum is analysed in Huygens' theory as resulting from the combination of "forces", one force drawing the pendulum toward the centre of the earth, another one toward the point in the ceiling where the thread holding the pendulum is fixed, etc. So, we accept Huygens' theory because we consider the concept of "force" and the mental construct described by the "parallelogram of forces" as legitimate. All it suffices is to consider the objections raised against such totally unempirical notions, from Descartes to Carnap (see Boudon 1997b), to see immediately that there are no criteria by which we could readily determine whether such concepts are acceptable, legitimate or not. Since we have no reason whatsoever to consider the case of Huygens' theory as exceptional rather than typical, it follows that we normally cannot define general criteria thanks to which a scientific theory can be held as valid or true. Descartes was convinced that the notion of "force" is unacceptable. We are convinced that it is acceptable. There are no easy criteria which we could use to judge it acceptable, though, except criteria which we would have identified and that Descartes had failed to identify. We accept it because it explains many things and has repeatedly been successfully used in the history of physics. So, when Kant states that there are no general criteria of truth, he is right.

If it is impossible to associate general criteria with the notions "true" or "false", why then would it be possible to associate general criteria with notions such as "fair", "good", "legitimate", etc. and their opposites? Of course there is a strong demand for such criteria. But, as the case of Popper's "falsification" criterion shows, the criteria which have been proposed to meet this demand are never sufficient. I have discussed these points more thoroughly elsewhere (Boudon, 1994b, 1997b).

Does this lead to an "intuitive" theory of truth, fairness, legitimacy or goodness? Evidently: no. We hold the notion of "force" to be acceptable in a scientific physical theory and the notion of "God" to be unacceptable, not for intuitive reasons, but because a historical Darwinian process has selected the first as adequate, given the aims pursued by scientists, and rejected the second as inadequate.

My claim here is then that the situation is basically the same, whether we have to explain the collective feeling that "X is true" or the collective feeling that "X is fair, legitimate, etc." Such statements are endorsed when they are grounded in people's minds on reasons perceived by them as strong, or as stronger than the reasons leading to the opposite conclusions. To this, it must be added that the empirical statements included in the system of reasons should satisfy the Tarskian criterion, i.e. be congruent with the relevant observations, but that in most cases the system of reasons will also include concepts and non-empirical statements the validity of which will not in the general case be reducible to the verdict of some well-defined criterion.

So, "cognitive rationality" and "axiological rationality" point to the fact that the feelings that "X is true" in the first case, "X is fair, legitimate, etc." in the second one are grounded in the mind of social subjects on systems of reasons perceived by them as strong; they differ by the fact that the "systems of reasons" include at least one prescriptive statement in the latter case.

The Universal and Contextual Dimensions of Axiological Feelings and Feelings of Justice in Particular

Besides having the shortcoming of wrongly assuming the existence of criteria of goodness, fairness, etc., the general theories of axiological feelings such as the ones I mentioned at the beginning of this paper, are unable to account satisfactorily for the contextual and historical variations of men's axiological and particularly feelings of justice.

The "cognitive model" I have presented allows us to capture more adequately than other models the combination of the contextual-historical dimension and the universal dimension characteristic of moral feelings.

Thus, in some contexts, people appear intolerant of any deviation from the principle according to which remuneration should reflect contributions, while in other contexts they appear to be very flexible in this respect, accepting without any protest wide deviations from the same principle, because strong reasons determine the two contrasted attitudes in the two cases. So, the point I made earlier about Rawls' "difference principle" can be held as general. Not only this principle, but also others can be rejected or accepted depending on the context.

On the whole, the cognitive theory of axiological feelings makes possible an accurate explanation of the observed variation of feelings of justice from one context to another, because it takes into account the parameters of the contexts responsible for the variation and assumes that these parameters are more or less consciously perceived by social actors. By so doing, the cognitive theory solves the apparent "contradiction" between the sensitiveness of the feelings of justice to the context, and the claim of coherence and objectivity more or less implicitly made by the social subjects who experience it.

This contextual variation of moral judgments is often presented as a proof of the basic inconsistency and contingency which govern the moral standpoints endorsed by individuals. Hochschild (1981) for example considers the fact that people accept different norms of justice depending on the characteristics of the contexts they are located in as a sign of the inconsistency of their standpoints. If so, the social scientist is invited to consider this inconsistency as justifying an investigation of psychological or social forces rather than of the reasons responsible for moral judgments. Alternatively, the inconsistency can be interpreted as supporting a strategic interpretation of the feelings of justice. Deutsch (1975) tried to follow this path, but his attempt turned out to be unsatisfactory (Deutsch, 1986).

By contrast, the cognitive model suggests that it is possible to reconcile the contextual character of the feelings of justice with their claim to "objectivity". When we express a moral judgment such as "this is fair, unfair, etc.", we expect other people to agree as soon as we feel that the reasons on which our judgment is based take into account the characteristics of the context, far from being merely derived from abstract moral precepts or from our own subjective inclinations. Again, it is not necessary to suppose that we can express these reasons clearly, but merely that we are vaguely aware of their existence. We normally have the impression that these reasons can be accepted as valid by any observer, provided he is informed of the characteristics of the context in which they emerged.

Of course, it is less easy to account for moral judgments in general or to ground our subjective axiological preferences. Also, it is possible – this is one of the sources of moral conflicts – that within certain limits an identical context is characterised in various fashions by various actors. The cognitive model can also take this possibility into account, however, as I have tried to show in the case of the several judgments proposed in Bazerman's experiment (Boudon, 2001).

On the whole, the model invites us to revise the received idea according to which the contextual variation of axiological judgments is incompatible both with the existence of general principles and with the idea that such judgments could be "objectively" valid.

A few additional examples will finally be sketchily described to illustrate the generality of the idea according to which, depending on the context, a principle can be adopted or rejected. These examples will also stress the point that the theoretical and empirical fruitfulness of the cognitive model derives from the fact that it reconciles rather than opposes singularity and universality, contextuality and universality, and by so doing possibly the sociology and philosophy of moral and of axiological feelings more generally.

Mills' *White Collar*

In his *White Collar*, C. W. Mills (1951) describes women clerks in a work environment where they all do the same tasks. They sit in a large room, all have the same desk, etc. Violent conflicts frequently occur among them on issues easily perceived from the outside as "minor": being seated closer to a source of heat or light, etc. The outside observer would readily see such conflicts as irrational, even as childish, because he would perceive them according to the principles of instrumental rationality: why such a violent reaction to such a minor issue with such minor *consequences*? As the women's behaviour would appear strange to him, he would easily turn to an irrational interpretation: childish behaviour. But such a diagnosis would leave many facts unexplained: that the conflicts appear repeatedly; that they are independent of the idiosyncratic characteristics of the persons; that the actors within the firm understand the conflicts; that they do not consider them "childish"; that they find them understandable rather than irrational; that they do not find the reaction out of proportion to its cause, etc. Any irrational explanation would fail to account for this set of facts.

By contrast, a cognitive interpretation can easily explain the recurrent conflicts. The fact that the clerks all do the same tasks in the same conditions has the consequence that any departure from a strict equality between contribution and remuneration can be immediately and easily perceived. Moreover, it is normally regarded as intolerable by those who are exposed to it. The white collar workers are all engaged in similar tasks, so that any minor advantage is immediately perceived as an illegitimate privilege. From an instrumental-consequential viewpoint, it effectively matters little to sit closer to the window. But, as soon as this advantage to the benefit of individual X results from an unjustified decision on the supervisor's part, it is perceived by Y, not as a disadvantage to her/himself, but as an injustice: I am here to get some remuneration for my contribution; I am in a situation of social contract with the firm; any unjustified advantage in favour of X, however minor, is a violation of this basic contract and consequently morally intolerable, even if materially of weak relevance. Again, any irrational analysis fails to account for the apparent disproportion between cause and effect. But a rational analysis in the instrumental sense is not better off here. It fails namely to account for the disproportion between the importance of the issue and the intensity of the reaction.

In other cases, people appear by contrast as extremely flexible with regard to the principle according to which remuneration should reflect contributions. Thus, educational investments are very unequally and unfairly rewarded. The income and social status distributions corresponding respectively, say, to x and x+k years of education generally overlap widely. This means that the probability for an individual with x years of education to get a higher status and a higher income than an individual with x+k years of education is normally very high. The lack of congruence between contributions (here: educational investment) and rewards (here: status and income) is massive. Still, nobody, even among the most extreme egalitarians, has ever suggested abolishing this form of inequality. Moreover, this inequality is not generally perceived as unfair, clearly because trying to correct it would be extremely costly if at all possible. It would suppose a general planning both of the educational and of the occupational systems which is properly inconceivable and certainly undesirable.

For the same reasons, inequalities between generations are rarely perceived as unacceptable and unfair, though they can be wider than any other form of inequality.

Many experiments on the feelings of justice have been conducted by psychologists. In most cases it would be easy to show that the cognitive model can provide an acceptable explanation of the findings. Thus, in a well-known study which was replicated in Switzerland and Germany respondents were proposed the following case (Kahneman *et al.*, 1986a; Frey, 1997):

> *A hardware store has been selling snow shovels for 30 Swiss Francs (or 30 German marks). The morning after a heavy snow storm, the store raises the price to 40 Swiss Francs/German marks. How do you evaluate the price rise?*

In Germany and Switzerland as well as in the US a very large majority perceived the behaviour of the firm as unfair. Should we be content to stress the fact that people do not always behave according to the utilitarian principles that are supposed to guide *homo oeconomicus*? Or would not it be more interesting to understand the reasons explaining the strongly structured distribution of answers? It can plausibly be assumed that they result from the respondents' application of a theory likely to be perceived as strong, according to which windfall profits should be accepted without guilt by a social actor provided this has no negative effects on other people; otherwise, the subject would gain his profit at the expense of others without justification.

Finally, an important remark should be introduced which I cannot develop to the extent it might deserve: in the various examples I have considered, the principle of equality between remuneration and contribution was frequently cited. One should not believe though that it is the only possible axiological ingredient of feelings of justice. Other arguments would for instance refer to the principle of the equal dignity of human beings or other principles.

An *a priori* frequently endorsed by sociologists is to consider that reasons are the causes of feelings only when they are objectively indubitable. This *a priori* accounts for the effort made by some sociologists to develop an instrumental theory of norms and values. Rationality, however, cannot be reduced to instrumental rationality in spite of the intellectual comfort gained by reducing the former to the latter. As well seen notably by Max Weber and before him by Adam Smith and others, axiological feelings cannot always be derived from instrumental, in other words from consequential considerations. A promising path to eliminate these difficulties is to consider axiological feelings in general and feelings of justice in particular as being generally the effects of systems of reasons perceived as strong by social actors. Sometimes these reasons belong to the consequential-instrumental type. Sometimes they do not and are rather of the cognitive type. As already seen by Durkheim observed (1979 [1912]), prescriptive and descriptive beliefs should be explained in the same way: because they are perceived as grounded.

French Doctors

I will briefly describe a final example aiming at suggesting that the cognitive approach I advocate is indispensable in the interpretation of data from field observation (such as Mills' observation of white collar workers), surveys or quasi-experiments (such as Frohlich's and Oppenheimer's), but also to decipher collective reactions in current social life.

In 1995, two French doctors were found guilty in a trial dealing with the transfusion of blood contaminated by the AIDS virus. A petition was signed all over the world by numerous doctors and scientists including thirty Nobel Prize winners. The petition made the point that the trial had been unfair and requested the French President to use his prerogative of presidential pardon, which legally can indeed be applied in this case, in order to release the doctors from jail. A large majority of people strongly disapproved of the proposal: in the press as well as in opinion surveys. Influential members of the government made clear they would not recommend the pardon. This is an example of these current collective sentiments of justice which the social sciences should be able to explain. I use this example because the collective negative sentiment produced in the public appeared unusually strong. Can theories proposing to analyse axiological sentiments as the effects of instrumental rationality satisfactorily explain this social fact? Is the classical sociological model which considers the internalisation of norms through socialisation as the basic mechanism able to explain all feelings, beliefs and reactions of any help here? Clearly not, while the cognitive model is: the petition signed by the Nobel laureates rested on the argument that the two doctors were only two among many other people who had also been responsible for the distribution of contaminated blood. So, the petition was based on the argument that nobody should be condemned until those equally guilty are condemned. If this rule was applied, nobody would ever be condemned. As this consequence is clearly unacceptable, the principles on which it is based are equally unacceptable. Thus, the collective rejection of the petition was based neither on the benefits to be derived from this rejection (which benefits?), nor on an aversion to the condemned doctors, but on the reason that it was grounded on a principle incompatible with the very existence of a system of justice.

Beyond Kantian, Utilitarian and Contractualist Theories

Some cognitive obstacles to the development of knowledge about axiological sentiments in general and justice sentiments in particular are easily identified. One of them is the attraction of simplicity. It explains the success of the Kantian, the Rawlsian or of the utilitarian theory of moral and axiological feelings generally. They provide easy criteria thanks to which a statement of form "X is good, fair, etc." could be validated. But this simplicity is the counterpart of a major weakness: these criteria often appear incongruent with people's axiological feelings. Rawls' theory is exposed to the same diagnosis as Kant's or Harsanyi's. It is simple. It provides in principle a criterion thanks to which fair inequalities could be distinguished from unfair inequalities as far as the distribution of primary goods is concerned. But this criterion does not correctly predict people's feelings. In fact, as we have seen with our discussion of the Frohlich–Oppenheimer study, people reject it in some circumstances.

Sociologists on their side often have a relativistic view of axiological feelings in general and of feelings of justice in particular. This attitude derives from many causes and notably from the positivistic tradition in which sociology is anchored. This tradition is full of suspicion toward the idea of seeing reasons as genuine causes and particularly as the genuine causes of axiological feelings. Sociologists with a positivist inclination traditionally prefer to introduce "material" causes, such as obscure psychological, cultural, social or biological forces, even if such forces appear very conjectural, rather than accepting the idea that reasons can be the causes of feelings. This explains why they are in most cases satisfied with the explanation that people feel in such and such way about some axiological issue because they have been socialised to feel so.

Still, a growing body of research starts from the view that axiological feelings are the effect of reasons. Thus, writers like Batson (1991) or Clark (1992) have shown that compassion and sympathy, far from being merely emotional reactions, are the effect of reasons: we feel less compassion for somebody's suffering if we have the impression that he is the cause of his suffering and that this cause was within his control than for somebody whose suffering appears to us as undeserved and beyond his control. We have no compassion for the taxpayer who groans that he is exploited if we accept the theory that the way the tax system is organised is fair. The study by Oppenheimer and Frohlich is another example of this new trend of research into axiological feelings. It remains to systematise the theory that could link such studies and to accept the idea that axiological feelings, far from deriving from the application of principles people would adhere to under the effect of socialisation or human nature or utilitarian calculations, are the product of more or less conscious and articulate theories or systems of reasons. Now, these theories will probably be different depending on the cognitive capacities of the subjects and other contextual parameters. The fact that the tax system is widely perceived as unfair in France, for instance, probably explains to a large extent the fact that evading taxes is considered by many people favourably rather than unfavourably: as a kind of "sport", as the French say.

On the whole, the theory most likely to link our growing body of knowledge on axiological feelings is the cognitive theory according to which these feelings are the product of more or less coherent systems of reasons perceived as valid. In a word, prescriptive and more generally axiological convictions are generated by processes which are exactly the same as the processes generating conviction on descriptive issues.

REFERENCES

Batson, C.D. (1991) *The Altruism Question*. Hillsdale, N.J., Lawrence Erlbaum.

Boudon, R. (1994) *The Art of Self-Persuasion*. London, Polity Press.

—— (1995) *Le Juste et le vrai, Études sur l'objectivité des valeurs et de la connaissance*. Paris, Fayard.

—— (1997a) "La rationalité axiologique". In: Mesure, S. (ed), *La rationalité des valeurs*, Paris, Presses Universitaires de France.

—— (1997b) "Peut-on être positiviste aujourd'hui". In: Cuin, Ch. H. (ed.), *Durkheim d'un siècle à l'autre*, Paris, Presses Universitaires de France: 265–288.

—— (1997c) "The Present Relevance of Max Weber's *Wertrationalität* (value rationality)". In: Koslowski, P. (ed.), *Methodology of the Social Sciences, Ethics, and Economics in the Newer Historical School: From Max Weber and Rickert to Sombart and Rothacker*, Berlin/New York, Springer: 4–29.

—— (2001) *The Origin of Values*. New Brunswick/London, Transaction.

Clark, C. (1992) *Misery and Company: Sympathy in Everyday Life*. Chicago, Chicago University Press.

Deutsch, M. (1975) "Equity, Equality, and Need: What Determines Which Value Will Be Used As the Basis of Distributive Justice?" *The Journal of Social Issues*, 31(3): 137–151.

—— (1986) "Cooperation, Conflict, and Justice". In: Bierhoff, H. W., Cohen, R. L., Greenberg, J. (eds), *Justice in Social Relations*, New York: Plenum Press: 3–17.

Durkheim, E. (1979[1912]) *Les Formes élémentaires de la vie religieuse*. Paris, Presses Universitaires de France.

Frey, B. S. (1997) *Not Just For the Money: An Economic Theory of Personal Motivation*. Cheltenham, Edward Elgar.

Frohlich, N. and Oppenheimer, J. A. (1992) *Choosing Justice: an Experimental Approach to Ethical Theory*. Oxford, University of California Press.

Habermas, J. (1981) *Theorie des kommunikativen Handelns*. Frankfurt, Suhrkamp.

Harsanyi, J. C. (1955) "Cardinal Welfare, Individualistic Ethics, and Interpersonal Comparisons of Utility". *Journal of Political Economy*, 63(4): 309–21.

Hochschild, J. L. (1981) *What's Fair? American Beliefs about Distributive Justice*. Cambridge/London, Harvard University Press.

Kahneman, D., Knetsch, J. and Thaler, R. (1986) "Fairness and the Assumption of Economics". *Journal of Business*, 59: 285–300.

Kant, I. (1787) *Kritik der reinen Vernunft*. Bibliographisches Institut, Leipzig/Vienna: Meyers Volksbücher, 2nd ed. [no date]; I, I, 2nd part (*Die transcendentale Logik*), III (*Von der Einteilung der allgemeinen Logik in Analytik und Dialektik*): 93, 1.

Kellerhals, J., Modak, M. and Sardi, M. (1995) "Justice, sens de la responsabilité et relations sociales". *L'Année sociologique*, 45 (2): 317–349.

Lukes, S. (1967) "Some Problems About Rationality". *Archives européennes de sociologie*, 8(2): 247–64.

Mead, G.-H. (1934) *Mind, Self and Society. From the Standpoint of a Social Behaviourist*. Chicago, The University of Chicago Press.

Mills, C. W. (1956) *White Collar: The American Middle Classes*. New York, Oxford University Press.

Mitchell, G., Tetlock, P. E., Mellers, B. A. and Ordonez, L. D. (1993) "Judgements of Social Justice: Compromise Between Equality and Efficiency". *Journal of Personality and Social Psychology*, 65(4): 629–639.

Pascal (1960[1670]) *Pensées*. Paris, Garnier.

Popper, K. R. (1968) *The Logic of Scientific Discovery*. London, Hutchinson, 1959. Original: *Logik der Forschung*, Vienna, 1934.

Radnitzky, G. (1987) "La perspective économique sur le progrès scientifique: application en philosophie des sciences de l'analyse coût-bénéfice". *Archives de philosophie*, 50: 177–198.

Rawls, J. (1971) *A Theory of Justice*. Cambridge, The Belknap Press of Harvard University Press.

Smith, A. (1976[1776]) *An Inquiry into the Nature and Causes of the Wealth of Nations*. Oxford, Todd W. B.

Sukale, M. (1995) *Max Weber, Schriften zur Soziologie*. Stuttgart, Reclam: Introduction.

—— (2002) *Max Weber, Leidenschaft und Disziplin*. Tübingen, Mohr Siebeck.

Tarski, A. (1936) "Der Wahrheitsbegriff in der formalisierten Sprache". *Studia philosophica*, 1.

Taylor, C. (1997) *La liberté des modernes*. Paris, Presses Universitaires de France.

Walzer, M. (1993) *Spheres of Justice. A Defense of Pluralism and Equality*. Oxford, Martin Robertson.

Weber, M. (1922) *Wirtschaft und Gesellschaft: Grundriss der Sozialökonomik*. Tübingen, Mohr.

5

The Objectivity of Artistic Values

I. ARTISTIC VALUES: BETWEEN PLATONISM AND CONVENTIONALISM

Contemporary thought on art often reveals, as it does on morality and on knowledge, a sceptical character: artistic values should be seen as collective illusions created either by anonymous social forces as put forward by the Marxist and Durkheimian traditions, or by the power of the "art worlds". For the first, such as Bourdieu (1979), I will judge a given work to be "great" because it is held to be such in the social class to which I belong, and hence in giving it such a status I confirm in my own eyes my membership of that class. This process develops in an entirely unconscious manner in my mind. It is only accessible to the sociologist. For others, such as Becker (1982), the "worlds of art" (made up of artists, collectors, art critics, gallery owners, museum curators, etc.) have the authority to impose their values on the public as a whole.

Such theories may be termed "conventionalist", since they deny the fact that these artistic values can be objectively justified and that they are the product of conventions. They have the merit of emphasising the weakness of platonic theories of aesthetic values, but they are not very persuasive. I will confine myself here to the observation that the conventions that are postulated as the bases of artistic conventions are of a very particular type, since they are not merely tacit, but completely unconscious. The art lover is convinced a given work is objectively sublime. It is nothing of the sort, according to the conventionalist theories: this feeling is a complete illusion, and its cause is not to be found in the qualities of the work, but in the unconscious and tacit agreement about it by the members of a social class or the networks of the art worlds.

It is proposed here that it is better to look at artistic values as the results of systems of sound reasoning: it is for objective reasons that art works are seen as great or minor. It is nonetheless necessary to point out that these reasons may not be immediately evident, as much in the domain of artistic values as in others. On the contrary, their appearance is most often the result of a social process that is not unlike that of a court case. The cognitive theory of artistic values that I propose here avoids, it seems to me, the deadends into which conventionalist and platonic theories of aesthetic sentiments lead us.

Good Weather for Protagoras

It is commonly thought nowadays that value judgements concerning works of art do not have any objectivity. I may believe that such a work of art is great. It is not in reality. I only have the illusion that it is, either because I am influenced, without knowing it, by the views of the "art worlds", or because I endorse without hesitation the values of my social class (Marxist version of aesthetic relativism), or of the society to which I belong, or just of my social milieu (Durkheimian version of aesthetic relativism).

The discovery of the importance of "art worlds" in artistic life is not new. Haskell (1976) provides an instructive analysis on the influence of networks, particularly those of art collectors, on artistic production and as a result develops an interesting chapter on the sociology of art. But the sub-title of his book (*Some aspects of taste, fashion and collecting in England and France*) emphasises explicitly that such networks are not alone sufficient to explain the phenomena of collective appreciation of a work of art. They only grasp superficial aspects of these phenomena that develop in the short term. In contrast with an assumption widely accepted in the milieux of the sociology of art, this field is not at all in opposition to aesthetics or indeed a substitution for it. Simmel's writings on art (1892, 1916) obtain, on the contrary, all their force of conviction because they harmoniously combine the two disciplines.

By contrast the work of Howard Becker (1982) declares explicitly that sociology, as he conceives of it, disqualifies all other forms of art theory, as is shown by the chapter in his *Art Worlds* on aesthetics, a discipline he adjudges illusory. In any event artistic values cannot be held to be objective, according to Becker. The social sciences should have the aim, he says, not of representing a point of view on aesthetics, but of replacing it.

In the view of these trends in social science that I have just mentioned, trends that can be variously termed post-modernist, conventionalist or relativist, aesthetics seems indeed to be based on a question that is enough to discredit it: how to determine the elements that create "beauty" in a work of art, how to determine the objective correlatives of its artistic value. Against this archaic way of posing a question on the origin of artistic values, the social sciences have tried to show that artistic values can be analysed in the same way as illusions. Aesthetics seems to be the manifestation of its illusions: it starts with the assumption that the value that is attributed to a work of art reflects its qualities. But this is not the case. The valorisation of a work of art is the result of anonymous social forces or of the power of the networks that constitute the art worlds.

Not all sociologists, of course, share this relativism. Referring to Simmel (1892) again, the great German sociologist points out that it is not possible to be moved by a work if there is not a conviction that this emotion is generated by qualities belonging to the work itself, and as a result capable of being revealed to anyone, or at least to those who have the cognitive resources that allow them to detect the qualities in question. As to Weber (1920–1921), he makes the point in his *Essays on the Sociology of Religion* that the institutionalisation of literary and artistic criticism can be explained by the richness and fertility of the postulate on which these disciplines are founded, to the effect that the emotions felt by the art lover are indeed generated by the objective characteristics of the work of art that it is the job of the art critic to detect. I believe that Weber and Simmel outline here a better and consequently more fertile approach than that of Becker.

That tastes vary according to class, milieux or society, that the "art worlds" play a role in the production of artistic values over the short term is a proven fact. It is well known that Lully used his influence to suppress Charpentier, confining him as far as posterity is concerned to religious music, so that he alone would receive public acclaim. This is why Charpentier was only rediscovered towards the end of the 20th century. Is it possible to conclude from the fact that the reputation of an artist may, over time, swing from high to low, that value judgements about artistic matters have no objective basis? Scientific truths, including those of mathematics, also vary over time. It does not mean that they have no objective basis. Nor does it mean accepting what I would call – in shorthand – platonic aesthetics, which argues that beauty is a property of the work analogous to its colour that can be grasped by the mysterious processes of intuition. But would it not be to throw the baby out with the bath water to draw from the obsolescence of the platonic theory of aesthetics the conclusion that the value of a work of art is only a matter of opinion or convention?

It is necessary to recognise, however, that this relativism is now securely anchored. There are many indications of this: one, for example, is that it now seems unremarkable that a director can interpret a dramatic work however he or she wishes. Not only has the value of a work of art become a matter of opinion, but even its meaning can be interpreted *ad libitum*. Why not see prejudice against homosexuals in Molière's *Tartuffe*? Doesn't just such a hypothesis explain the blinding of Orgon? Why shouldn't *Le Misanthrope* be interpreted as a treatise on social mobility in the 17th century? Isn't it possible to read in the fact that Célimène looks out for Arsinoé's carriage an indication of acute class consciousness and a compulsive desire for social climbing? Roland Barthes owed his success to the fact that he gave himself in full measure both the right and the duty of interpreting and evaluating literary works by following his own singular inspiration, as shown so brilliantly by Pommier (1986, 1994).

These liberties of interpretation are based on the post-modernist principles that I described earlier: the meaning of a work of art, and artistic values more generally, are not contained in the work of art itself, they emanate from the consciousness of the individual who appreciates it, or from the collective consciousness of the groups that it pleases. The tenets of Barthes confer a creative consciousness on the spectator. It is this consciousness that produces the light which illuminates the work of art. For sociologists of a neo-marxist or neo-Durkheimian per-suasion, this light comes from either the collective consciousness that is implanted in any individual belonging to a given class (neo-marxist version) or a given collectivity (neo-Durkheimian version). As to indi-vidual consciousness, they see it as passive and reduced to being merely a receptacle of the forces emitted by the collective consciousness.

Heresy, the Basis (Source) of Relativism
False theories frequently owe their credibility to the fact that they have the status of metonyms or hyperbolae. They take the part for the whole,

and allot a greater generality to their principles than they deserve. In general they have the status of "heresies" in the literal sense of the word (*hairein* = to choose): they choose the parts that suit them and ignore the others; they extrapolate from the particular to the general; they exaggerate the relevance of an observation; they choose the facts that support and ignore those that contradict.

Another basis for the credibility of false ideas comes from the principle that if "A is false", then "non-A is true", by applying the law of the excluded middle. I have proposed elsewhere, in *L'Art de se persuader*, a catalogue of these errors (Boudon, 1990) and emphasise in chapter 1 the importance of the mistaken use of the law of the excluded middle (*principe du tiers exclu*). The law of the excluded middle states that [X or not X] is true for any statement X, i.e. any statement is either true or not true; there is no third possibility. Here, because platonic aesthetics are disqualified, and because it is impossible to identify the elements that constitute the beauty of a work of art, it is too readily concluded that its value is a matter of either individual taste or of collective convention.

The fact that the processes of valorisation might be associated with the phenomena of snobbery goes without saying. It may be that someone likes a certain category of objects because they are liked in the social class to which they belong. That is exactly what Veblen (1960) saw so clearly. Some people like formal gardens because they are evidence of their membership of the "leisure class". The formal garden became a sign of distinction, positively valued by the leisure class because no profit could be drawn from it. It required much care and attention, but had no use. It had value as a sign: it indicated that its owner was sufficiently wealthy to be able to use his time in any way that he wanted. Its value was symbolic, although the owner of the formal garden saw it as aesthetic. But Veblen was careful to reduce the artistic sensitivity of the garden lover to the phenomenon of false consciousness. He could see that certain formal gardens were successful, while others were not. Symbolic and aesthetic values may thus peacefully co-exist, far from it being the case that the one must be seen as the truth of the other. There is a brilliant extension of Veblen's thesis by Quentin Bell (1976). In the past, crinolines and corsets were seen as enhancing women's value. In reality, this value was highly symbolic: because of their appearance and their inconvenience, such accessories demonstrated the impossibility for the woman who wore them to do anything with her hands, and even to dress and undress herself unaided. Such signs of dependence functioned as symbols of superiority: corsets, crinolines and complicated hairstyles implied attentive servants.

In a similar way it is possible to like classical music for snobbish reasons, because this is a sign that one belongs to the elite. As Roquentin suggests in Sartre's *La Nausée* one *believes* in liking classical music rather than actually liking it. The master of suspicion himself would not be taken in: he sees that music lovers are fools, as Sartre puts it, who are caught in their own trap. What Sartre does not see is that snobbery can only explain the taste for classical music in certain cases. Snobbery unquestionably exists. But it is clearly absurd to see the phenomenon of snobbery as the key to artistic values. That is exactly what Simmel (1900) saw so well, when he insisted on the distinction between the snob and the amateur. It is not generally because a cultural product is appreciated by the elite that it is thought to be superior. It can be appreciated by the elite without that being the cause of its superiority. Without doubt, certain correlations can be observed between cultural consumption and social origin. But to find in that the proof that cultural preferences are explained by class membership is a step too far. On the other hand it is very clear that many types of cultural products are widely accepted, that are not in any sense to the taste of the "elites" or the "dominant class".

It also happens that the "art worlds" are able for a time to value or devalue an artist who does not merit it. But no work has been consistently recognised as a result of the activity of the "art worlds" alone. Despite the grants and other efforts to promote it, much of the output of avant-garde music is rightly seen as having little value.

On artistic matters as in other areas, relativist theories often use an argument that seems compelling, although it has little justification, to the effect that aesthetic canons vary with cultures. It is possible to observe that the same thing can be said of other values. What is thought to be good here is thought to be bad there. Even in the matter of truth, the fact that there is a history of science is enough to show that what was held to be true yesterday is no longer the case today, and vice-versa. It is appropriate that one cannot draw from the variability of judgements of the form, "X is true", or "X is false" the conclusion that no scientific truth exists or from the variability in time and space of judgements such as "X is good" or "X is bad", that moral judgements are cultural conventions. The fact that the Greeks refused to consider $\sqrt{2}$ as a number only shows that they had reasons to do so that we do not have any longer, and not that it is impossible to decide whether they were right or wrong.

The variation in time and space of the beliefs attached to value judgements does not in any event mean that it is necessary to explain them in a conventionalist or subjectivist manner.

Beyond Platonism and Conventionalism

Why cannot "conventionalist" theories be considered general theories of artistic values? Firstly, as we have just seen, because they put forward hypotheses that are both questionable and non-restrictive. Then, because it is easy to refer to many types of facts for which they are not able to account; for instance, that there are artists and works of art considered "classic", or some relatively stable hierarchies of artists and art works, or that it is relatively easy to export some works of art from one culture to another. It would be readily accepted that such facts are not mere curiosities. They are inseparable from art itself.

If the effects of socialisation that are so widely used by culturalists of all forms, the class determinisms of neo-marxist theorists, or the influences of the art worlds, represented the ultimate sources of artistic valorisation, it could only be fragile and changeable. The culturalists who make rather liberal use of Durkheim want artistic values to appear to be in concordance with the condition of a society or a culture: it is because a given work appears to express for me the *essence* of the society in which I live that I take it to be valid. The neo-marxists want me to see a given work as beautiful because it is thought to be so in the class to which I belong. But how does it come about then that we continue to value those works that appeared in earlier cultures, that we might be sensitive to works of exotic art or even that so many transgressions of the boundaries of class cultures can be observed?

If values are secreted by the art worlds, where does the stability of these hierarchies come from? Why is it that artistic values, if they are the reflections of temporary states of a society, appear to be stable while societies change? All the research shows that absolute rediscoveries are rare (Milo, 1986). *The Barber of Seville* and *Pelléas et Mélisande* were whistled off the stage on their first nights. But that did not mean that Rossini and Debussy were unknown in their time. During his lifetime, Stendhal did not enjoy a reputation comparable to that of Balzac, but the contemporary "art worlds" had not failed to notice him. The statuses of works of art and artists in particular appears to be very stable over time.

More stable even than it might seem, because certain variations in their values are not incompatible with the stability of their reputations.

For instance, in the United States prior to the second world war, Mozart's standing among composers and music critics was lower than that of Beethoven. This only shows that the weightings of the criteria of evaluation on which the reputation of an artist is judged may vary. Before the second world war, a particular importance was attached to creative artists who had made a major impact on the "language" of their art. This criterion became the most important: only those "creative artists" who had made a contribution to the renewal of the language were worthy of the title. This is why Boulez declared that Shostakovitch was a composer of minor importance, because he wrote in a language that was close to that of Mahler; a language "superseded" by Schoenberg, Alban Berg and Anton Webern. From the point of view of the renewal of the language, Beethoven seemed readily superior to Mozart. Nowadays, this hierarchy is no longer accepted. Nobody any longer follows the evolutionism of Boulez, according to which a great composer can only be someone who has shown himself capable of renewing the language of music. Such changes in the reputations of Beethoven and Mozart reflect the fact that the relative weightings of criteria have changed, and not that the standing of the two composers on these given criteria has in any way altered.

The hypothesis that snobbery and more generally *convention* (in the most general sense of the term) is the basis of artistic values cannot easily respond to certain questions. If it was true, the appeal of works of art would be much more variable than it is. If they are classics simply because they are signs of distinction, why do they continue to be classics? Why does the work of Rembrandt retain all of its power and its appeal to us, despite the fact that it was made in a society that has very little in common with our own? How can conventionalist theories account for the fine gradations and the precise adjectives that are coupled with both works of art and artists?

I leave on one side the fact that conventionalist theories are not merely powerless to explain what they claim to explain. Worse, they generate hypotheses that are both unwieldy and fragile. The person who likes classical music, does not really like it, but only *believes* that he or she likes it, as the conventionalists of all types would tell us. How is it possible to distinguish between them? Is it possible at this point to ignore the facts of consciousness? With what justification and on what bases may this false consciousness be presumed?

In short, conventionalist theories of artistic value do not pass the standard tests used to judge the validity of a scientific theory.

The subject of artistic values brings us straight back to the questions raised about other values. It is important to note this because of the stakes involved in the present discussion. In the same way, conventionalist theories of moral values rest just as much on unwieldy hypotheses that have little relevance to the facts. The conventionalists explain that I believe "X is good" because the others believe it too. But they cannot explain why I must be automatically in agreement with the judgement "X is good" simply because others are. Nor can they explain why I have the feeling that "X *is* good" rather than the feeling that I *believe* that "X is good". If moral values can be explained by convention why do I find it so difficult to change them? I have no difficulty in substituting "how are you?" for the hand-shake as soon as I leave France for the United States. On the other hand, I would find it a lot harder to get used to the idea that fraud is a good thing. What is the difference? Because the first case but not the second can be analysed in conventionalist terms. At its simplest, it is not possible to lump moral beliefs with conventions, without mistaking the particular for the general. This very costly "heresy" can only be maintained by ignoring many distinctions and by using hypotheses that are both clumsy and gratuitous. Finally, conventionalist theories cannot explain the phenomena of irreversibility that appear in the normative domain, (introduction of universal suffrage, abolition of the death penalty).

All of these observations may be transposed to the case of judgements of the form, "X is beautiful" (I am using the word "Beautiful" here, following Baudelaire, as expressing the fact that X creates an overwhelming feeling of positive valuation). Conventionalist theories are confronted here with exactly the same objections as in the case of the normative domain. Is what is beautiful - because it is taken to be so by the art worlds – also perceived as *being* beautiful? Why are collective tastes mistaken for value judgements? I prefer red wine to white wine. I do not conclude from this that the former is intrinsically better, and I would readily admit that my next door neighbour has quite the opposite preference. By contrast, I would be very surprised if an art lover was unmoved by a particular work by Dürer or Rembrandt. I could conceive that he might have difficulty in accepting it. I will admit that he might not like it. But I would be astonished if he said that it was totally without value. It is readily accepted that the judgement, "I like X" has a different meaning from " X is beautiful"; it is also accepted that the two do not always coincide. It is very difficult to explain these distinctions in the framework of a theory inspired by conventionalism.

This is not to say, of course, that the Beautiful exists in the same sense as blue or green. The Beautiful is not an attribute of a work of art. Any "platonism" is definitively excluded here. The same observation can be made about the Good. There are no general criteria that enable the judgement that a norm is good or that a work of art is beautiful. But that does not mean that the evaluation of a work of art is subjective, as the conventionalists conclude. In short "conventionalism" does not explain artistic values any better than "platonism".

How can we avoid the impasses of "platonism" on the one hand and of conventionalism (in other words sociologism) on the other? Quite simply, by looking at the roots of sociology. Weber argued that in terms of the good there was an axiological rationality. This idea can be interpreted in the following way: we judge that "X is good (or bad)", not because we have an inner perception that X contains the attribute "good" (or "bad") or because there are general criteria making it possible to affirm that "X is good" (or "bad"), but because we have sound reasons to believe that "X is "good" (or "bad"). Deception, then, is "bad" because it destroys the very basis of social exchange. That is why we have strong reason to value it negatively. But it is on the basis of other types of reason that we see a particular policy for reducing unemployment as good or bad, to take that example.

Thus understood the idea of "axiological rationality" is a way out of the platonic world of essences, where the True, the Good, and the Beautiful are defined by groups of canons or of attributes. It suggests that we estimate that "X Is right, true, good or beautiful" when we have strong reasons for making that judgement. To which it must immediately be added that a reason will not seem strong to us unless we perceive it to be *objectively* so. We cannot like an object that we do not think is likeable, as Simmel (1989) pointed out.

Let us call this the "postulate of meaning", or "postulate of significance", making clear immediately that the word "meaning" must be taken here as designating the systems of strong reasons that are perceived as objective by social actors.

II. ARTISTIC VALUES ARE BASED ON OBJECTIVE REASONS

Tartuffe

Why is Molière's play *Tartuffe* currently considered a "classic"? Why does the play regularly return to the stage? Why is it interesting to many different audiences?

The curtain falls on a performance of *Tartuffe*. Audiences share almost all the same moral feelings towards the main character (Boudon, 1995). It is possible then to refer to them as "collective sentiments". These "sentiments" are themselves based on normative beliefs, translated into collective value judgements. Moreover, all audiences have the impression that their sentiments *are* right. Nearly all of them feel a certain admiration for the main character, for his aplomb, for his manipulative and dissimulating style, for his ability to achieve the ends he has set himself. At the same time, all feel a moral repulsion towards him. This *collective* reaction is not a result of the processes of influence: there is no social contagion here. Nor does it come from any process of inculcation. It is clearly insufficient to claim that the reaction follows from the application by the member of the audience of norms that he or she has internalised. The fine modulation of normative reactions ("admirable from some points of view, but repugnant"), the fact that they are experienced in an objective way (not "I feel that he is repugnant", but "he *is* repugnant") is easily explained, however, if they are seen as the result of reasons: trust is a fundamental resource of social life; it is displayed through certain signs (Tartuffe tries to show the purity of his intentions by signs of *piety*); the impostor betrays the confidence of those that he deceives by sending them deceiving signs; as a result he hurts innocent victims, and in particular he uses a basic mechanism of social life for his own profit.

To this it may be added that the collective *interest* expressed in relation to Tartuffe can be understood readily by the reasons that are its basis. Deception constantly undermines and threatens social life. As a result the politician whose aim is to be elected owes it to himself to be popular, and a way of doing so is to support the "great causes"; professionally, then, he is encouraged to hide his personal ambitions behind a posture of altruism. But on this the electorate is often wary. This is why it is so difficult for a politician to convince people of the sincerity of his lack of personal interest. Less easily forgiven, when it comes to light, is the deception typical of an intellectual or a scientist, for it contradicts the very essence of intellectual or scientific activity.

Deception is threatening because it is a common temptation. At the same time this threat is particularly serious because it is aimed at the very essence of social life. In the case of Tartuffe, he personifies a type of extreme deception, absolute deception if you will, which is to hide immoral intentions under the cloak of respect for moral values.

This is why the play is considered a masterpiece: any sensitive member of an audience will find it completely absorbing

The collective character of the reaction is explained by the fact that obviousness is based on objective reasons. The feeling of it, the moral certainty experienced by every member of the audience, the fact that each tends to have the same reaction as the person in the next seat, and this irrespective of their cultural background, are the consequence of the reasons on which these sentiments are based.

Hence the processes responsible for the formation of collective beliefs about artistic values are no different in principle from the processes that create collective beliefs on other subjects. In every case, certainty emerges from strong reasons. In every case cognitive processes are the source of certitude. That is why what I set out here I term a "cognitive" theory.

Molière puts on stage a threat that runs through social life. He emphasises the dominance of personality. Two consenting victims, Orgon and his mother, allow Tartuffe to terrorise a whole family of powerful characters. His dominance is so great that only a "coup de théâtre" could neutralise it. Put simply, *Tartuffe* is widely thought to be a masterpiece because it exposes one of the great cancers of social life and anyone who is able to understand the meaning of the play tends also to be sensitive to this threat. There are thus many reasons to recognise a great work in this comedy.

The Limits of Understanding

The greatness of an artist often derives from the fact that he or she is able to express something that it has not been possible to express as well before. Of course, it also necessary that what he or she expresses is itself valued.

This is the case of the painter Paul Klee. *Die Grenzen des Verstandes* ("The limits of understanding"), the title of one of his paintings (1927), would not surprise anybody if it were a philosophical work, that is a work normally expressed in words. Here, knowledge is represented by a round, beige spot that suggests the sun. Such a close relation between knowledge and light suggests the most classical form of symbolism. It calls to mind the work of Puvis de Chavannes. But Klee goes much further. His aim is not to represent knowledge, but the limits of understanding. We cannot draw on the arsenal of classical symbolism. Neither understanding, nor *a fortiori* the limits of understanding permit ready depiction. However, Klee manages to succeed. The tension of understanding

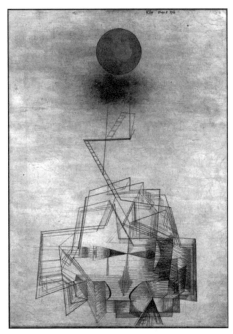

Paul Klee, *Die Grenzen des Verstandes* (1927)

towards knowledge is represented by a series of zigzag lines that describe an upward movement, towards the sun. The geometric form of these bent lines suggests the articulated, logical and simplifying nature of philosophical and scientific theories. Klee opts for a "constructivist" theory of knowledge, of a Kantian type. He sees knowledge as being efficacious. Indeed, the ladders made up from the zigzag lines reach towards the sun. At the same time, and this line is emphasised again by Kant, they appear to be blocked by an impassable barrier.

In short, it is a whole treatise on philosophy that Klee has managed to depict. There is not merely performance, but also efficacity. The painter expresses with the aid of line and colour a problem that has preoccupied not just western philosophy since the time of Plato, but human thought itself.

I am not concerned with the false "naïveté" of the style. It is often used by Klee. It might however allow the viewer to think that the painter has been able to represent the unrepresentable because, as the "naïveté" of the drawing suggests, he has a child's conception of the world. As Gombrich (1972) points out, from the 1920s children's drawings were no longer seen as scribbles but more exactly as "children's drawings" because they were felt to be imbued with a power of expression that adults could no longer achieve. This is because the adult is obsessed by the reductive view that sees painting as something that must aim at the representation of appearances.

It should be noted that the (Jacob's?) ladder that disappears into dark cloud protecting the sun suggests the continuity both of religious tradition and of philosophical speculation. Each is based in universal concerns.

There are then some precise reasons for seeing this painting as "great" in the aesthetic sense and "beautiful" (in the Baudelairian sense), even if it is impossible to list them all as with any great work of art. It expresses an object that is theoretically inexpressible in the language of painting. In one fell swoop it extends the expressive domain of painting.

It can be seen that the greatness of Klee is not the result of snobbery (although there are doubtless some Klee snobs), but of the exemplary success of a project that is, on the face of it, unrealisable. There are objective reasons to affirm that *Die Grenzen des Verstandes* is a great work. It maps out a new continent for painting. Klee assiduously explored it in many other works which also seem to express clearly what seems at first sight inexpressible, as with his *Brüderlichkeit* ("Brotherly love"), which depicts an abstract virtue in a non-allegorical manner, or his *Zur Gruppe geschlungen* ("Part of the group"), that expresses the hold of the group over the individual.

Die Grenzen des Verstandes, it may be emphasised, deals with an eternal problem in a time when scientific progress seemed suddenly to have come to a full stop in the two key sciences of the era, mathematics and physics.

Madame Bovary

The explanation Baudelaire (1980[1857]) gives for the greatness of *Madame Bovary* is an exemplary fragment worthy of inclusion in a collected volume of the great texts in the sociology of art.

This masterpiece commands respect for objective reasons, argues Baudelaire.

Max Weber would say of Baudelaire that his greatness as an artist came from the fact that he extended the limits of poetry by arguing that the poet describes mediocrity, moral turpitude, degeneration, laxity, and in short sings the praises of all that is normally considered of negative value, but which is human none the less. The unusual but fruitful nature of this project, and its exceptional and ambitious character, meant that for Weber the Baudelairian project was perfectly described by the title of his work, *Les Fleurs du mal* (Weber, 1995[1919]).

Baudelaire understands the greatness of *Madame Bovary* so well because he had undoubtedly opened up poetry to the world of negative values. That is how he reads Flaubert. His aim is to paint a picture of mediocrity and vulgarity, which could be "beautiful" (in the Baudelarian sense, that is, imbued with artistic power). Baudelaire argues that it was because of his artistic power that the magistrates found Flaubert innocent at his trial for obscenity in 1857.

> *this remarkable concern for Beauty, in men whose faculties are not engaged unless it be for the Just and the True, is one of the most touching symptoms, compared with the ardent lusts of this society that has definitively abandoned any spiritual love and which, neglecting its ancient roots, only cares for its own guts. All in all it can be said that this decision, through its great poetic significance, was definitive, that the Muse had won the case.*

> [*ce souci remarquable de la Beauté, en des hommes dont les facultés ne sont mises en réquisition que pour le Juste et le Vrai, est un symptôme des plus touchants, comparé avec les convoitises ardentes de cette société qui a définitivement abjuré tout amour spirituel et qui, négligeant ses anciennes entrailles, n'a plus cure que de ses viscères. En somme on peut dire que cet arrêt, par sa haute tendance poétique, fut définitif, que gain de cause a été donné à la Muse.*] (Baudelaire, (1980[1857]: 477–483).

This passage tells us that even in a materialist era the power of Beauty wins out even with those who are thought to be concerned only with the Just and the True. And there is more: artistic creations must express their time in what is essential, and by so doing enlarge the expressive register of art in an irreversible way.

Moreover, Baudelaire shows that if the Beauty of *Madame Bovary* is objective, it cannot be interpreted in a Platonic way. It cannot be reduced to any group of attributes. It is misplaced to cite the notions of harmony or coherence that would be employed by anyone adhering to the Platonic idea of beauty. The greatness of *Madame Bovary* lies in its novel project: to show the "power" of "vulgarity" in an era characterised by a distaste for the noble and the grand; to show the vulgar by using the fact that vulgarity is a value that is part and parcel of its time.

Everything is told, suggests Baudelaire, as if Flaubert had thought out his project with total clarity:

We lay out a vigorous, picturesque, subtle style on an ordinary canvas. We enclose the warmest and most explosive feelings in the most trivial sort of adventure. The most important, the most decisive statements issue from the mouths of the most stupid characters.

[*Nous étendrons un style nerveux, pittoresque, subtil, exact sur un canevas banal. Nous enfermerons les sentiments les plus chauds et les plus bouillants dans l'aventure la plus triviale. Les paroles les plus solennelles, les plus décisives, s'échapperont des bouches les plus sottes.*] (Baudelaire, *ibid.*).

Banality, triviality are thus deliberately chosen as vehicles of description:

Where is the land of stupidity, the world most productive of absurdities, the most populated with intolerant imbeciles? The provinces. Who are the worst actors there? The little people who concern themselves with petty posts whose exercise warps their thinking.

[*Quel est le terrain de sottise, le milieu le plus productif en absurdités, le plus abondant en imbéciles intolérants? La province. Quels y sont les acteurs les plus insupportables? Les petites gens qui s'agitent dans de petites fonctions dont l'exercice fausse leurs idées.*] (Baudelaire, *ibid.*).

The weak character of Charles Bovary is clearly presented in a cruel way in the very first lines of the novel: he is so sure of his own insignificance that even as a young schoolboy, he is so ashamed of his name that he mumbles it almost inaudibly: *Charbovary.*

What subject is worn-out, sold-out, the barrel-organ that has been played until it groans? Adultery.

[*Quelle est la donnée la plus usée, la plus prostituée, l'orgue de Barbarie la plus éreintée? L'Adultère.*] (Baudelaire, *ibid.*).

The greatness of *Madame Bovary* consists in the impossible nature of the project: to depict the vulgar and the trivial, and also in the fact that Flaubert manages to make the reader feel that the vulgar and the trivial, so characteristic of his time, are also timeless dimensions of the human condition.

This is a project that cannot be understood, as Baudelaire emphasises, unless it is situated in its own time. The vulgarity that Baudelaire refers to is also that which attracted the attention of Tocqueville and that he expresses in a different way: the transition from aristocratic to democratic society (that prefigures Tocquevillian America) makes banality into a positive value. It is because these changes were felt more or less confusedly and in a wide and diffuse way that Flaubert (like Tocqueville before him) was read and appreciated.

Flaubert's project is then profoundly original; it aims to express something that has not yet been expressed. At the same time it resonates with feelings that were widespread at the time. There were reasons why it was formulated at this particular moment. Baudelaire sets out a superb analysis in the sociology of art. Despite its originality and paradoxical character, celebrating the vulgar, Flaubert expresses a reversal in values that struck many observers. That is why it is placed so high in the history of literature. Despite his superhuman power, Balzac continues to depict the great human emotions as described by the moralists. He weaves his novels around intrigues. Flaubert works the "miracle" of describing

> *this poor little provincial adulteress whose entire story apart from the imbroglio is made up of sorrow, disgust, sighs, and several febrile swoons, drawn from a life cut short by suicide.*

> [*cette pauvre petite provinciale adultère, dont toute l'histoire sans imbroglio se compose de tristesses, de dégoûts, de soupirs et de quelques pâmoisons fébriles arrachées à une vie barrée par le suicide.*]

Baudelaire underlines here that the work of art should be directly related to its time, that it should be inspired by its time. But at the same time the exploitation by the artist of this singularity allows him to conquer new territory to the benefit of art, to push back the limits of artistic expression, and thus acquire the dimension of universality.

In this sense it is possible to speak of artistic "progress". Not that Flaubert might be thought superior to Shakespeare, to Cervantès or to Molière. Flaubert, amongst others, opened the way irreversibly to a new continent of artistic expression. In his memoirs, Shostakovitch regrets that Haydn was not born later. What he means by that is that his genius would have had a richer palette on which to draw (Volkov, 1980).

The existence of this progress is correlative with the appearance of irreversibilities in the history of art (as in that of science and of morality). After Flaubert and Baudelaire, art had at its disposal the means of expressing essential dimensions of man and of human history such as the ugly, the vulgar and the trivial. That is why an Otto Dix or a Max Beckmann speak about war in a way that is totally different to that of Callot, of Goya, or even the Picasso of *Guernica* (which remains very close to Callot). There is no longer an insistence on cruelty, horror, the denunciation of barbarism, but on the stinking wounds, the atrocious injuries, amputated members, dehumanising invalidity, dirty bandages. Similarly Shostakovitch's *Lady Macbeth* owes its artistic grandeur to the fact that it makes Shakespeare's monstrous heroine into a heroine *à la* Flaubert.

The exploration of the continent discovered by Flaubert continues long after him. Not that Flaubert had the slightest direct influence on Otto Dix. But he made possible what was not before. In the same way, the composer who manages to give a meaning to a dissonance or a rhythm that was previously thought "unacceptable", "ugly", etc, contributes irreversibly to the expressive resources of artists to come.

Rembrandt's Portraits

It is possible to follow here one of the great classical sociologists, certainly one of the great sociologists of art, Georg Simmel, even though his work in this domain is, as in so many others, more suggestive than definitive. Simmel's writings on art do not have the systematic aspect that is in Hegel, for instance. But in his work on Rodin and especially Rembrandt, he shows quite clearly the routes down which a sociology of art worthy of that name should proceed (Simmel, 1916).

As with Flaubert, Rembrandt was sensitive to the values of his time. Durkheim, Weber, Burckhardt, Simmel himself and many others have analysed the upheaval of values that occurred during the great changes of the sixteenth century. The intensification of the division of labour and diversification of social roles, the lengthening of the processes of production and exchange linking individuals to each other, increasing relations between distant regions, the discovery of other ways of life and of thinking, and increasing mobility lead to a valorisation of the individual and the development of individualism in the moral sense of the term.

It is this development, one Simmel himself studied for the *Philosophy of Money*, that he finds expressed in the portraits of Rembrandt. By contrast with the painters who precede him, Rembrandt the portraitist tries to depict individuals rather than types. More exactly, the portraits of Rembrandt express the idea of individuality through the individual; the personality that is painted has an interest for the painter not because he is a particular individual, and even less that he represents a human *type*, but because he is an *individual*. It is not the content of individual singularity that interests Rembrandt, but the fact that this singularity affirms the interest of the individual as an individual. In short, as with Klee much later, it is a very abstract idea that had not been expressed to anything like the same extent before Rembrandt painted his self-portraits. By contrast with the portraits of Dürer, who depicted general traits of character (nobility, intelligence, pride, etc.), those of Rembrandt represent the individual in all his banal singularity. Banality is a reminder that the singular features of the individual have no importance and that all that counts is singularity itself. The individual is interesting only as an individual, not because he is Durand or Dupont, but because in being Dupont, he is different from Durand. The painter makes us aware, here, of a complete and historic change in values.

The few lines of Baudelaire on Flaubert make the many treatises written later on the author of *Madame Bovary* seem mostly pointless. It is not by chance that the great historian-sociologist of art, Gombrich, refers so closely to Simmel when he describes Rembrandt's portraits. The principal source of Rembrandt's greatness lies where Simmel locates him; in his project to paint the individual as an individual. Frans Hals also created something not achieved before him, to grasp fleeting and marked expressions, such as those associated with surprise. In this sense he is worthy of being considered an artist of the first rank. But he does not have the exceptional historical significance of Rembrandt, because even though he grasped with blinding virtuosity the fleeting expression, his painting continued to be based on a psychology of human types and on the classical theory of the emotions. Although his paintings are as lifelike and individualised as is possible, it is man in general who explodes with joy under the features of any particular Amsterdam merchant.

So Simmel and Gombrich agree about the essential point that comes through their analyses; not just the status of "classic" but also the fine gradations that distinguish between works and artists can only be explained if we see them as the result of strong reasons, that is reasons on which it is easy to agree. It is true that the originality of Rembrandt the portraitist lies where Simmel located it. It was because he was right that Gombrich follows him. On the other hand it is easy to see why a painter who manages in apparently prosaic paintings to express a phenomenon as great as a sea-change in values is exceptionally important. The reasons why we count Rembrandt amongst the greatest are of the same order as those that explain why Newton or Einstein become such emblematic figures of the man of science.

I note merely for the record that Simmel brilliantly extended his programme in the sociology of art to other examples, notably that of Rodin; the question is the same as that about Rembrandt, that is: why does Rodin occupy such an eminent position in the modern history of sculpture? The direct line of explanation is the same; behind the *feeling* of power and grandeur that Rodin's sculptures generate, we can find precise and objective reasons. It is because these reasons are precise and objective that they are shared and that there is general agreement to place Rodin very high in the hierarchy of sculptors.

It should be added that consensus can take some time to appear. Socrates' nominalism was so in advance of its time, explains Simmel (1990), that he was condemned to death by his judges. What they saw as moral worthlessness, a lack of respect for institutions, was in reality a manifestation of the value of the critical mind. Centuries had to go past before the idea developed that economic value is not an attribute of things but an equilibrium resulting from supply and demand. Such delays are normal currency in the realm of ideas, and appear frequently in the domain of art. Schubert was seen for a long period as simply a pleasant composer. Even if Rembrandt's greatness was recognised quite early, the reasons for this were not clear until Simmel.

What in particular should be noted is that good sociologist as he is Simmel starts from the basis that it is a good idea to turn his back on any conventionalism, whether direct or indirect, implicit or explicit. The consensus on Rodin or on Rembrandt is the effect of objective reasons. There is no reason to suppose that these reasons will always be understood, or that they will be immediately. In the best case, they are understood in an intuitive way, and they only become clearly evident with time.

The Place of Sociology Between Platonism and Sociologism

Sociology and in a more general way contemporary social science often appear to be ideologies of legitimation. Under the pretext of showing the deep mechanisms hidden under surface appearances, they end up transforming into appearances the most unimpeachable realities.

All of contemporary sociology of science strives to explain the collective beliefs of scientists in the same way as anthropologists analyse the rituals of the "savage". We are informed that behind scientific certitude, it is necessary to unmask an unacknowledged and unacknowledgeable desire for power, or the result of an equally unacknowledged and unacknowledgeable set of individual and collective interests. Feyerabend (1975) tried to convince his reader that Galileo was in particular driven by his desire for power and that he owed his success purely to his rhetorical and strategic abilities. In the same manner, the sociology of norms sees its vocation at present in revealing the interests or the emotions that lie *behind* the acceptance of norms and ignores by this the fact that they are experienced by actors as based on objective reasons. This perception is declared to be "false". Such an unwieldy hypothesis is readily invoked, because the party line, drawn from Nietzsche, Freud, Marx and from Durkheim (or at least the part of his work read by many neo-Durkheimians) says that consciousness is "false" by its very nature. Rather curiously the major hypothesis of these authors, who have been called the *masters of suspicion*, more exactly the hypothesis that consciousness is naturally false, is considered as a major discovery of the human sciences.

There is here an apt and spectacular illustration of the metonymies that I described earlier. That consciousness can be blinded, for instance by emotion, can be readily accepted. But the masters of suspicion go well beyond such a platitude. They argue that consciousness is "false" on every subject, and of course that it is so in all innocence, I mean that it is completely unaware of this falsity. That consciousness may be sometimes false in a precise sense, as in the case of confusion or error, is undeniable. That it is by its very essence and that the vocation of the social sciences and more generally the human sciences is to reveal to the actor the meaning of his beliefs, meanings that escape him but that the sociologist has the power to reveal to him, is by contrast an unacceptable postulate.

The post-modern sociology of art even argues that artistic values are illusions. We believe we like a work of art because it is great. In truth, it bores us and we only say we like it because *that is what is done* in the milieu to which we belong. We think we are dealing with the masterpiece of the century. In reality, the "art worlds" have managed to sell us this idea, much as a travel agency sells us Tunisia or Sri Lanka.

Post-modern sociologists of art and of science insist strongly in general on the fact that their approach represents a radical rupture with earlier approaches. Some argue that anthropology should replace philosophy as the only legitimate form of thinking about art, science or morality. This is because beliefs about art, ethics or science cannot be objectively based. Hence Welsch (1987), a good historian-sociologist of art, sees postmodernist relativism as a revolution that is irresistible and major, as a form of progress that can only be accepted.

The influence exercised by this type of sociology makes it necessary to remind ourselves that there is another sociology, whose advantage is not to impose on its subject these types of mutilations. I have mentioned Simmel and Gombrich. Both pose the most interesting questions that there can be in the sociology of art; why does Rembrandt permanently occupy the top of the scale? Where does this enduring interest that he produces derive from? Why did it appear in the 17th century and not in an earlier period? Others pose equally fascinating questions: why is there a vogue for landscape and still-life in 17th-century Holland? The answer is that Calvinist iconoclasm had suggested to painters that they should give up trying to represent of the divine and find ways of showing how it could be found in the realm of "beings", to borrow Heidegger's term. This divine may be found in the landscapes of Caspar David Friedrich. Such a conjecture leads on to other questions: for example, why was a Friedrich unlikely to be found in France (Besançon, 1994)?

The questions about the sociology of art that I have raised here concern either comparative sociology ("why is spiritualism missing from French painting of the 18th and 19th centuries?"), or the sociology of creativity and its reception ("why is Rembrandt given such high rank?"). A thousand other questions might be envisaged, of course, to begin with how to find why this or that work was produced.

In short, writers such as Gombrich (1989[1972]) Raynaud (1998) and Simmel before them are there to show that the sociology of art can both pose interesting questions and escape the reductionist trap. The same is true of normative sociology. Contractualist and functionalist theories have their drawbacks. But they provide theories that are useful in accounting for normative phenomena without any recourse to reductionism.

These non-reductionist theories of the sociology of art or of the normative share a characteristic. They begin with the principle that to account for aesthetic sentiments ("this work is great") or for normative sentiments ("this decision is just"), it is necessary to understand the outcomes of strong reasons that are seen correctly by the subject as having objective validity. It is because social subjects wish to base their views on strong reasons that the phenomena of consensus appear. These non-reductionist sociologies do not require the postulate of false consciousness and avoid that of conventionalism.

Once again consensus is not always something that immediately appears on every subject. The meaning of the work of art is not designed always to be understood in a clear and immediate manner. On the contrary if it is true that the given meaning, far from being indescribable corresponds to a system of strong reasons, it is necessary for it to appear that these reasons should be made clear, understood and accepted. It will be the same for innovations in other domains; interest bearing loans, life insurance, agrarian capitalism, universal suffrage were all subject to a long period of "resistance" because their meaning was not comprehended, and this was due to the fact that they were seen in the context of limiting "frameworks", such as the idea that putting a price on a life is immoral. The processes of production and diffusion of these systems of reasons represent the place of articulation between criticism, and the sociology and philosophy of art (Boudon, 1995).

But when consensus does appear – for instance on the matter of the greatness of Rembrandt, or the morally unacceptable nature of a given act – it is based on strong reasons.

The Incommensurability of Artistic Programmes

I will allow myself to mention another important problem. Simmel starts from the principle that the artist gives himself a "programme", in the sense that Lakatos (Lakatos, Musgrave, 1974) would later use this term. And throughout his discussion he shows that such programmes may be more or less fruitful and viable. This notion of an expressive programme, which is situated at the heart of Simmel's sociology of art, is perhaps that which best defines, it might seem, the work of art. Abstract art does not appear viable to him because it is too distant from the real. Expressionism and impressionism, at least if we consider the doctrines espoused by these movements, rather than the works that are placed under such labels and which are a long way from them, do not seem any more acceptable to him because, as they aim to reproduce the real in a textual form they abolish the very idea of a programme (Simmel uses the term "point of view", but by its familiarity this term may pass the reader by and that is why I prefer to speak of the "programme").

By contrast Danto (1964) starts with the idea that artistic programmes are incommensurable. The platonic programme (to copy the real), Malevitch's programme of the "black square" (to arouse the aesthetic senses by avoiding all representation of whatever sort), the theosophical programme of Mondrian (to represent divine powers) would all be acceptable programmes. After that it is a matter of the painter finishing his canvasses. Every programme can lead to masterpieces, Danto suggests. He explains how any work labelled as such by the artist is thus artistic. Duchamp's urinal, the beer cans and the star spangled banners of Jasper Johns are works of art because they are created in artistic programmes. No art programme can be judged. It appears that Danto wants to use here, in the domain of art, Kuhn's idea (1962) that scientific paradigms are incommensurable.

It would seem that in this imaginary debate between Simmel and Danto, it is more likely that Simmel is right. The great artist is someone who 1) has something to express, 2) this something is important, and who 3) succeeds in expressing it. By comparison with the landscapes of Friedrich, the rigorously geometric forms and pure colours of Mondrian do not succeed in sending the spiritual message that, despite his pretensions, he wants to express. They have a value that is mostly decorative. This aspect of his work has been particularly valued by interior and fashion designers.

From another point of view the relations between programme and work are complex. Rather strangely, Simmel appears to ignore this when, in contradiction with his usual aversion to any form of substantialism, he appears to substantialise impressionism and expressionism. Who cannot see that Zola's naturalism does not exclude the lyricism also found in his work? Or that the expressionism of Max Beckmann has little in common with that of Egon Schiele? A programme may sometimes involuntarily express a message that is more powerful than the programme in question would wish. This is the reverse of the case of Mondrian. In wanting to copy reality directly, the hyperrealists have contrived to give ordinary objects, such as the Volkswagen Beetle, an unreal dimension which seems a reminder of the mystery found in Friedrich's landscapes.

Programmes may also be followed in a rather vague fashion, and as a result of this fuzziness they display a Simmelian distance that ordinarily they would reject. This is of course the case with the impressionists. It is the case of Messiaen. He patiently recorded bird song. He even went as far as Polynesia to collect the warbling of a native species. But he also introduced the indispensable distance between original and music that Simmel describes and thus managed to create combinations of rhythms and sounds that are valued for the complexity and the sense of feeling that they are able to express: the feeling of wellbeing, the disappointments of pleasure, optimism, faith in the meaning of life. The programme of "concrete music" seems far distant here.

By contrast it is most unlikely that Andy Warhol expresses any more than platitudes on the place of the cartoon or advertising in the contemporary world, or on the cult of celebrity. Perhaps he attracted attention to himself because he managed to make the most ordinary object into a work of art.

It may also happen that the declared programme is completely different from that which is actually followed. Quite often the painting of Wassily Kandinsky or Hans Arp is not "abstract"; it expresses in an idealised way primitive forms of life and thus reminds the observer of the fragile assemblage of cells that make up his own organism. The "spiritual" is indeed present "in art", but less because the art termed "abstract" is indeed abstract, than because it is on the contrary, figurative.

In short, while it may be necessary to clarify and correct the approach, it seems better to follow Simmel than Danto. Viable programmes are those which are located at a reasonable distance from the real. Too close to the real, they deprive the artist of any creative power. Work that follows the programme cannot have expressive value except by accident, as in the case of the hyperrealists. Too far from the real, it no longer expresses anything. That is the case with Mondrian, whose spiritual message remains an intention rather than being effectively expressed in the painting itself. Simmel puts his finger here on the reasons for the failures of "abstract" painting and "concrete" music, as soon as the artist follows his programme to the letter, and of course for the programmes, such as that of Manzoni, that confuse art with the hoax.

The "Death of Art"

The post-modernists see in their diagnosis of the "death of art" some sort of unimpeachable empirical proof of their nihilism. The postmodern era is characterised, as we know from Nietzsche, by an empty heaven. An art that is congruent with the time, must then be nihilist. Hence the greatness of Duchamp's urinal: it expresses post-modernist nihilism. Simmel's theorem may be applied here: art is linked too closely here to the real to be able to express anything.

However, it is possible to be reassured that artistic activity is so essential that the "death of art" is unlikely. This impression of the "death of art" is a perceptual distortion fed by postmodernism. Lacking by definition any theory of values, post-modernist nihilism tends to place the hoax, mystification and innovative work on the same level, as is seen by the Duchamp urinal being made the modern equivalent of Rembrandt's self-portraits.

It is still necessary to explain why works that seem insignificant at first sight can appear to be significant. It is for this other important question for the sociology of art that I will try to outline an answer.

III. FROM REMBRANDT TO DUCHAMP

Tocqueville suggested that "democratic" societies were destined to produce a somewhat unwholesome by-product: the encouragement of vulgarity. He foresaw the decline of the arts and literature. More precisely, he attributed to the democratic character of the American society of his time the fact that its arts and literature could not thrive, and suggested that as similar causes lead to similar effects, the condition of the arts and literature was also likely to decline in the societies of the old European nations, to the extent that they became more "democratic". Liberalism would be hostile to art: the market would kill all artistic creativity.

This forecast was evidently too pessimistic. But it is true that the processes described by Tocqueville on this matter carry a certain power of conviction; it may even be possible to identify other mechanisms alongside those he suggests to support his predictions, and that lead in the same direction.

Reality TV

I want to refer to a more anecdotal example than those Tocqueville considered, but which is far from being without interest and intriguing for the sociologist: the appearance and relative success of a certain type of TV programme that it seems hard to like, such as "reality TV". Let us be clear at the outset: they are shocking in their vulgarity.

These programmes are effectively the product of the market forces that characterise "democratic" societies. The public likes to see celebrities. Now the celebrities who owe their popularity to authentic performances are too few to satisfy demand, and to populate the screens of the innumerable TV channels that operate 24 hours per day. Great sportspeople who practise media-friendly and mediatised sports are not legion. The stock of artists whose work can touch a vast audience or the scientists responsible for inventions or discoveries that are televisual is smaller still. In France the great telegenic scientists can be counted on the fingers of one hand; taken as a whole they could not create more than a few hours of programming per year. Televisual saints are even less numerous. This is no doubt why the abbé Pierre has occupied for so long the top spot in the *hit parade* of French celebrities. Televisual politicians are more numerous. But they are seen a lot. And they cannot really satisfy the need in question because they are inevitably without exception unable to hide the fact that they want to be elected or re-elected, and thus convince the viewers that they are only interested in the common good.

So this is the source of the idea, one whose remarkable ingenuity should be applauded, of fabricating celebrities whose visibility is not based on *any particular merit* and the stock of which is in consequence inexhaustible. This is the stroke of genius that presided over the birth of reality TV.

The Success of the Fictional Masterpiece

In the same order of ideas, and one of the most interesting enigmas which the sociology of art should concern, and which it has not succeeded so far in resolving, is to explain why a work created by using a sponge of the sort that can be bought at the chemist's shop is sold at Christie's for millions of dollars, when it is full of blue paint and signed by an artist, Yves Klein as it happens, and who is recognised by a particular art museum (*Herald Tribune*, 14–15 June 2003).

Both sociology and philosophy take account of the explosion of cultural production, the growing eclecticism of cultural consumption, the diversification of the places in which cultural products are made, the democratic invasion that characterises culture, and they insist justifiably on the fact that this situation greatly complicates the cultural transmission function given to the school. They recognise – following Simmel – that culture is composed of products to which the consumer can only have access after having made a more or less lengthy investment. They also observe the increasing tendency for products to be put on the market that require less investment (Michaud, 1997; Coulangeon, 2003).

But the social sciences rarely pose the question of the origins of this phenomenon which is situated in the logic that governs the behaviour of the social actors concerned and particularly actors on the supply side, while the behaviour of actors on the demand side is modified by different factors which notably include the diffusion of the means of mass communication.

It is possible – a thesis I submit to specialists in the sociology of art – that it might be necessary to explain this phenomenon by the same schema as reality TV, by the considerable increase in demand for works of art by a public which does not know what to do with its money or by decision makers whose role is to spend other people's money on "culture" (banks, insurance companies, public cultural agencies, etc.) and by the correlative lack of a sufficient numbers of works of art that are objectively innovative and significant. We are no longer in the time when Dürer recounts – in one of his letters – that he has been advised not to dine with Italian painters in Venice, because he was in danger of being poisoned due to the fact that he had begun to encroach too greatly on the clientele of the local artists (Gombrich, 1992). The supply of masterpieces was then greater than the demand from princely courts and rich individuals. Today the opposite is true: demand is greater than supply.

The disequilibrium between supply and demand in favour of demand encourages galleries, museums, art critics and cultural "administrators" to promote fictional masterpieces which have the advantage over authentic masterpieces of being produced on demand. Once an artist's reputation is established, it is confirmed by many authorising sources. Museum directors can fill their walls or have something to "install" in their galleries and the directors of commercial galleries have something to sell. Art critics need works of art to fill their columns. Insofar as philosophers of art are concerned they need not shrug their shoulders at a body of work that provides them with the subject for a dissertation. This is why a philosopher who wished to explain the success of Duchamp's urinal declared:

> *Why not appreciate the ordinary qualities of the Fountain; its sparkling white surface, its pretty oval form: it has some analogies with certain works of Brancusi or Moore ...* (quoted in Becker, 1982).

Finally, the entire public will agree that just as there is no smoke without fire, there is no glory without talent, even without genius. From which it may be concluded that whereas the Renaissance produced the smile of the Mona Lisa, Postmodernity produced the smudge of the blue sponges.

The geniuses in question often acquired their status not through their work but thanks to a clever *mise en scène* of their own personality, or even more simply through some naughtiness or escapade exploitable in the celebrity media. Baselitz, celebrated some while ago in Paris by an exhibition that they did not hesitate to call "De Dürer à Baselitz" (*From Durer to Baselitz*), became an overnight success in 1963 thanks to a work called "The big night in the bucket" (*Die grosse Nacht im Eimer*), where one can contemplate a young man with an oversized penis occupied with conscientious masturbation. It also true that both Jean-Jacques Rousseau and Salvador Dali also organised the *mise en scène* of their personality. But they *also* produced significant works.

Marcel Duchamp was perhaps a real *creative* artist, but in particular an authentic innovator. Riding on the surrealist wave he managed to his great surprise to pass off a hoax as a work of art. Having done so he registered a sort of "patent" in the art worlds that could be exploited indefinitely. Following this painters registered other patents inspired by the same idea but that did not represent innovations as radical as Duchamp's urinal. Yves Klein, artist of the blue sponges, Manzoni, author of *Artist's Shit*, ("it is from me, therefore it is a work of art") were content to exploit these diverse "patents". As these fictional masterpieces fulfil a demand from art lovers and eventually a wider audience, a self-maintaining process develops where demand leads to supply and supply generates demand.

I am well aware that this analysis cannot in any way account for the evolution of contemporary art. It should be made clear once more that Yves Klein would not have been possible if Malevitch and others had not opened the route for him. And it must be added that Malevitch and Kandinsky gave themselves the task of expressing the unexpressable, the "spiritual in art", and that it is thought nowadays without question that everyone can find in any work a hidden meaning – even an unsuspected "profundity". On the subject of *reality TV* it is possible to see in it not just a response to a demand but a concern with showing people "as they are" and with criticising in a Rousseau-like fashion what "society" has done.

But this allows me to think – and this is something on which I would like to insist – that this analysis in terms of supply and demand is more satisfactory than that which attributes to the "art worlds", or the "networks" that generate artistic life (artists, directors of museums and galleries, art critics, etc.) the power to *impose its values* on the public. The "art worlds" have been there all the time, whereas the proliferation of fictional masterpieces is characteristic of ours. Where does the power come from attributed to them by Becker (1982), who is certainly one of the most important sociologists of art of our time? Becker accepts this explanatory model that sees no problems in according to such a network the power to impose its values on the public, and to represent the public as if it were made up of heteronomic individuals who allow themselves to be readily manipulated without their knowledge.

If the reactions of visitors to any exhibition is observed, however, it is easy to see that the public can distinguish without difficulty between a hoax and a work of art. I observed this very thing myself during an exhibition devoted to Christian Schad at the Musée Maillol in Paris in 2002. Alongside its temporary exhibitions, the museum also shows a permanent exhibition devoted to Maillol, of course, but also to Duchamp. It was easy from the first glance to see that the visitors tended to display a reaction of curiosity (somewhat relative, fleeting and a little disenchanted) in front of Duchamp's urinal and a strong emotional reaction to the spellbinding portraits of Schad: the public can quite easily distinguish between a real and a fictional masterpiece.

To formulate the same proposition differently, by contrast with the view of the relativist sociology of art, which cannot accept that artistic values may be objectively based, the art lover is not necessarily a *snob* exclusively concerned with distinction and of course unconscious of his motivations or a *simpleton* – just as much unconscious of the forces which he passively obeys – who let themselves be taken in by the "art worlds".

Such theories are now standard references in the teaching of the sociology of art, nearly everywhere in the world. They have a corollary whose power and audacity might be admired, even if its veracity is questionable, that is to say that since aesthetic emotion is an illusion of social origin nobody can have ever felt authentic aesthetic pleasure.

The other question that this explanation by the power of the network finds it difficult to answer is why does the phenomenon of the proliferation of fictional masterpieces occur at the same time as the development of "mass culture"? For Marcel Duchamp is a near contemporary of Matisse, Picasso, Beckmann, Schiele and other authors of authentic masterpieces. It is only in recent decades, with the explosion of demand for works of art, that the fictional masterpieces have become so commonplace.

In the same way we can explain the proliferation of a literature concerned with the experiences of real false heroes or real false martyrs. In 1999, a prestigious German publishing house published the autobiography of Benjamin Wilkomirski. The author tells of his terrible experiences as a child in the Auschwitz extermination camp. The book was immediately translated into a dozen languages and acclaimed by critics as a "classic of the literature of the Holocaust". In reality the author's name was Bruno Dössekker and he had never been to Auschwitz. This is to cross the boundary separating the vulgar from the nauseating.

Another publishing house of note launched, with the help of a massive advertising campaign, the confessions of a secret agent in post-war Germany. The author hid his identity under a pseudonym, but gave interviews to the television, back turned to the camera. Strangely enough nobody, neither the western secret services, the *Stasi*, nor even the ordinary citizen had noticed at the time what he said he had done, that is to blow up a petrol refinery on the border between the two Germanies, an event that is quite unlikely to have passed unnoticed. A university professor who acted as "reader" for the publishing house warned the editor that these pseudo-souvenirs could only be *Quatsch*: junk. This opinion did not convince the editor to stop the launch (*Der Spiegel*, 21 July 2003, 44–46). Here again we see the result of the surplus of demand over supply.

The examples that I have cited above suggest that the underlying mechanism driving them has a certain generality.

REFERENCES

Baudelaire, C. (1980[1857]) "*Madame Bovary* par Gustave Flaubert". *L'Artiste*, 18 October 1857; In: *Œuvres complètes*. Paris, R. Laffont, 1980.

Becker, H. S. (1982) *Art Worlds*. Berkeley, London, University of California Press.

Bell, Q. (1976) *On Human Finery*. London, The Hogarth Press.

Besançon, A. (1994) *L'image interdite: une histoire intellectuelle de l'iconoclasme*. Paris, Fayard.

Boudon, R. (1990) *L'Art de se persuader*. Paris, Fayard/Seuil.

—— (1995) *Le juste et le vrai, études sur l'objectivité des valeurs et de la connaissance*. Paris, Fayard.

——— (1994) "Les deux sociologies de la connaissance scientifique". In: Boudon, R., Clavelin, M. (eds), *Le relativisme est-il résistible? Regards sur la sociologie des sciences*, Paris, Presses Universitaires de France.

Bourdieu, P. (1979) *La Distinction: critique sociale du jugement*. Paris, Editions de Minuit.

Cluzel, J. (2003) *Propos impertinents sur le cinéma français*. Paris, Presses Universitaires de France.

Coulangeon, P. (2003) "Le rôle de l'école dans la démocratisation de l'accès aux arts". *Revue de l'Observatoire Français des Conjonctures Économiques*, 86: 155–169.

Danto, A. (1964) "The Art World". *Journal of Philosophy*, 61: 571–84.

Feyerabend, P. (1975) *Against Method*. London, N.L.B.

Gombrich, E. (1989[1972]) *The Story of Art*. Phaidon, London.

Haskell, F. (1976) *Rediscoveries in Art. Some Aspects of Taste, Fashion and Collecting in England and France*. London, Phaidon.

Kuhn, T. S. (1962) *The Structure of Scientific Revolutions*. Chicago, University of Chicago Press.

Lakatos, I. and Musgrave, A. (eds.) (1974) *Criticism and the Growth of Knowledge*. London, Cambridge University Press.

Michaud, Y. (1997) *La Crise de l'art contemporain*. Paris, Presses Universitaires de France.

Milo, D. (1986) "Le phénix culturel, de la résurrection dans l'histoire de l'art; l'exemple des peintres français (1650–1750)". *Revue française de sociologie*, 38(3): 481–504.

Pommier, R. (1986) *Un marchand de salades qui se prend pour un prince: réponse du petit Pommier au grand Barbéris*. Paris, G. Roblot.

——— (1994) *Études sur 'le Tartuffe'*. Paris, Sedes.

Raynaud, D. (1998) *L'Hypothèse d'Oxford: essai sur les origines de la perspective*. Paris, Presses Universitaires de France.

Simmel, G. (1916) *Rembrandt, ein kunstphilosophischer Versuch*. Leipzig.

——— (1900) *Philosophie des Geldes*. Leipzig, Duncker & Humblot.

——— (1989) *Gesammelte Schriften zur Religionssoziologie*. Berlin, Duncker & Humblot.

——— (1892) *Die Probleme der Geschichtsphilosophie*. Munich, Duncker & Humblot.

Veblen, T. (1960) *The Theory of the Leisure Class*. New York, Mentor.

Volkov, S. (1980) *Témoignage: les mémoires de Dimitri Chostakovitch*. Paris, Albin Michel.

Weber, M. (1995[1919]) *Wissenschaft als Beruf*. Munich, Duncker & Humblot.

——— (1920–1921) *Gesammelte Aufsätze zur Religionssoziologie*. Tübingen, Mohr.

Welsch, P. (1987) *Ästhetisches Denken*. Stuttgart, Reclam.

6

An Archaeology of the Modern Concept of Common Sense

I. THE DEVALUATION OF COMMON SENSE

Under this heading I want to suggest some thoughts about a fact that until now has not seemed to attract much attention from the historians and sociologists of ideas, that is the devaluation of common sense that is widely observed in many areas within the social sciences. This devaluation of common sense can be explained by the same causes that explain the spread of relativism. Relativism and devaluation of common sense are in other words two sides of the same coin. Each follows from the attempt to naturalise the human being that characterises the human sciences. Interpreting his actions, beliefs, feelings as being primarily the effects of psychological, biological or socio-cultural forces, they are not interested in the reasons he might give for such actions, beliefs, or feelings. More precisely they tend to treat these reasons as effects rather than causes, and to see these reasons as unimportant or fallacious.

It is not difficult to find examples of these attempts at naturalisation. Cognitive psychologists tell us that ordinary thought is "magical", and that intuition is normally subject to many types of bias; while even some eminent anthropologists and sociologists support the contention that social subjects under the influence of *cultural* or *psychological forces* make real those representations that they believe to be founded in reality, but which are unconscious effects of their socialisation. Moreover, that these social subjects believe in the objectivity of many

165

types of ideas that are in fact *constructions*, and that if these individuals believe what they believe, it is essentially because they are under the effect of these forces. And, that the reasons that the subject has should not be taken into account, that they can only have the function of *justification* or *rationalisation*. Sociobiology tells us that moral sentiments are the effect of mechanisms described by the neo-Darwinian theory of evolution; that evolution required, for reasons of efficiency, that these mechanisms should be unconscious; and that ordinary thought is generated by phylogenetic factors. Economists appear to have avoided this *naturalisation* of the human subject, but this is only because, as Milton Friedman (1953) pointed out, the real motivations and reasons why people do things are not of interest to economics because they do not constitute a scientific debate. The only thing which counts is that an economic theory should lead to consequences that are congruent with reality. It is of little concern how it represents the content of human consciousness.

There is a rupture here with classical philosophy, which saw common sense as naturally right, even if it might be disturbed by the emotions. There is no reason to suppose that the famous declaration that begins the *Discours de la méthode* of Descartes and according to which "good sense is the one thing in the world best shared" might have been intended as an irony. The everyday expression "that is contrary to common sense" still reflects this classical idea. It implies that common sense and good sense are the same. Molière provides a perfect example of this idea when he constructs a play around two types of character, the leading characters whose good sense is corrupted by their emotions, and the secondary characters, always sensible, whose function is to emphasise the ridicule to which the leading characters are subject and who are meant to represent public attitudes. That they make the audience laugh means that the public shares the good sense of ordinary people. That they should continue to make audiences laugh is a sign perhaps that the classical theory is still valid.

By contrast the idea of common sense is treated by wide sectors of the human sciences as if it were an antonym rather than a synonym of good sense.

If I mention here the concept of archaeology, it is because this devaluation of common sense seems to me to rest on *a priori* that are mostly metaconscious and whose origins would, I believe, be interesting to identify. In the preceding chapters I have had the opportunity to refer to some of these *a priori*. As this chapter is in the nature of a conclusion, I feel justified in referring to them again summarily at the same time as I will identify some others.

The Influence of Marx and Nietzsche

This modern scepticism about good sense comes mainly, and this is a point so well known that there is no need to labour it, from the "masters of suspicion" who have taught us to beware of the evidence of common sense. I have already referred to this in chapters 2 and 5.

Nietzsche taught us that values were constructions, that they could be the outcome of various psychic forces and notably that of *ressentiment*. Marx taught us that social structures were able to generate forces that could invert the image of reality in the mind of the social subject. It is certainly the case that following them and under their influence an important tradition of thought appeared that we call *critical sociology*, which took on the task of extracting common sense from its false premises.

The influence of the masters of suspicion tends nowadays to be in decline. While it is recognised that the mechanisms that they described exist, there is general agreement in thinking that they were given a generality that was far too excessive. Even then, Weber categorically refused to follow Nietzsche when he proposed explaining the success of Christianity through the process of *ressentiment*. We tend to follow Weber on this, nowadays. It survives in the work of Scheler (1978[1912]), for whom the process of *ressentiment* explains some circumscribed examples such as the bitterness of the retired politician, who like Bismarck finds himself deprived of the only thing – power – that interests him. But it cannot in any way be considered sufficient to explain more complex phenomena.

If the devaluation of common sense persists despite the declining influence of Nietzsche and Marx in the human sciences, that is because it has another source. The conjecture that I would like to develop now is that this persistence is due to other factors, less visible than the teachings of the masters of suspicion, but whose influence on the human sciences – and as result on the modern view of common sense – is perhaps deeper and longer lasting.

The Influence of Hume and Comte

The first is Hume. I will only mention him briefly here, as I have already discussed this in detail in chapters 1 and 2. According to Hume, it is not possible to infer the imperative from the indicative. No argument from the indicative can generate an imperative conclusion: an unshakeable theorem. From this theorem have been derived the ideas that there is a gulf dividing the positive from the normative, the descriptive from the prescriptive, the factual from the axiological; that support for these normative judgements could not come from them being objectively based, because they cannot be in principle, as the imperative cannot be concluded from the indicative. As I tried to show earlier, it seems to me that this idea has had considerable influence on the explanations of norms and values in the human sciences and especially in anthropology and sociology.

The examples of research projects that take a culturalist vision of normative beliefs and that take up as a result Hume's notion that prescriptive beliefs cannot in principle be objectively based and that they should be seen as a result of habit can be indefinitely multiplied. A major discovery by Hume, according to the culturalists, was to have proved that where common sense sees major differences between the categories of norms, values and customs, the only pertinent category would be the latter. It is as a result of tradition or habit that we believe such an institution or such a norm are good, or that such a value is sound. The reader will find several illustrations in chapter 1 of what I call culturalist theory, in other words the paradigm in which the beliefs of the social actor must be considered as the result of forces emanating from the culture to which he belongs.

The "archaeological" perspective I have adopted leads me to the conjecture that the culturalist theory is only credible to those who are totally convinced that axiological beliefs (beliefs concerning norms and values) cannot be objectively based. If this idea is not accepted, it is hard to accept three propositions that seem to become more unlikely at each stage, for instance (1) that the distinctions that common sense would make between customs, norms and values, are worthless, (2) that the certainties of the subjects observed are based in their view on *illusory reasons*, whilst at the same time (3) the researcher is able to identify their *true causes*, and by so doing is exercising a power whose origin is mysterious.

How can we explain that it is possible to readily accept such postulates that are both radical and odd at the same time? It would be easier to endorse them if it can be accepted that axiological beliefs cannot be objectively based. And this is a readily accepted corollary of Hume's theorem, even though it is in fact a *paralogism*.

I will now turn to another writer that I have not had an opportunity to mention in the previous chapters, and who I think has a great significance for explaining the emergence of relativism: Auguste Comte. He was responsible for two central ideas that can be infinitely modified and that have had a long term influence on the social and human sciences. These are perhaps the two idea that have made the biggest contribution to the doubtful thesis that the human sciences cannot be true sciences unless they succeed in naturalising the human subject.

As with the case of Hume's theorem these two ideas are not necessarily perceived at a conscious level by practitioners in the social sciences. I have taken the opportunity elsewhere to put forward, under the title of "Simmel's model", the idea that any argument implies the mobilisation of ideas that are not explicitly perceived by the subject because they are *self-evident* (Boudon, 1990). This model draws attention to the fact that an explicit system of true arguments can lead to a false conclusion that is held to be true, the falsity of the conclusion resulting from premises unperceived because they are treated implicitly as self-evident.

I do not believe that the idea of "Simmel's model" poses any difficulties of principle in itself nor that it reintroduces in its train the undesirable concept of an unconscious *force*. It simply records processes that can be easily illustrated. When Pythagoras's theorem is demonstrated, axioms of Euclidean geometry are mobilised but without being explicitly acknowledged.

The key ideas described here seem to me to follow this schema. They are present in the minds of many practitioners in the social sciences but as notions that are *self-evident*, which like familiar furniture end up being invisible.

Variations in the Rules of Philosophy

Auguste Comtc invented the idea that human thought would only be objective and capable of accounting for reality with the appearance of positivism. As we know, the positivist state is preceded by two earlier ones, theological and metaphysical. In the periods characterised by these two states, human thought was subject to illusions.

It is good form to deride the simplism of the *law of the three states*. But that does not mean that the idea underlying this law is rejected, according to which the rules of thought and of inference, far from being universal, are subject to variation; a proposition that was surely revolutionary when Comte put it on the market.

Now while Comte's law of the three states appears obviously simplistic, the idea of the variability of the rules of thought is on the contrary generally accepted to the point of being taken for granted.

This idea was taken over at the beginning of the 20th century by many writers, and in particular by Lévy-Bruhl (1960 [1922]), who argued that only within modern societies did thought obey the rules of valid inference that enabled it to grasp reality.

The British anthropologist R. Needham (1972) had great admiration for the work of Lévy-Bruhl. At first sight this was somewhat surprising in an anthropologist who had not only little nostalgic attachment to the past, but who was moreover someone who saw himself as resolutely modern. He shared the general view that Lévy-Bruhl's evolutionism was outdated, for was it not of course a 19th century conception? But if time was replaced by space, or more precisely the concept of the *phases* of history that Lévy-Bruhl inherited from Comte, by that of *culture* and if instead of arguing that the rules of thought vary from one of these phases to the next, it is argued that the rules of thought can be distinguished from one *culture* to another, it is possible to administer a useful face-lift, so to speak, to Lévy-Bruhl. It makes him compatible with the modern viewpoint that sees the world composed of cultures that are more or less the same as monads, a perspective (possibly and illusory one) illustrated with brilliance by Huntington (1996).

Finally, from all of Lévy-Bruhl's work, Needham places most emphasis on the Comtian idea of the variability of the rules of thought. By transposing the hypothesis of the variability of the rules of thought from time to space, from the *historical phases* identified by Comte to the *cultures* of the modern culturalists, Needham inverts the meaning of an essential point. While the evolutionism of Comte and Lévy-Bruhl led these writers to forecast the triumph of science in the last stage of the evolution of human thought, the culturalism of Needham leads him on the contrary to elevate *relativism* to the level of a fundamental truth. However important this difference, it is understandable that Needham praises the merits of Lévy-Bruhl. Needham departs from the fact that, following Comte, it was Lévy-Bruhl who implanted the idea that the rules of thought might be variable in the sciences of man. Once the truth and novelty of this idea are accepted all that is necessary to make it compatible with postmodern relativism is to clarify that the rules of thought are variable according to culture and to add that no culture can claim to represent "true thought". Hence, according to postmodern relativism the category of the universal is a category particular to western civilisation that the West imagines is objectively valid, an illusion that the cultural anthropologist is keen to denounce.

On this point Needham comes close to Geertz. The rules of thought are culturally variable, they are seen as valid or invalid as a result of the action of cultural forces that mean that they must be treated as such in a given culture. Lévi-Strauss (1962) also takes over this perspective when he identifies "la pensée sauvage" (the "savage mind") as a form of thinking with its own rules.

Many cognitive psychologists (Nisbett and Ross, 1980) seem to follow the same line of thought inspired by Comte, Lévy-Bruhl and Needham, when they describe everyday thinking as *magical*. Only the thinking of the scientist follows the valid rules of inference. In everyday life the Westerner, even if educated, allows himself to be guided by rules of inference that derive from "magical thought" (Shweder, 1977).

The cognitive anthropology displayed in other works by Shweder (1991) or by d'Andrade (1995) also belongs to the same line of thought, that each culture has its own cognitive framework. These cognitive frameworks are incommensurable.

Some writers have tried to go further and have felt it necessary to detail the mechanisms that link rules of thought considered valid in a culture to some specific elements of the culture in question. It is on such a basis that Granet (1990) or Whorf (1969) argued that language inflects thought. As it is not possible to think without words or sentences, and as the words that are available to describe the same reality are not the same from one language to another, and as sentences are not constructed in the same way, they tell us, we cannot think about the world in the same way from one culture to another.

The variety of these examples, that I could multiply almost indefinitely, suggest that even if Comte is no longer read one of his ideas seems to have become established fact in a wide swathe of the human sciences.

The Content of Consciousness is Excluded from Sociological Thought

Comte is also the source of a second idea, that scientific thought must exclude intentions and reasons and more generally the content of the consciousness of actors from sociological thought. In particular it must be on guard against making the intentions and reasons that social actors describe to themselves the explaining factors of their actions, their attitudes and their beliefs. The movement from the theological state to the metaphysical state and then to the positive state is characterised by the fact that phenomena that were explained in the earlier state by *final causes* are explained in the later state by *material causes*. Positivism draws the conclusion that it is only material causes that science should recognise as valid.

The objection to this point would be that it is not non-scientific to see immaterial *reasons* as the *cause* of the behaviour that the subject describes. The fact that inanimate nature does not follow final causes does not imply that the human subject might not be motivated by final causes. The ban on explaining natural phenomena by *mind* (*esprits*) does not mean that the *human mind* should be excluded from the explanation of human phenomena. But this distinction did not seem to occur to the positivists.

Gellner (1987) suggests that the positivist idea that scientific thinking must ignore the content of consciousness has also had considerable influence. *Behaviourism* in psychology, *structuralism* and some variants of *functionalism* in the social sciences, *instrumentalism* in Milton Friedman's sense of the term in economics, are all intellectual movements that attribute decisive importance to the principle that the exclusion of all subjective data is a fundamental trait of science.

It is actually Comte's idea that sociology should avoid all considerations dealing with the subjectivity of actors that the behaviourists are using when they define scientific *psychology* as dealing with the relations between two observables: *stimuli* and *responses*. It is what Malinowski's functionalism uses when he argues that the *anthropologist* is concerned with the relations between institutions. It is what Murdock's structuralism (1949) is using when, for instance, he discusses whether there is a relation between residential rules, rules of alliance and rules of filiation. It is again evident in Milton Friedman's work when he argues that an *economic* theory dealing with the psychology of actors is not worthy of debate. If the results of a theory are congruent with reality, it does not matter whether the content of consciousness that is imputed to the actor is realistic or not. In any event, there are no ways of knowing this content.

Friedman's instrumentalism (1953) had great influence not just in economics but in political science as well. The huge literature on the voting paradox produced by *political scientists* cannot be explained without taking it into account. There is a voting paradox because "rational choice theory" (RCT) has problems with explaining voting behaviour. According to this theory actors behave according to the consequences of their actions. Now the elector's vote has no effect on the outcome of an election. The paradox disappears if it is accepted that the actor votes not because he thinks he is able to influence the result of the election with his single vote, but because he believes that democracy is a good system and that elections are a fundamental institution of democracy. But the partisans of RCT do not accept this explanation based on good sense because as followers of positivism they see the consciousness of subjects as of no importance. As they are convinced that RCT is a theory of general validity, they are on the contrary constantly seeking ways of reconciling the theory with the facts of voting. The flood of articles produced by this false question is only explicable if it is *taken for granted* that the thought processes of subjects are of no relevance (Boudon, 1997).

On the whole, in the positivist principle, whereby the content of consciousness is excluded from the data of the human sciences, the ban on making the intentions and reasons of actors the real cause of their actions or their beliefs seems to be well entrenched in the practice of the social sciences.

At the same time this principle raises considerable problems, because it runs contrary to other principles. If we do not have access to the internal workings of the parrot, and if as a result we must accept the idea that they must not be mentioned, the same is not true of the human being. What people say are also facts, but specific facts that have the property of expressing their state of consciousness. The same is true of all behaviour; it expresses states of consciousness. Is it really possible for the human sciences to ignore the states of consciousness of the subjects that they observe?

One example is enough to illustrate the difficulties that come about if this line is followed. Horton (1993) argues against Wittgenstein's theory of magic, in which the rain dance does not express a *belief* in the efficacy of the ritual, but a *desire* that rain will come. It cannot be accepted, he suggests, because the subjects when questioned all affirm and are convinced, that without these rituals rain will not come. The expression of these states of consciousness is part of reality. Can they just be ignored? The scientist should not in principle arbitrarily exclude one part of reality from the rest.

How can this duty be reconciled with the Comtian disqualification of subjective data?

The conjecture I introduce at this point is that the human sciences have invented a particular class of concepts, that I will call *naturalising concepts*, mainly in order to avoid this contradiction between the fact that they cannot ignore that the *declarations* and *behaviours* of social actors are the results of states of consciousness, and the positivist principle that the human sciences cannot take on board the states of consciousness of individuals if they wish to be "true" sciences. These concepts are currently seen and treated as "basic" concepts, precisely because they are thought to resolve a major contradiction between principles that are equally important.

These concepts have a *functional* value, to legitimate the exclusion of the content of consciousness from the universe of facts of which the observer must take account. The difficulty is that they have little *explanatory* value. Before coming to this point I will suggest some examples of these concepts.

The first idea is that of *false consciousness* (Mehring), a concept whose importance I have referred to in several preceding chapters. It can be thought of as the prototype of the naturalising concepts. If consciousness is false, states of consciousness are necessarily caused by another thing than the reasons that the subject attributes to them. They are necessarily caused by factors external to the subject. The idea of false consciousness makes it possible to separate the content of consciousness from the analysis in the name of science, and more precisely it allows the analyst to treat them as *facts to be explained*, and prevents him from treating them as *explanatory factors*. This is because it is contradictory with the principles of positivism to make them the causes of anything, even if their existence cannot be denied.

The idea of false consciousness is given little credence nowadays, but less because of the result of critique than because it was carried away with the tide amongst the other concepts that made up the Marxist tradition. There are numerous alternatives or even functional substitutes today.

It is easy to find many types of ideas that fulfil exactly the same *naturalising* function and which are still seen as perfectly admissible.

A concept such as that of *frame*, or *framework* fulfils the same needs. It argues that the subject is the support for various cognitive schema that are imposed on him by external forces. The subject imagines in the majority of cases that he has reasons for accepting them, but these reasons have no relevance, because they are not the cause of the so-called representations. The idea leads to the same conclusion as that of false consciousness: the causes of states of consciousness of the subject are not to be found in the reasons he gives for them, in the meaning he gives them, in the reasons he has for accepting them, but in the action of invisible cultural forces.

The idea of *bias* is widely used by social psychologists and cognitive psychologists to explain for example why the subject evaluates inaccurately the probability of certain events or why he perceives relations of causality where they do not exist (Kahneman and Tversky, 1973; Nisbett and Ross, 1980). It has the same logic as the concepts of *framework*, or of *false consciousness*. As with these other ideas it is frequently mentioned but rarely debated. It justifies the idea of looking for the causes of errors or intuitive mistakes in forces external to the subject.

The concept of *social representation* which is also much used, is close to that of framework, its value more functional than explanatory.

Bourdieu's concept of *habitus* owes its success to its functional virtues. Reynaud (2002) shows this clearly when he provided as an epitaph for his *in memoriam* a quotation from the French sociologist where he gives sociology a primordial role: to give back to people who play a game the rules of which they do not know, the meaning of their actions. If they do not know the meaning of their actions, it is because they emanate from their *habitus*. Once more we find this idea that meaning of his action escapes the actor, and that it is the sociologist who will find it, an idea that some sociologists regard as taken for granted.

A similar *a priori* can be seen in the work of Lévi-Strauss, but it is submerged within a far more complex theory. The different marriage systems adopted by non-literate societies are solutions to the problem of the exchange of women. Everything is presented as if each of these societies had chosen one of the *n* solutions mathematically possible for this problem. This theory assumes that in a collective unconscious that reminds us of Jung, the non-literate societies had posed and solved a complex mathematical problem and by a throw of the dice had chosen one of these *n* possible solutions. As soon as this solution dictates that Ego could not marry his parallel cousin, the individual belonging to a society having adopted the solution in question is protected from being in any way attracted to her.

Parodi (2004) has shown that one of the reasons for the success of this type of structuralism is because this form of analysis allows a *naturalisation* of the human subject; his behaviours, including those which involve sexual attraction, are the effect of functional demands that can be represented in a mathematical form. In the work of Lévi-Strauss any trace of the subjectivity of the actor completely disappears.

The idea of *socialisation* is also part of this conceptual arsenal. It implies that the ideas endorsed by the subject are taken on under the effect of forces to which he is thought to be passively exposed.

Amongst the classic writers Pareto (1964–1988[1916]) was the first to have put forward a schema that eliminates the subjective from sociology and thus satisfies Comte's second principle. For him, two types of beliefs and actions exist, those that are "logico-experimental" first of all. They are accepted because they are based on objectively valid reasons, hence Pythagoras's theorem is believed because it is true; and we row to make a boat move because, by doing so we use a means objectively adapted to the end in mind. On the other hand to account for the fact that a Greek sailor made a sacrifice to Poseidon before boarding, it is necessary to point to *cultural forces* acting on his mind and at his own will, forces that can only be apprehended indirectly and through their effects, that Pareto termed *residues*. As to the meanings that the Greeks gave to these beliefs, to the reasons that they saw for believing them, they must be analysed as rationalisations (or as *derivations*, in the terminology of Pareto).

All these ideas have in common that they suggest that the actors' beliefs are imposed on him through the action of external forces. The reasons he might give are only *rationalisations* or *justifications*. As they are not the true cause of these beliefs, their causes must be sought elsewhere.

To clarify: I am not saying that ideas such as *bias*, *social representation, socialisation*, etc, do not describe any reality. It is true that the mind may wander into error or that we carry around ideas that were drummed into us during childhood. I am only denying that the ideas and beliefs of social subjects can and should be analysed in principle in the same way that gravitational forces affect physical objects.

Finally, the implicit argument from Hume that is used in the social sciences and that I have mentioned above can be schematised in the following manner: an imperative conclusion cannot be drawn from indicative reasoning, for normative beliefs are not based on facts; however, social subjects believe that their normative beliefs are soundly based; the meaning that they give to their beliefs or in other words the reasons they believe they have to endorse them are not their causes, which are to be found in elsewhere, in psychological, biological or cultural forces.

As to the implicit argument taken from the first key idea of Comte, as it was updated by Needham, it may also be easily restated: the rules of thought are variable, and if we retain this idea underlying that of the law of three states and if we also detach it from Comte's evolutionism (a form of surgery that presents no fundamental difficulty) it is concluded that these rules are empty of objective universality and validity; in consequence, they are the result of psychological, biological or cultural forces.

The implicit argument drawn from Comte's second principle is as follows: a science is only a science if it abstains from invoking subjective data as explanatory factors. States of consciousness are facts. But if it is accepted that the reasons that the subject gives for them are illusions and that the reasons for these so-called states of consciousness may be imputed to psychological, biological or cultural forces, it is possible to avoid explaining the phenomena in question by imputing subjective causes. By declaring for instance that bad mental habits are due to the bias that results from biological evolution or to cerebral processes that are still to be discovered, the human sciences are put on an equal footing with the natural sciences.

This exclusion of the subjective is congruent with the consequence drawn from Hume's key idea and from the first key idea of Comte: that the cause of beliefs of all types, normative and non-normative alike, is to be sought in psychological, biological or cultural forces.

If this archaeology, these *a priori*, are not exposed it is difficult to understand that the human sciences are in the main characterised by theories that have for several decades explained behaviour by psychological, biological or cultural forces. It is difficult to see why concepts such as *framework*, or *bias* might be accepted with such little resistance, and that they pass as easily for valid *explanations* of phenomena observed by the sociologist, psychologist or anthropologist; it is difficult to understand the vogue for culturalism, for constructivism (a modernised version of the culturalism that colours cultural relativism), for structuralism and several other currents of thought; it is difficult to understand the objections that may be addressed to these concepts and why they have had so little influence.

It is these *a priori* that explain, or at least this is the conjecture I put forward here, that the devaluation of common sense has been imposed without question in so many areas of the human sciences, leading to their support for a *naturalist* programme that treats the human subject as motivated by psychological, biological or cultural forces.

In fact, the arguments that I have rehearsed here are little more than a house of cards.

II. WEAKNESS YET SUCCESS OF THE NATURALIST PROJECT: WHY?

I will confine myself to summary remarks on this point because my aim is to not to provide a full critique of the ideas I have just mentioned, but simply to make their fragility more evident.

Frame: Popper (1976) criticised the mythical character of *framework* and *frame* with some weighty arguments but little attention seems to have been paid to them. His article is rarely cited. Why? Because he demolishes an argument that underpins many of the products of the social sciences.

His critique consists of emphasising that a subject embraces an idea or a system of ideas only when it is acceptable to him. If doubts begin to occur in his mind, for example because this idea or system of ideas – this framework, if this term is preferable – appears to be incompatible with what he observes, he will question the framework and look for a better one. The image of the framework has in other words an inconvenience, for it suggests that it is accepted irrevocably by the subject, rather than being accepted because he has reasons to accept it and to stop doing so if he is convinced that there are better alternatives.

Bias: the concept assumes that the intellect is subject to *reasons* when it leads the subject to a true idea, but to psychological *forces* when it leads to a false idea.

Why not assume that in the second case the subject also obeys reasons, but false reasons that the subject believes to be, if not true, at the least valid conjectures? There are propositions that are held to be scientific truths and others that are erroneous but which were believed by scientists in the past. Must it be assumed that the scientists who believed in what we now know as errors were motivated by cultural forces? Is it not simpler to assume that they followed reasons which they had reason to suppose were valid, and that we have reasons to suppose are invalid (Boudon, 2003)? Would it not be simpler also to assume that intuitional mistakes are due to invalid conjectures?

Social representations: the same comments can be made here as for the two previous ideas.

Habitus: as used by Bourdieu, this concept has little in common with Aristotle's *hexis*. Thomas Aquinas, who followed Aristotle's work very closely, translated *hexis* as *habitus*. He distinguished between the *habitus a corpore* and the *habitus ab anima* and put the second under the control of the will. There is indeed a difference between corporal habitus that means we know how to ride a bicycle and the mental habitus that means we believe in this or that proposition. Tomorrow we will still know how to ride a bicycle. It is impossible even to unlearn how to ride one. On the other hand we may stop believing in the proposition tomorrow if there are reasons to do so. By bringing the *habitus ab anima* within the *habitus a corpore*, a *trick* is performed that makes it possible to attribute behaviour to external forces. Moreover these new types of *habitus* have a function that nobody can see except the piercing eye of the sociologist, that of reproducing social classes.

Here is another example of a concept that, just like *framework*, meets with some immediate objections, but which can be seen as a "discovery" by what Pascal called the semi-intelligent because it enables the sociologist who manipulates it to believe that it satisfies the positivist demand for the naturalisation of man.

The method through which Lévi-Strauss naturalises the human subject is, as I have pointed out, much more subtle. It attempts to explain the marriage rules that are imposed on individuals by showing that the possible rule systems are of a finite number and by assuming that individuals accept this mathematical reality, much in the same way as they accept the rules of geometry. The relations that Ego maintains for example with his female cousins follow from the unconscious application of these rules.

On the matter of the different feelings generated for Ego by his female cousins, according to whether they are parallel or cross, Homans and Schneider (1955) have shown quite pertinently that they can be explained without recourse to a Jungian-type unconscious, but by simple psychological mechanisms. Ego feels closer to his female cousin if she is the daughter of a parent to whom tradition dictates that Ego owes allegiance, and hence that Ego has authority over the person's children. Lévi-Strauss – perhaps quite sincerely – dismissed this objection with one word. Because it was inspired by *psychologism*, it had no merit, for the interpretation that it put forward had the disadvantage of taking account of the content of individual consciousness and thus could not be *scientific*.

Other authors refer to forces that are more *biological* than cultural to explain certain social phenomena. Thus, according to the sociobiologist Ruse (1993), moral sentiments are the result of the play of the processes of natural selection. These processes are not part of the actor's consciousness because they can act more effectively as a result.

Tooby and Cosmides (1992) refer to phylogenetic processes to explain intuitional errors. All these explanations are purely conjectural. But they have the advantage of respecting Hume's principle, together with the two principles of Comte.

Why have these rather weak explanations been so successful, these notions that deserve to be described as somewhat verbose? They have a *descriptive* value, a *functional* value (they legitimise pseudo-explanations that satisfy principles derived from empiricism and positivism) but no *explanatory* value (since the causes that they attribute to the phenomena they explore have no greater status than that of words). However, they are often seen as having explanatory value.

I will not return to the idea that the main reason for this success is due to their functional value, in the fact that they conform to the three principles that are seen to define the necessary conditions for a *truly scientific* explanation. But there is more.

An idea cannot become dominant unless it contains some truth. False ideas are often either *hyperboles* or *heresies* (from the Greek *hairein*= to choose) derived from true ideas. I have already referred to these in chapter 1.

An example of a *hyperbole*: *ressentiment* explains *any* attitude. This hyperbole is grafted on to an irrefutable proposition ("*certain* attitudes are the result of the mechanism of *ressentiment*"). It is false, but it may seem to be true since it is the hyperbole of a true proposition.

An example of a *heresy*: poor social conditions are *the* cause of crime. We should say, *one* cause of crime. But the slip from one to the other is easy to make.

The concepts that I have analysed earlier are all movements of a hyperbolic or heretical nature.

The concept of *false consciousness* may describe irrefutable states of affairs. The *Junker* described by Karl Mannheim (1954), who sees his activities as very different from those of the industrialist while there is no real difference between them, may be seen as in a state of *false consciousness*. The concept describes in this case an *understandable* state of affairs. The *Junker* has reasons for wanting to retain the old image of radical difference between town and country, and he has not realised that he manages his enterprise using the same principles as the industrialist.

But there is a gulf between these examples and the idea that consciousness will *always* be false. This *hyperbole* is established because on the one hand there are ready examples to point to and on the other because the process of hyperbolisation has great *functional* value here. It is only when the idea that consciousness *can* be false and that it is false *in certain cases* is transformed into a postulate (consciousness *is* false, is false *in all cases*) that it enables the sociologist to ignore any interpretation given by the subject of his actions and to propose a true interpretation, that has no relation to the reasons of the subject himself, which are thus seen as *rationalisations* or as *justifications*. The second of these concepts tends to be preferred nowadays because it has the advantage of not referring to the psychoanalytic tradition and of presenting the behaviour of the subject as the result of *cultural forces* and *strategies* that pursuit the objective of justification.

It seems difficult to me to understand the establishment of these concepts and the importance they now command unless we assume that the three principles drawn from Hume and Comte have acquired the status of "proven fact" in the minds of many people, an application of what I term "Simmel's model". All these concepts are scientifically weak, but have the *functional* virtue of leading to a theory of behaviour that satisfies the three principles.

All these concepts contain a promise, somewhat like the idea of finding the "North West Passage", that of making the human sciences into *hard science*.

Today, structuralism is dead. More generally the human sciences are seen as going through a difficult time. The concepts that they have exploited to naturalise man and as a result to become "true" sciences look at best like something that has not really progressed knowledge, and in many ways has slowed it down. This is the main reason why such a pronounced scepticism is spreading through the human sciences. It is felt that time is up for the human sciences, and that the record of recent decades is hardly a glorious one. Evidence of such doubts is readily found.

Outside the discipline, the German weekly magazine *Die Zeit* (March 2002) noted that the discredit of the human sciences is so great in Germany that the government had decided to transfer a significant amount of grants for the *Geisteswissenschaften* to research projects concerned with biological cognitivism. The "cognitive sciences" had the advantage of their vocation being the treatment of the human subject as a natural being, with no need to invoke the tortuous processes I mentioned earlier.

Within the discipline, many researchers and in some cases those of considerable standing appear to be highly sceptical as to whether the human sciences have made much contribution to human knowledge in the last two or three. Several examples can be mentioned: those of Horowitz (1994), Dahrendorf (1995) or Turner and Turner (1990). Almost everywhere the social sciences are seen as at best in a fallow period, at worst as disciplines that have become sterile.

In fact the account is only in debit in the matter of the programme which attempted to naturalise man in order to make him an object of science. Because there is also another project, although one that has been rather forgotten for the last thirty years, that is best illustrated by the work of a Tocqueville, a Weber or a Durkheim and which, although somewhat overrun by the *naturalist* project remains vigorous and continues to demonstrate its fertility.

III. IS IT NECESSARY TO ACCEPT THE CONCLUSIONS DRAWN FROM HUME AND COMTE?

The long-term failure of the naturalist project is due, it seems to me, in large part to the weakness of the concepts and theories conceived by the human sciences to naturalise man. They did not lead to the discovery of the North West Passage, quite simply because this idea was no more than a theory.

I mean by this that it is possible to construct authentically scientific theories without following the *a priori* drawn from Hume and Comte.

Hume and the Discontinuity Between Descriptive and Prescriptive

I will remind the reader of a point developed in chapter 1. The correct formulation of Hume's theorem is as follows. An imperative conclusion cannot be drawn from premises that are *all* indicative. Or: in general a prescriptive conclusion is the result of a series of reasons only certain of which are indicative, while others are imperative. All that is necessary, in effect, is that a *single reason* should be imperative in order to draw an imperative conclusion from a system of reasons.

Functionalist sociology (in its scientifically useful forms) takes on the project of showing that people positively or negatively value an institution because the institution in question leads to consequences that they see as positive or negative for the functioning of a given social system. Thus the functionalist sociology of inequality has shown that people readily accept inequalities when they see them as functional. Here, social actors' attitudes are explained by reasons that they have for adopting them, an explanation of the phenomenon under study that there is no reason to suppose could not be perfectly scientific. It accounts for the facts by a series of propositions that are quite reasonable. Moreover the actors concerned are most likely to approve the explanation.

In the same way, collective beliefs about the organisation of political life can be explained in relation to whether a given regime can satisfy certain criteria, such as respect for the citizen.

These remarks are obvious facts. If their relevance cannot be appreciated it is because there is commitment to the idea that normative beliefs cannot be explained by reasons but must be explained by causes which are not reasons.

It is perhaps through a dramatic and hyperbolic reading of Hume that the particular forms of the human sciences I have described here have endorsed the idea of the wide gulf between the factual and the normative.

Comte's First Principle and its Variant: The Idea of Cultural Variation in the Rules of Thought

Lévy-Bruhl had virtually abandoned the hypothesis of a primitive mentality in his *Carnets* (1949). Nonetheless Needham praised the power of this hypothesis as soon as he had dispensed with the evolutionist vision that Lévy-Bruhl had associated with it: beliefs that are observed in different places are variable because they derive from cultural forces.

Now it is possible to analyse variation in beliefs without endorsing culturalism. This can be seen in the analysis of scientific beliefs. Nobody would explain that we do not believe today what we believed yesterday by using a hypothesis about variation in the laws of thought or the action of cultural forces. Recognised scientific beliefs and also invalid *false scientific beliefs* are straightforwardly explained in a rational way. To return to the classic examples I have already mentioned, as long as the principle of inertia could not be conceived, there were readily intelligible reasons to continue to wonder endlessly about the forces that maintain the movement of the arrow in flight. As soon as the principle of inertia was conceived, such questions appear ridiculous. But there were no reasons to think them so before the discovery of the principle of inertia. There is here an example of a sudden change in the answers given by scientists to certain questions. Now these changes in scientific beliefs do not involve in any way a variation in the rules of thought.

A vital source of the scientific power of the analyses of Tocqueville, Durkheim and Weber lies in the fact that when they analyse beliefs they start without any hesitation with the principle affirmed by Descartes at the beginning of the *Discours de la méthode*, that good sense is the one thing in the world that is best shared. The rules of thought are in effect universal, the mechanisms of belief formation are the same everywhere, while one must still bear in mind the contextual parameters of those who believe in this or that idea.

For Durkheim (1979[1912]), magical thought follows the same rules as scientific thought. The magician's beliefs are not explained by cultural, psychological or biological forces, but by perfectly understandable reasons. Why does the magician believe in causal relations that are false? Why does he not abandon a practice that has failed? Not because he is unaware of the contradictions between fact and theory. He is aware, because he tries to explain them. How? By recourse to auxiliary hypotheses, exactly as an astronomer would do who observes that such a planet is not to be found where the astronomical theory he believes would predict. The astronomer does not allow himself to reject a theory that enables him to predict many phenomena. He will try instead to eliminate the contradiction with reality by introducing an auxiliary hypothesis that allows him to reconcile the theory with observed facts. The magician obeys in a similar way the "holistic thesis of Duhem–Quine": he behaves just as normally as a scientist. Not being able to determine the points at which the theory is defective, he constructs the hypothesis that the heart of the theory is not wrong and invents auxiliary hypotheses to explain his failures. Moreover, Durkheim says, since rain dances are not performed except in periods when there is a chance of rain, it would be expected that rain would fall with greater likelihood the days when the ritual is performed than the days when it is not (Boudon, 2000). The existence of a *correlation* will confirm the magician's belief in a relationship of *causality:* no rain without a rain ritual. Confirming the "rationalist" principle of Durkheim, Evans Pritchard (1972[1937]) showed in his studies of the Azande that they master both propositional calculus and probability as well as us. Weber (1922) explains magic in a similar way to Durkheim.

For Weber, religious beliefs are rational (Boudon, 2001). This is evident in his study of theodicy. From the moment that a single god is proposed, a theoretical difficulty becomes evident. How is it possible to explain evil in a world subject to the will of a unique God, the supposed source of good? Weber shows how the world religions have put forward three solutions to this problem. I do not need to discuss them. These indications are enough to show that Weber treats the production and diffusion of religious beliefs in the same way as the production and diffusion of scientific beliefs are usually handled. For Weber as for Durkheim, religious theories aim at explaining the world. They put forward the postulate that phenomena derive from the spiritual realm. Scientists, by contrast, do not allow themselves such a postulate. Theology and science thus define two explanatory programmes about the world that rely upon different axiomatic bases. Apart from that, the theologian follows the same rules as the scientist. Weber greatly emphasises the fact that theology, just like science, is careful to eliminate contradictions, to produce explanations of the world that are as general, elegant and convincing, etc., as possible.

Even though it sees the sidelining of religion to the profit of science, Weber's theory of *disenchantment* sets out an analysis that is very different from Comte's *law of the three states*. For Weber, disenchantment tends to eliminate explanation of the world by final causes, by the spiritual. But that does not mean that the rules of thought have evolved. Quite simply the "theological programme" for the explanation of the world has progressively ceded ground to the efficiency of the "scientific programme". For Weber as for Durkheim, the rules of thought are invariables: they are valid for all eternity. They are observed as much by theology as science. Theology is no less rational than science. It simply applies different axiomatic principles. If the scientific explanation of the world has overwhelmed the non-scientific explanations of natural phenomena, it is because the scientific programme has proved to be more efficient. This explains why in those areas that science has not occupied or that it cannot occupy, religious thought is able to remain active. Now this is exactly what can be observed, for the progress of science has not abolished religion.

Tocqueville always saw collective beliefs as rational. In the 18th century, the French had more reason than the English to create a cult of Reason, he remarks. The French had more reason to be irreligious than the Americans (Boudon, 2003). Tocqueville, like Durkheim and Weber, starts from the principle that individuals believe in an idea as soon as they have sound reasons to do so. If collective beliefs vary from one context to another, its is because the contextual parameters are different from one context to another. Tocqueville, in the same way as Durkheim and Weber, never makes collective beliefs the product of cultural forces.

I have suggested that the concern of cognitive psychology with the idea of *bias* is of no use. There is no reason to believe that ordinary thought obeys different rules to more ordered thinking, that everyday thought might be "magical", as the cognitive psychologists like to say, and that only scientific thought is rational (Boudon, 1995).

In an experiment, Tversky and Kahneman (1973) asked psychiatrists if they believe in a cause and effect relationship between depression and suicide. The majority of psychiatrists replied in the affirmative. Tversky and Kahneman asked them on what bases they had answered in the affirmative. All replied that they had often seen depressive patients attempt suicide. For the statistician, the reply is not sufficient, for it is based on *one* datum, where in fact *four* are necessary. The responses of the psychiatrists then were based on a major error. This is the source of the idea that ordinary thought is based on invalid rules, or "magic". But it might be said in objection that in fact the doctors were right: in cases where the marginal numbers of a binary contingent table are asymmetric, the fact of being able to observe a *respectable* number of cases of convergence may legitimately lead to a strong presumption of causality. If 20% of a psychiatrist's patients are depressives and if 20% attempt suicide, it means that as soon as the percentage of patients presenting the two characteristics is significantly more than 4% it would be valid to see a causal relation between the two variables: the fact of using only one datum where statistical theory would want four, does not mean a gross error but a valid intuition.

Although the great sociologists had no use for the idea of cultural forces to explain variations in beliefs from one culture to another, many anthropologists, psychologists, political scientist and sociologists of today believe that one cannot abandon Comte's *first* principle, as it was updated by Needham, and also believe that a serious science cannot allot to reasons the status of causes that follow from Comte's *second* principle.

Comte's Second Principle: Exclusion of the Content of Consciousness

Nonetheless, a scientific theory does not in any way imply that the idea of causality must be identical with that of material causality.

The criteria for the scientificity of a theory are as follows: a scientific theory is defined as composed of a series of propositions all equally acceptable and compatible; it must allow (first criterion) with the greatest precision possible the deduction of the state of things within its jurisdiction. Moreover, it must only contain acceptable propositions and concepts.

Thus Huygens's theory allows us to deduce the behaviour of all pendulums in all conditions. Moreover (*second criterion*) it only contains acceptable propositions. The ideas of force or of the parallelogram of forces are acceptable, in the sense that they allow us to organise all our knowledge of mechanics. Durkheim's theory of magic is in the same way composed of psychological propositions that are immediately acceptable and of empirical propositions that are immediately verifiable. The fact that the magician may be sensitive to contradiction is not observable. But, just like the idea of *force*, an idea such as that of *sensitivity to contradiction* allows us to organise many types of knowledge. It does not correspond to immediately observable data, but it is based on the fact that human subjects exhibit, everywhere and always, behaviour indicating that they negatively value any contradiction and try to avoid it.

As to the states of consciousness of the subject, their determination is part of the habitual procedures used in the construction of theories. If I see someone cutting wood in his yard in 45°C in the shade, I can with certainty state that he is not cutting it to keep warm. I do not even need to ask him to confirm my diagnosis. In other cases, the subject's statements may allow us to reject a theory. Wittgenstein's theory of magic, that interprets magic rituals as having an expressive and non-instrumental function in the mind of the subject, would seem unacceptable as soon as subjects state that their rituals have an instrumental function. Unless we introduce the idea of *false consciousness* at this point and begin the impossible mission of explaining why this should exist.

IV. THE FAILURE OF THE NATURALIST PROGRAMME

The effective analyses produced by the social sciences begin from the idea that good sense is the one thing in the world that is best shared, but that the reasons for behaviour and beliefs depend on contextual parameters. Aristotelian physicians had an interpretation of why mercury rises in a barometer that would appear strange to us. Their thought was not obscured by psychological or cultural forces. At its simplest, they had not found a better theory in the market.

But empiricism (or more exactly, a corollary erroneously drawn from Hume's theorem) and positivism (or more exactly, two central ideas from Comte) have generated ideas that have been seen as the evidence for the discontinuity between the is and the ought; on what science is and what it should be. This is why sociologists, anthropologists, psychologists and economists have finished up by believing that it is indispensable to naturalise man, to deprive him of his most evident characteristics, the faculties of judgement, imagination, intentionality, if we want to take the human sciences to the same level as the sciences of nature.

Culturalism and structuralism are slowing down, but the *a priori* on which their ambitions were founded continue, and there is no shortage of strategies for the naturalisation of man. These stratagems always return to the supposition that the meanings that man gives his actions and his beliefs are null and void, and that in any event these meanings are not the causes of his actions and beliefs. All that remains, then, is to seek the "genuine" causes and to see the reasons given by the subject as dependent variables.

The result of an exemplary unintended consequence is that nothing has distanced the human sciences from their objective of becoming true sciences more than the idea that in order to do so they should naturalise their object. Only certain areas of the human sciences have followed this naturalist programme but they have been the most visible ones. And it remains current in its gentler forms as is shown by the explanatory virtue allotted to concepts such as *bias* and *framework*.

The measure of the importance of the *naturalist* programme is shown by the fact that certain epistemologists have no hesitation in remarking that there are two fundamental types of explanation of behaviour: the explanation via "norms" (that which explains behaviour as the result of norms internalised by the subject) and the explanation via "reasons". This rather strange denomination assumes that it is not possible to have reasons for accepting a norm. The extravagant nature of this distinction establishes the fact that the social sciences are divided between, in effect, *naturalist* and *rationalist* programmes.

The preferred programme of the classic theorists, the *rationalist* programme, or as we should perhaps distinguish it from classical rationalism, the *neo-rationalist* programme, what I have sometimes called here the *cognitive*, embraces the idea that good sense is the one thing in the world that is best shared.

REFERENCES

d'Andrade, R. (1995) *The Development of Cognitive Anthropology*. Cambridge, Cambridge University Press.

Boudon, R. (1990) *L'Art de se persuader*. Paris, Fayard/Seuil.

—— (1995), *Le Juste et le vrai; études sur l'objectivité des valeurs et de la connaissance*. Paris, Fayard.

—— (1997) "Le 'paradoxe du vote' et la théorie de la rationalité". *Revue française de sociologie*, 38(2): 217–227.

—— (2000) *Études sur les sociologues classiques, II*. Paris, Presses Universitaires de France.

—— (2001) "La rationalité du religieux selon Max Weber". *L'Année sociologique*, 51(1): 9–50.

—— (2003) *Raison, bonnes raisons?* Paris, Presses Universitaires de France.

Dahrendorf, R.(1995) *Whither Social Sciences? The 6th Economic and Social Research Council Annual Lecture*. Economic and Social Research Council, Swindon, UK.

Durkheim, E. (1979[1912]) *Les Formes élémentaires de la vie religieuse*. Paris, Presses Universitaires de France.

Evans-Pritchard, E. E. (1968[1937]) *Witchcraft, Oracles and Magic among the Azande*. Oxford, Clarendon Press.

Friedman, M. (1953) *Essays in Positive Economics*. Chicago, Chicago University Press.

Geertz, C. (1984) "Distinguished Lecture: Anti anti-relativism". *American Anthropologist*, 86(2): 263–278.

Gellner, E. (1987) "Zeno of Cracow", In: *Culture, Identity and Politics*, Cambridge, Cambridge University Press: 47–74.

Granet, M. (1990) *Études sociologiques sur la Chine*. Paris, Presses Universitaires de France.

Homans, G. and Schneider, D. (1955) *Marriage, Authority and Final Causes. A Study of Unilateral Cross-cousin Marriage*. Glencoe, The Free Press.

Horowitz, I. (1994) *The Decomposition of Sociology*. New York, Oxford University Press.

Horton, R. (1993) *Patterns of Thought in Africa and the West*. Cambridge, Cambridge University Press

Huntington, S. (1996) *The Clash of Civilizations and the Remaking of the World Order*. New York, Shuster and Shuster.

Kahneman, D. and Tversky, A. (1973) "Availability: a Heuristic for Judging Frequency and Probability". *Cognitive Psychology*, 5: 207–232.

Lévi-Strauss, C. (1962) *La Pensée sauvage*. Paris, Plon.

Lévy-Bruhl, L. (1960[1922]) *La Mentalité primitive*. Paris, Presses Universitaires de France.

—— (1949) *Les Carnets de Lévy-Bruhl*. Paris, Presses Universitaires de France.

Mannheim, K. (1954) *Ideology and Utopia*. London, Routledge and Kegan Paul.

Needham, R. (1972) *Belief, Language and Experience*. Oxford, Blackwell.

Nisbett, R. and Ross, L. (1980) *Human Inference*. Englewood Cliffs, N.J., Prentice-Hall.

Murdock, G. (1949) *Social Structure*. New York, Macmillan.

Pareto, V. (1964–1988 [1916]) *Traité de sociologie générale*. In: *Oeuvres complètes*, vol. 12. Geneva, Droz.

Parodi, M. (2004) *La Modernité manquée du structuralisme*. Paris, Presses Universitaires de France.

Popper, K. (1976) "The Myth of the Framework". In: Freeman, E. (ed.), *The Abdication of Philosophy: Philosophy and the Public Good,* La Salle, Ill., Open Court: 23–48.

Reynaud, J.-D. (2002) "Pierre Bourdieu (1930–2002): restituer aux hommes le sens de leurs actes". *Revue française de sociologie*, 43(1): I–V.

Ruse, M. (1993) "Une défense de l'éthique évolutionniste". In: Changeux, J.-P. (ed), *Fondements naturels de l'éthique*, Paris, Odile Jacob: 35–64.

Scheler, M. (1978[1912]) *Das Ressentiment im Aufbau der Moralen*. Frankfurt, Klostermann. From *Gesammelte Werke*, Bd. 3 *Vom Umsturz der Werte*. Bern, Francke: 33–147.

Shweder, R. A. (1977) "Likeliness and Likelihood in Everyday Thought: Magical Thinking in Judgments about Personality". *Current Anthropology*, 18(4): 637–659.

—— (1991) *Thinking through Cultures: Expeditions in Cultural Anthropology*. Cambridge, Harvard University Press.

Tooby, J. and Cosmides, L. (1992) "The Psychological Foundations of Culture". In: Barkow, J., Cosmides, L. and Tooby, J. (eds.), *The Adapted Mind: Evolutionary Psychology and the Generation of Culture*, New York, Oxford University Press.

Turner, S. P. and Turner, J. H. (1990) *The Impossible Science. An Institutional Analysis of American Sociology*. London, Sage.

Weber, M. (1922) *Wirtschaft und Gesellschaft: Grundriss der Sozialökonomik*. Tübingen, Mohr.

Whorf, B. L. (1969) *Linguistique et anthropologie. Les origines de la sémiologie*. Paris, Denoël.

Bibliography

Albert, H. (1975) *Traktat über kritische Vernunft*. Tübingen, J. C. B. Mohr.

Aya, R. (2001) "The Curse of Cognitive Cultural Relativism". In: Lindo, F., van Niekerk, M. (eds), *Dedication and Detachment: Essays in Honour of Hans Vermeulen*, Amsterdam, Aksant: 33–41.

Ayer, A. J. (1960 [1946]) *Language, Truth and Logic*. London, V. Gollancz.

Batson, C.D. (1991) *The Altruism Question*. Hillsdale, N.J., Lawrence Erlbaum.

Baudelaire, C. (1980[1857]) *"Madame Bovary par Gustave Flaubert". L'Artiste*, 18 October 1857. Reprinted in: *Œuvres complètes*. Paris, R. Laffont, 1980.

Becker, H. S. (1982) *Art Worlds*. Berkeley, London, University of California Press.

Bell, Q. (1976) *On Human Finery*. London, Hogarth Press.

Ben David, J., Zloczower, A. (1962) "Universities and Academic Systems in Modern Societies". *Archives européennes de sociologie*, III: 45–84.

Besançon, A. (1994) *L'image interdite: une histoire intellectuelle de l'iconoclasme*. Paris, Fayard.

Blumer, H. (1969[1930]) "Science without Concept". In: *Symbolic Interactionism: Perspective and Method*. Berkekey, University of California Press: 153–170.

Boltanski, L., Thévenot, L. (1991) *De la justification: Les économies de la grandeur*. Paris, Gallimard.

Boudon, R. (1990) *L'Art de se persuader*. Paris, Fayard/Seuil.

—— (1992a) "Le pouvoir social: variations sur un thème de Tocqueville". *Revue des Sciences Morales et Politiques*, 531–558. Reprinted in *Études sur les sociologues classiques, I*. Paris, Presses Universitaires de France, 1998.

—— (1992b) "Should we Believe in Relativism?" In: Bohnen, A., Musgrave, A. (eds), *Wege der Vernunft. Festschrift zum siebzigsten Geburtstag von Hans Albert*. Tübingen, J. C. B. Mohr (Paul Siebeck): 113–129.

—— (1994) "Les deux sociologies de la connaissance scientifique". In: Boudon, R., Clavelin, M. (eds), *Le Relativisme est-il résistible? Regards sur la sociologie des sciences*, Paris, Presses Universitaires de France.

—— (1994) *The Art of Self-Persuasion*. London, Polity Press.

—— (1995) *Le Juste et le vrai: études sur l'objectivité des valeurs et de la connaissance*. Paris, Fayard.

—— (1997) "Le 'paradoxe du vote' et la théorie de la rationalité". *Revue française de sociologie*, 38(2): 217–227.

—— (1997a) "La rationalité axiologique". In: Mesure, S. (ed.), *La rationalité des valeurs*. Paris, Presses Universitaires de France.

—— (1997b) "Peut-on être positiviste aujourd'hui". In: Cuin, Ch. H. (ed.), *Durkheim d'un siècle à l'autre*. Paris, Presses Universitaires de France: 265–288.

—— (1997c) "The Present Relevance of Max Weber's *Wertrationalität* (Value Rationality)". In: Koslowski, P. (ed.), *Methodology of the Social Sciences, Ethics, and Economics in the Newer Historical School: From Max Weber and Rickert to Sombart and Rothacker*, Berlin/New York, Springer: 4–29.

—— (1999) "*Les Formes élémentaires de la vie religieuse:* une théorie toujours vivante". *Année sociologique*, 49(1): 149–198.

—— (2000) *Études sur les sociologues classiques, II*. Paris, Presses Universitaires de France.

—— (2001) "La rationalité du religieux selon Max Weber". *L'Année sociologique*, 51(1): 9–50.

—— (2001) *The Origin of Values*. New Brunswick/London, Transaction.

—— (2002) *Déclin de la morale? Déclin des valeurs?* Paris, Presses Universitaires de France and Québec, Nota Bene.

—— (2003) *Raison, bonnes raisons*. Paris, Presses Universitaires de France.

—— (2003a) "Beyond Rational Choice Theory". *Annual Review of Sociology*, 29: 1–21.

—— (2003b) *Y a-t-il encore une sociologie?* Paris, Odile Jacob.

—— (2004) *Pourquoi les intellectuels n'aiment pas le libéralisme*. Paris, Odile Jacob.

Boudon, R., Betton, E. (1999) "Explaining the Feelings of Justice". *Ethical Theory and Moral Practice: An International Forum*, 2(4): 365–398. Reproduced in Boudon, R., Cherkaoui, M. (eds), *Central Currents in Social Theory*. London, Russell Sage Foundation, 2000, Vol. VI: 453–484.

Bourdieu, P. (1979) *La Distinction: critique sociale du jugement*. Paris, Editions de Minuit.

—— (1980[1973]) "L'opinion publique n'existe pas". *Les temps modernes*. Reprinted in: *Questions de sociologie*, Paris, Minuit, 1980: 222–235.

Buchanan, J. and Tullock, G. (1965) *The Calculus of Consent*. Ann Arbor, University of Michigan Press.

Buican, D. (1984) *Histoire de la génétique et de l'évolutionnisme en France*. Paris, Presses Universitaires de France.

Bunge, M. (1999) *The Sociology-Philosophy Connection*. London/New Brunswick (USA), Transaction.

Caplovitz, D. (1967) *The Poor Pay More*. London, Macmillan/New York, Free Press.

Clark, C. (1992) *Misery and Company: Sympathy in Everyday Life*. Chicago, University of Chicago Press.

Cluzel, J. (2003) *Propos impertinents sur le cinéma français*. Paris, Presses Universitaires de France.

Cohen, D. (1999) *Le Droit à..., Mélanges offerts à F. Terré*. Dalloz, Presses Universitaires de France: 393–400.

Coulangeon, P. (2003) "Le rôle de l'école dans la démocratisation de l'accès aux arts". *Revue de l'Observatoire Français des Conjonctures Économiques*, 86: 155–169.

d'Andrade, R. (1995) *The Development of Cognitive Anthropology*. Cambridge, Cambridge University Press.

Dahrendorf, R. (1995) *Whither Social Sciences? The 6th Economic and Social Research Council Annual Lecture*. Swindon, UK, Economic and Social Research Council.

Danto, A. (1964) "The Art World". *Journal of Philosophy*, 61: 571–84.

Dawkins, R. (1989) *The Selfish Gene*. Oxford, Oxford University Press.

Deutsch, M. (1975) "Equity, Equality, and Need, What Determine Which Value Will Be Used As the Basis of Distributive Justice?" *The Journal of Social Issues*, 31(3): 137–151.

—— (1986) "Cooperation, Conflict, and Justice". In: Bierhoff, H. W., Cohen, R. L., Greenberg, J. (eds), *Justice in Social Relations*. New York, Plenum Press: 3–17.

Douglas, M., Ney, S. (1998) *Missing Persons: a Critique of Personhood in the Social Sciences*. London, Sage.

Durkheim, E. (1960[1893]) *De la division du travail social*. Paris, Presses Universitaires de France.

—— (1979[1912]) *Les Formes élémentaires de la vie religieuse*. Paris, Presses Universitaires de France.

Eisenstadt, S. (2002) "The Construction of Collective Identities and the Continual Construction of Primordiality". In: Maleševic, S. , Haugaard, M. (eds), *Making Sense of Collectivity: Ethnicity, Nationalism and Globalisation*. London, Pluto Press: 33–87.

Evans-Pritchard, E. E. (1968[1937]) *Witchcraft, Oracles and Magic among the Azande*. Oxford, Clarendon Press.

Feyerabend, P. (1975) *Against Method*. London, N.L.B.

Frey, B. S. (1997) *Not Just for the Money: An Economic Theory of Personal Motivation*. Cheltenham, Edward Elgar.

Friedman, M. (1953) *Essays in Positive Economics*. Chicago, Chicago University Press.

Frohlich, N. and Oppenheimer, J. A. (1992) *Choosing Justice, an Experimental Approach to Ethical Theory*. Oxford, University of California Press.

Geertz, C. (1973) *The Interpretation of Culture*. New York, Basic Books.

—— (1984) "Distinguished Lecture: Anti Anti-relativism". *American Anthropologist*, 86(2): 263–278.

Gellner, E. (1987) "Zeno of Cracow". In: *Culture, Identity and Politics*, Cambridge, Cambridge University Press: 47–74.

Glendon, M. A. (1996) *A Nation under Lawyers*. Cambridge (Mass.), Harvard University Press.

Goldhagen, D. J. (1997) *Hitler's Willing Executioners: Ordinary Germans and the Holocaust*. New York, A. Knopf.

Gombrich, E. (1989[1972]) *The Story of Art*. London, Phaidon.

Goyard Fabre, S. (2002) *Les Embarras philosophiques du droit naturel*. Paris, Vrin.

Granet, M. (1990) *Études sociologiques sur la Chine*. Paris, Presses Universitaires de France.

Gusfield, J. (1981) *Drinking, Driving and the Symbolic Order*. Chicago, University of Chicago Press.

Habermas, J. (1981) *Theorie des kommunikativen Handelns*. Frankfurt, Suhrkamp.

Harsanyi, J. C. (1955) "Cardinal Welfare, Individualistic Ethics, and Interpersonal Comparisons of Utility". *The Journal of Political Economy*, 63(4): 309–21.

Haskell, F. (1976) *Rediscoveries in Art: Some Aspects of Taste, Fashion and Collecting in England and France*. London, Phaidon.

Hayek, F. von (1973–1979) *Law, Legislation and Liberty*. London, Routledge and Kegan Paul.

Henrich, J., Boyd, R., Bowles, S., Camerer, C., Fehr, E., Gintis, H., McElreath, R. (2001) "In Search of *Homo Economicus*: Behavioral Experiments in Fifteen Small-Scale Societies". *American Economic Review*, 91(2): 73–78.

Hochschild, J. L. (1981) *What's Fair? American Beliefs about Distributive Justice*. Cambridge, MA/London, Harvard University Press.

Homans, G., Schneider, D. (1955) *Marriage, Authority and Final Causes: A Study of Unilateral Cross-cousin Marriage*. Glencoe, The Free Press.

Horowitz, I. (1994) *The Decomposition of Sociology*. New York, Oxford University Press.

Horton, R. (1993) *Patterns of Thought in Africa and the West*. Cambridge, Cambridge University Press

Hübner, K. (1985) *Die Wahrheit des Mythos*. Munich, Beck.

Hume, D. (1972[1741]) *Essais politiques*. Vrin, Paris. Tr. from *Essays Moral and Political*. London, printed for A. Millar, 3rd edn., 1748.

Huntington, S. (1996) *The Clash of Civilizations and the Remaking of the World Order*. New York, Shuster and Shuster.

Inglehart, R., Basañez, M., Moreno, A. (1998) *Human Values and Beliefs: a Cross-cultural Sourcebook*. Ann Arbor, The University of Michigan Press.

Kahneman, D., Tversky, A. (1973) "Availability: a Heuristic for Judging Frequency and Probability". *Cognitive Psychology*, 5: 207–232.

Kahneman, D., Knetsch, J., Thaler, R. (1986) "Fairness and the Assumption of Economics". *Journal of Business*, 59: 285–300.

Kant, I. (1787) *Kritik der reinen Vernunft*. Bibliographisches Institut, Leipzig/Vienna: Meyers Volksbücher, 2nd edn. [no date]; I, I, 2nd part (Die transcendentale Logik), III (Von der Einteilung der allgemeinen Logik in Analytik und Dialektik): 93, 1.

Kellerhals, J., Modak, M., Sardi, M. (1995) "Justice, sens de la responsabilité et relations sociales". *L'Année sociologique*, 45 (2): 317–349.

Kuhn, T. S. (1962) *The Structure of Scientific Revolutions*. Chicago, University of Chicago Press.

Kuran, T. (1995) *Private Truths, Public Lies: The Social Consequences of Preference Falsification*. Cambridge, Mass., Harvard University Press.

Lakatos, I. and Musgrave, A. (eds) (1974) *Criticism and the Growth of Knowledge*. London, Cambridge University Press.

Latour, B., Woolgar, S. (1978) *Laboratory Life*. London, Sage.

Lévi-Strauss, C. (1952) *Race et histoire*. Paris, UNESCO. Repr.: Paris, Gonthier.

—— (1962) *La Pensée sauvage*. Paris, Plon.

Lévy-Bruhl, L. (1949) *Les Carnets de Lévy-Bruhl*. Paris, Presses Universitaires de France.

—— (1960 [1922]) *La Mentalité primitive*. Paris, Presses Universitaires de France.

Lukes, S. (1967) "Some Problems about Rationality". *Archives européennes de socio-logie*, 8(2): 247–64.

MacIntyre, A. (1981) *After Virtue*. London, Duckworth.

Mandeville, B. de (1728–1729) *The Fable of the Bees, or Private Vices, Publick Benefits*. With an essay on charity and charity-schools, and a search into the nature of society [by Mandeville]. The 5th edition, London: J. Tonson (J. Roberts).

Mannheim, K. (1954) *Ideology and Utopia*. London, Routledge and Kegan Paul.

Marshall, T. H. (1964) *Class, Citizenship and Social Development*. Garden City, New York, Doubleday.

Mead, G. H. (1934) *Mind, Self and Society: From the Standpoint of a Social Behaviorist*. Chicago, University of Chicago Press.

Merton, R. (1970[1938]) *Science, Technology and Society in Seventeenth Century England*. New York, Howard Fertig. Original version: "Studies on the History and Philosophy of Science", *Osiris* 4(2); 1938.

Michaud, Y. (1997) *La Crise de l'art contemporain*. Paris, Presses Universitaires de France.

Mills, C. W. (1956) *White Collar: The American Middle Classes*. New York, Oxford University Press.

Milo, D. (1986) "Le phénix culturel, de la résurrection dans l'histoire de l'art; l'exemple des peintres français (1650–1750)". *Revue française de sociologie*, 38(3): 481–504.

Mitchell, G., Tetlock, P. E., Mellers, B. A., Ordonez, L. D. (1993) "Judgements of Social Justice: Compromise Between Equality and Efficiency". *Journal of Personality and Social Psychology*, 65(4): 629–639.

Moore, G. E. (1954[1903]) *Principia ethica*. Cambridge, Cambridge University Press.

Moulin, L. (1953) "Les Origines religieuses des techniques électorales et délibératives modernes". *Revue internationale d'histoire politique et constitutionnelle*, April–June: 106–148.

Murdock, G. (1949) *Social Structure*. New York, Macmillan.

Nadeau, R. (2003) "Cultural Evolution True and False: A Debunking of Hayek's Critics". *Cahiers d'épistémologie*, Montréal, UQAM.

Needham, R. (1972) *Belief, Language and Experience*. Oxford, Blackwell.

Nietzsche, F. (1969) *Götzendämmerung*. Werke, Bd 2, Munich, hrsg. v. K. Schlechta.

Nisbett, R., Ross, L. (1980) *Human Inference*. Englewood Cliffs, N.J., Prentice-Hall.

Oberschall, A. (1994) "Règles, normes, morale: émergence et sanction", *L'Année sociologique*, 44(Argumentation et Sciences Sociales): 357–384.

Opp, K. D. (1983) *Die Entstehung sozialer Normen*. Tübingen, J. C. B. Mohr.

Pareto, V. (1988 [1916]) *Traité de sociologie générale*. In: *Oeuvres complètes*, vol. 12. Genève, Droz.

Parodi, M. (2004) *La Modernité manquée du structuralisme*. Paris, Presses Universitaires de France.

Pascal (1960[1670]) *Pensées*. Paris, Garnier.

Piaget, J. (1985[1932]) *Le Jugement moral chez l'enfant*. Paris, Presses Universitaires de France.

Pommier, R. (1986) *Un marchand de salades qui se prend pour un prince: réponse du petit Pommier au grand Barbéris*. Paris, G. Roblot.

195

Pommier, R. (1994) *Études sur "le Tartuffe"*. Paris, Sedes.

Popkin, R. H. (1979) *The History of Scepticism from Erasmus to Spinoza*. Berkeley, University of California Press.

Popkin, S. L. (1979) *The Rational Peasant: The Political Economy of Rural Society in Vietnam*. Berkeley, University of California Press.

Popper, K. R. (1945) *The Open Society and Its Enemies*. London, Routledge and Kegan Paul.

—— (1957) *The Poverty of Historicism*. London, Routledge and Kegan Paul.

—— (1959) *The Logic of Scientific Discovery*. London, Hutchinson. Original: *Logik der Forschung*, Vienna, 1934.

—— (1963) *Conjectures and Refutations: The Growth of Scientific Knowledge*. London, Routledge.

—— (1976) "The Myth of the Framework". In: Freeman, E. (ed.), *The Abdication of Philosophy: Philosophy and the Public Good,* La Salle, Ill., Open Court: 23–48.

Radnitzky, G. (1987) "La perspective économique sur le progrès scientifique: application en philosophie des sciences de l'analyse coût-bénéfice". *Archives de philosophie*, 50: 177–198.

Rawls, J. (1971) *A Theory of Justice*. Cambridge, The Belknap Press of Harvard University Press.

Raynaud, D. (1998) *L'Hypothèse d'Oxford: essai sur les origines de la perspective*. Paris, Presses Universitaires de France.

Reynaud, J.-D. (2002) "Pierre Bourdieu (1930–2002): restituer aux hommes le sens de leurs actes". *Revue française de sociologie*, 43(1): I–V.

Rorty, R. (1979) *Philosophy and the Mirror of Nature*. Princeton, Princeton University Press.

—— (1989) *Contingency, Irony and Solidarity*. Cambridge/New York, Cambridge University Press.

Ruse, M. (1993) "Une défense de l'éthique évolutionniste". In: Changeux, J.-P. (ed.), *Fondements naturels de l'éthique*. Paris, Odile Jacob: 35–64.

Scheler, M. (1926) *Die Wissensformen und die Gesellschaft*. Leipzig, Der Neue-Geist.

—— (1955) *Le formalisme en éthique et l'éthique matériale des valeurs*. Paris, Gallimard, 6th edn.

Scheler, M. (1978[1912]) *Das Ressentiment im Aufbau der Moralen*. Frankfurt, Klostermann. From *Gesammelte Werke*, Bd. 3 *Vom Umsturz der Werte*. Bern, Francke: 33–147.

Sen, A. (1999) *Employment, Technology and Development*. Oxford, Oxford University Press.

Shweder, R. A. (1977) "Likeliness and Likelihood in Everyday Thought: Magical Thinking in Judgments about Personality". *Current Anthropology*, 18(4): 637–659.

—— (1991) *Thinking through Cultures: Expeditions in Cultural Anthropology*. Cambridge, Harvard University Press.

—— (2000) "What About 'Female Genital Mutilation' and Why Understanding Culture Matters in the First Place", *Daedalus*, 129 (4): 209–232.

Simmel, G. (1892) *Die Probleme der Geschichtsphilosophie*. Munich, Duncker & Humblot.

—— (1900) *Philosophie des Geldes*. Leipzig, Duncker & Humblot.

—— (1916) *Rembrandt: ein kunstphilosophischer Versuch*. Leipzig, Wolff.

—— (1989) *Gesammelte Schriften zur Religionssoziologie*. Berlin, Duncker & Humblot.

Smith, A. (1976[1776]) *An Inquiry Into the Nature and Causes of the Wealth of Nations*. Oxford, Oxford University Press.

Sokal, A., Bricmont, J. (1997) *Impostures intellectuelles*. Paris, O. Jacob.

Sperber, D. (1996) *La Contagion des idées*. Paris, Odile Jacob.

Strauss, L. (1953) *Natural Right and History*. Chicago, University of Chicago Press.

Sukale, M. (1995) *Max Weber: Schriften zur Soziologie*. Stuttgart, Reclam: Introduction.

Sukale, M. (2002) *Max Weber: Leidenschaft und Disziplin*. Tübingen, Mohr Siebeck.

Tarski, A. (1936) "Der Wahrheitsbegriff in der formalisierten Sprache". *Studia philosophica*, 1.

Taylor, C. (1997) *La liberté des modernes*. Paris, Presses Universitaires de France.

Tocqueville, A. de (1986a) *L'Ancien Régime et la Révolution*. In: *Tocqueville. De la démocratie en Amérique, Souvenirs, l'Ancien Régime et la Révolution*. Introduction and notes by Lamberti, J.-C., Mélonio, F. Paris, Laffont, Bouquins.

—— (1986b) *De la démocratie en Amérique*. (1835–1840). In: *Tocqueville. De la démocratie en Amérique, Souvenirs, l'Ancien Régime et la Révolution*. Paris, Laffont.

Tooby, J. and Cosmides, L. (1992) "The Psychological Foundations of Culture". In: Barkow, J., Cosmides, L., Tooby, J. (eds), *The Adapted Mind: Evolutionary Psychology and the Generation of Culture*, New York, Oxford University Press.

Trevelyan, G. M. (1942) *English Social History; A Survey of Six Centuries, Chaucer to Queen Victoria*. London/New York, Longmans/Green.

Turner, B. S. (1992) *Max Weber: from History to Modernity*. London, Routledge.

Turner, S. P., Turner, J. H. (1990) *The Impossible Science: An Institutional Analysis of American Sociology*. London, Sage.

Urmson, J. O. (1968) *The Emotive Theory of Ethics*. London, Hutchinson.

Veblen, T. (1960) *The Theory of the Leisure Class*. New York, Mentor.

Voegelin, E. (1952) *Toward a New Science of Politics*. Chicago, University of Chicago Press.

Volkov, S. (1980) *Témoignage: les mémoires de Dimitri Chostakovitch*. Paris, Albin Michel.

Walzer, M. (1993) *Spheres of Justice: A Defense of Pluralism and Equality*. Oxford, Martin Robertson.

Weber, M. (1995[1919]) *Wissenschaft als Beruf*. Stuttgart, Reklam.

—— (1920–1921) *Gesammelte Aufsätze zur Religionssoziologie*. Tübingen, Mohr.

—— (1922) *Wirtschaft und Gesellschaft: Grundriss der Sozialökonomik*. Tübingen, Mohr.

Welsch, P. (1987) *Ästhetisches Denken*. Stuttgart, Reclam.

Whorf, B. L. (1969) *Linguistique et anthropologie. Les origines de la sémiologie*. Paris, Denoël.

Wilson, J. Q. (1993) *The Moral Sense*. New York, Macmillan/The Free Press.

Index

Index compiled by Annie Devinant,
Institut des Sciences Humaines
Appliquées, Université Paris-Sorbonne